POLYPHILO or The Dark Forest Revisited

An Erotic Epiphany of Architecture

Alberto Pérez-Gómez

The MIT Press
Cambridge, Massachusetts
London, England

First MIT Press paperback edition, 1994
© 1992 Massachusetts Institute of Technology

This book was set in Univers and Palatino by DEKR Corporation and was printed and bound in the United States of America.

Library of Congress Cataloging-in-Publication Data

Pérez Gómez, Alberto, 1949–
    Polyphilo, or, The dark forest revisited : an erotic epiphany of
architecture / Alberto Pérez Gómez.
        p.   cm.
    Based on: Hypnerotomachia Poliphili / Francesco Colonna.
    ISBN 0-262-16129-X (HB), 0-262-66090-3 (PB)
    I. Colonna, Francesco, d. 1527.   Hypnerotomachia Poliphili.
II. Title.   III. Title: Polyphilo.   IV. Title: Dark forest
revisited.
PR9200.9.P4P6   1992
853'.3—dc20   91-4518
                                                           CIP

For my brothers and sisters,
poets,
fliers,
demiurges;
makers of order and form who have
cast spells and incantations
of the time,
prophetic
arrested gestures
for our myth in the future
to discover its
place

CONTENTS

ACKNOWLEDGMENTS

This book was conceived as a collaborative project, implicitly questioning traditional assumptions about authorship. Its realization would not have been possible without the help of a remarkable group of colleagues and students. The first draft of the text was read enthusiastically by Steve Parcell, Donald Kunze, Gregory Henriquez, Mary Alice Dixon-Hinson, and Katsuhiko Muramoto. Steve Parcell made a detailed criticism and offered very important suggestions. The text was then fully rewritten. Terri Fuglem subsequently edited Hours Three to Seventeen, Twenty-three and Twenty-four. Terrance Galvin edited Hours One and Two, and Eighteen to Twenty-two. The three Polya chapters, Hours Eighteen to Twenty, were subsequently rewritten by Louise Pelletier, who introduced a contemporary feminine perspective and also helped with final revisions of the whole text, graphic design, and format.

For typesetting and formatting, and many hours in front of the computer screen, my gratitude goes to Susie Spurdens, secretary of the History and Theory of Architecture program at McGill University.

The images were initially made possible by the kind permission of Aerospatiale in Toulouse, France, and Construcciones Aeronauticas S.A. in Madrid, Spain, to photograph inside their respective factories. Special thanks to the representatives of Mexico, France, and Spain in the International Civil Aviation Organization in Montreal and to the authorities of Aerospatiale for their hospitality and assistance.

Natalija Subotincic was responsible for the airplane photography, with my help and that of Mara Subotincic. The final photographic images from Hours Three to Eight and from Hours Ten to Fifteen are the work of Natalija Subotincic. Those for the remaining chapters were conceived and realized by Louise Pelletier. The collages in Hours Eighteen, Nineteen, and Twenty are the result of a close collaboration between Ms. Pelletier and myself.

In Memoriam Frances C. Lonna, whose inspiration and original work were the point of departure for this project.

Our common sense tells us that the things
of this earth barely exist, that actual
reality is
only in
our
dreams.

Charles Baudelaire, *Les Paradis Artificiels*

"You should know that Poliphilo dreamed about being in a threatening dark forest and narrates the myriad things he saw, a veritable strife for love, which is the meaning of the Greek words in the title. With elegant style and great care, he tells of many ancient marvels deserving of a place in the theater of memory, architectural monuments encountered in his search for Polia, his beloved: a pyramid and obelisks; the great ruins of classical buildings; the precise measurement and characteristics of columns, their capitals, bases, entablatures with their diverse architraves, friezes, and cornices, and their respective moldings and ornaments; a great horse; a magnificent elephant; a hollow colossus; and a triumphal gateway with its harmonic measurements and ornamentation. After suffering a major scare behind the threshold, passing the test of a frightening tunnel, and being brought back to life by a wonderful encounter with the five senses in the form of five nymphs, he describes how he is shown several fountains and quenches his thirst by drinking the tepid water springing from a stone nymph's breasts. He is then taken to a munificent bath where he is teased by the five senses before eventually arriving at the palace of the queen, who is the embodiment of free will, and being invited by her to partake of a splendid meal. He expresses his admiration for the variety of precious stones and materials worn by all present, and describes a game in dance and other measurements of sound. After the festivities, he is taken to visit three gardens, the first made of glass, the second of silk, and the third a labyrinth, which is human life. In its midst was trinity itself, expressed through hieroglyphs, as in sacred Egyptian sculpture. He describes three important doors of where one must choose and how, behind one, Polia awaits him. Without either realizing the meaning of their physical proximity, she takes him to admire the four triumphs of Jove: four processions whose chariots and artifacts celebrate the stories of the classical poets explaining the effects of various kinds of love. Then follow the triumph of Vertuno and Pomona, the ancient sacrifice of Priapus, and the description of a magnificent temple of great beauty where the sacrifices of miraculous rites and ancient religion once took place. It is here that the couple fully acknowledge their loving encounter. Poliphilo then proceeds to narrate how he and Polia arrive at the coast to wait for Cupid at the site of a ruined temple, where she persuades him to explore in search of admirable ancient things. There he finds, among many enlightening epitaphs, a mosaic mural depicting hell. Scared again, he returns to Polia, just in time to meet Cupid, who has arrived in his ship propelled by beautiful rowing nymphs. Both climb aboard, and Love uses his wings as sails. Sea gods, goddesses, and nymphs pay tribute to Cupid and the vessel arrives triumphantly at the island of Cytherea. Poliphilo then tells about the forests, gardens, fountains, and rivers on the island, as well as the procession of triumphal chariots and nymphs in honor of Cupid. In the center of the island, the final place of arrival, he describes the veneral fountain with its precious columns and the actions that take place after the appearance of Mars, followed by a visit to the innermost enclosure containing the tomb of Adonis, where the nymphs tell the story of the hero's death and of the sad celebration of his anniversary commemorated every year by Venus, the lover.

"The nymphs finally ask Polia to tell the story of her own love, its origins and difficulties. Polia acquiesces and her words fill the second book, giving a genealogy of her family, explaining her initial inclination to ignore Poliphilo, and providing a detailed account of the final success of their love. Following Polia's account, Poliphilo concludes by describing their embrace in the happy place of dwelling, until he is awakened, sad and alone, by the song of the nightingale."

Thus reads the synopsis that appears as a preface to the original edition of *Hypnerotomachia Poliphili*, published in Venice by Aldus Manutius in 1499. We will never know with certainty who the author was. From the beginning his identity

was clouded with mystery, his name only revealed through an anagram. It could have been the friar Francesco Colonna (1433–1527), a Franciscan from Venice. This is, indeed, the most widely held hypothesis, one argued admirably by Claudius Popelin, the translator and author of a vast and learned introduction to a terse French edition of the work (Paris, 1883). Many questions have been raised about this hypothesis, particularly in relation to the themes, interests, and the intense erotic content of the book. More recently Maurizio Calvesi, in *Il Sogno di Polifilo Prenestino* (Rome, 1983), argues that the author was a Roman also named Francesco Colonna, lord of Palestrina after 1484 and member not of a religious order but of a pagan confraternity, the Roman academy of Pomponio Leto. Equally controversial is the authorship of the out-standing woodcuts that accompany the text, although it has often been stated that they were most probably the work of an artist from the Veneto. These images, representing the places, monuments, and fragments visited in the dream, exerted a profound influence on the architecture of Europe from the sixteenth century on. Synthesizing love, geometry, and imagination through a vision of ancient architecture, the book became a source of architectural ideas in Europe for at least 300 years. *Hypnerotomachia* was translated into French in 1546 and published in 1551, 1554, and 1561. Transformed French versions with different titles appeared in 1600, 1657, and 1772. More recent free translations appeared in 1803, 1811, and 1883. A large section of the first part was translated into English under the title *The Strife of Love in a Dream*, published in 1592 and 1890.

Architectural treatises throughout history have clarified the meaning of built work and, perhaps more important, have since Vitruvius articulated the possibilities of an ethical practice, addressing the issue of the appropriateness of forms to certain cultural situations. Renaissance treatises are of course no exception, and while *Hypnerotomachia Poliphili* fulfills this role, it is my contention that it opens up further possibilities for architectural discourse.

The Renaissance was a seminal time for our own architectural practice. Architecture was "promoted" to acquire the status of a liberal art. Its theory, in the tradition of the Greek *techné* and articulated through *mathemata*, became a potentially prescriptive set of rules, the origin of later scientific and technological methodologies. Yet the Renaissance also developed potential alternatives to this sort of theory, the most significant one being *Hypnerotomachia*.

The theocentric universe had already been exhausted by the late fifteenth century. Cleverly, the hero of *Hypnerotomachia* reveals that architectural creation could no longer be directly inspired by the gods through contemplation as a mere liberal art, in the sense of Alberti, nor could it come about as the *ars* or craft of the medieval mason, acting as the hand of God the Augustinian Architect. The answer lay somewhere in between yet in a different place, where a radically different role for the personal imagination might emerge, one that was "no longer" the Aristotelian-medieval passive function of mimesis, and "not yet" the imagination of the Romantic "genius," deluded by the possibility of creation ex nihilo.

Indeed, *Hypnerotomachia* is the first narrative articulation of architectural practice, at the very inception of the modern age. It already expounds a poetic vision that sets a temporal boundary to the experience of architecture, showing that architecture is not only about form and space but about time, about the presence  of man on earth. Architecture had always fulfilled its inveterate cultural task of disclosing a symbolic order at the intersection between a "situation," a ritual or liturgy, and its material, constructed frame. Both aspects were perceived as indispensable and intimately related, yet traditionally they were never, even remotely, assumed to be related in an absolute and permanent fashion as two terms in an unambiguous

equation. Ritual actions were obviously narrative (temporal) forms that articulated, together and within their architectural (spatial) sites, the order of human purpose in the gap between a mortal humanity and an overwhelming external reality. At the time of the Renaissance, sacred and profane rituals remained a fundamental part of the culture, and this is clearly reflected in *Hypnerotomachia*. The effective public function of ritual would be questioned eventually as a result of both the scientific revolution and its political consequence, the emergence of democracy at the end of the *ancien régime*. Therefore, the issue of "situation" was not to become an explicit problem for architecture until the mid-eighteenth century, when it appears in the form of questions about "character" and "type" related to architectural meaning in the theoretical writings of Jacques-François Blondel, Germain Boffrand, Sebastien Le Camus de Mézières, and others. It became a crucial theoretical problem during the late eighteenth century in the works of Etienne-Louis Boullée and Claude-Nicolas Ledoux and has remained so until our own time.

However, given the dominant instrumental turn taken by architectural theories in the last two hundred years, it is easy to understand that our historical tradition has maintained in high regard Alberti's *De re aedificatoria* and Palladio's *Quattro libri* and has practically ignored *Hypnerotomachia*. Indeed, it could be argued that European architecture followed the models of Alberti, Palladio, and Vignola, architecture as a liberal art guided by mathematical and geometric principles, precisely because these treatises were the precursors of a "scientific" theory of architecture that allowed for the objectification of form. Nevertheless, as I have shown in my *Architecture and the Crisis of Modern Science*, this simplistic reading disregards the question of intention. Architectural treatises of this type, from the Renaissance to the end of the eighteenth century, served as articulations of the metaphysical dimension of architecture in the traditional world; referring the generation of forms to a coherent cosmos and its transcendent values, they elucidated the meaning of an architecture that was itself beyond question. In retrospect, these works can be read as anticipations of a theory that eventually became obsessed with prescription and instrumentality, culminating in the work of Jean-Nicolas-Louis Durand, and nineteenth- and twentieth-century rationalism.

Today, in the wake of modernism, after witnessing the failures of instrumental theories and functionalism to generate meaningful architecture, we are better prepared to appreciate the great relevance of the original *Hypnerotomachia*, a text that should find its place in the architectural history curricula of our schools. *Hypnerotomachia* is the telling of a dream, a "didactic" dream, a narrative that articulates the appropriateness and ethical values implicit in the making of "classical" architecture in a way more convincing for us than the canonic treatises of the Renaissance. Its narrative form itself prevents us from reducing its "content" to an instrumental reading and thus opens up ways to articulate ethical questions pertinent to our own architectural practice.

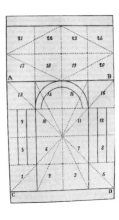

Hypnerotomachia fulfills its objective by demonstrating how architectural meaning is not something intellectual, a "formal" question of proportional relationships or abstract aesthetic values, but rather originates in the erotic impulse itself, in the need to quench our physical thirst: the existential condition to which humanity can only be reconciled within the realm of *poiesis* (the making of culture, i.e., art and architecture) and its metaphoric imagination. Poliphilo first experiences the overwhelming harmony of classical architecture and then, as soon as he measures the wonderful monuments he encounters, discloses the presence of precise proportional relationships. In his sensuous narrative this discovery of *mathemata* is constantly synthesized with a recollection of love; the effect of architecture is always beyond the purely visual, evoking the memory and expectation of erotic fulfillment. The harmony of architecture is always mater-ial (related to the Mother of All) and tactile, the formal exactness of number coinciding with the sensuous qualities of the materials, akin to the harmony that stems from our wholeness as human beings in love and analogous to the experience of wholeness that is prompted by the beautiful melodies often accompanying Poliphilo's encounters. Poli-philo is, indeed, the lover of Polia, the absent woman, whose name stands for the city (*polis*) and perhaps also for multiple knowledge or wisdom (in the Biblical sense of carnal knowledge) and thus alludes to the primordial existential orientation conveyed by architecture to one's embodied consciousness. She is represented as the missing "sixth sense" in the episode in which Poliphilo, after

experiencing the mortal threat of the laby-rinth, encounters five nymphs whose names are those of the senses. The whole-ness of love and architecture is sensuous yet beyond the senses, it is a wholeness underscored by alchemical themes and operations of fragmentation and union that structure the narrative.

The emphasis on desire as the "origin" of meaning cannot be discounted, even in our skeptical times. The architectural meanings to which we have access, those that touch us and leave us in awe, do not occur as "associations" in the mind alone, despite our Cartesian "common sense." This understanding of mean-ing is, indeed, a seventeenth-century prejudice first articulated for architecture in the theoretical works of Claude Perrault. Architectural meaning, like erotic knowl-edge, is primarily of the body and happens in the world, in that prereflective ground of existence where reality is first "given," and as such it can never be reduced to pure objectivity or subjectivity.

In Poliphilo's Renaissance world of magic and alchemy the primacy of the

prereflective ground as the origin of meaning is even more explicit. The elements of nature are never stable and *physis* is alive, con-stantly transforming. In alchemy the process is more important than its products, because the world of nature is in perpetual motion and change, never fully objectified and stable. The alchemist/architect must strive to find the primordial unity yet understands that the end is never fully attainable. Architecture is a verb rather than a noun.

In *Hypnerotomachia* the work of architecture was perceived to have a propitiatory role, its purpose to bring about good fortune and a happy life. Fortune is identified with Fortuna Primigenia and also with Venus Physizoa, the primordial mother, Earth. Architecture is a propitiation of Fortuna, which in our context could be translated as the Heideggerian "earth," an element ever present in the work of art that reminds mankind of its mortal nature and discloses Being as being-toward-death. This theme, in line with the necessity of cultivating prudence to develop a sound architectural practice, is constant throughout *Hypnerotomachia*. When Poliphilo arrives at the palace of Free Will, the question of individual freedom against predestination becomes

explicit. The power of architecture as a form of white astral magic is evidenced in the astrological ordering of the Queen's abode. As a result, a number of relevant questions, eminently modern in their implications, can then be articulated: What are the limitations and responsibilities of the new man, whose newly acquired dignity was being celebrated by the Renaissance? What is the role of the individual imagination in a world that recognizes the need for man to transform the order of creation and celebrates its artifacts while demanding that such acts of human *poiesis* be reconciled with the "given" order of experience? In this context, where is architecture? Where is the beloved Polia?

These fundamental questions are eventually confronted at the three doors, where Poliphilo must make his most important choice. Neither of two nymphs that accompany him, Logistica (Reason) nor Thelemia (Desire/Will/Fulfillment), manage to convince him to take either the right or the left door. Poliphilo, at the crossroads, chooses neither *vita contemplativa*, a life of contemplation associated with classical metaphysics and theology but also with architecture as a liberal art and science, nor *vita activa*, the world of human action and "being as production" in the old medieval sense, associated with architecture as a mechanical art but that, undergoing secularization, would lead to technology as the physical fulfillment of material desires through a will-to-power and its male-oriented, punctual cycle of toil, pleasurable reward, and endless disillusion. Rather, Poliphilo's choice leads him through the middle door to *vita voluptuaria*, a life of desire where fulfillment is never fully present nor fully absent. A life of desire as both recollection and projection and of ethical responsibility and respect for the otherness of his beloved, leading to an architecture mindful of its necessary appropriateness and wholeness: this, we thus learn, is the life that the good architect must pursue.

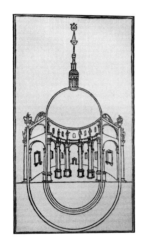

Indeed, Poliphilo meets Polia beyond that central door. She carries a lighted torch, and they walk together. After witnessing the divine effects of love through many works of human creation and ritual processions, they eventually recognize each other in the circular Temple of Venus, the place where the architecture is most perfect. Under the dome an eternally glowing lamp and a well mark the *axis mundi* where a priestess of Venus performs rites that lead to a miraculous germination of life, while Poliphilo extinguishes Polia's fiery torch in the water.

Although the only extant English edition "happily" ends with the alchemical fusion of water and fire, in the original we soon learn that in order to fulfill their desire the couple must still cross the sea of death. In fact, immediately after acknowledging the wholeness brought about by love, Poliphilo must visit, alone, a cemetery under a ruined temple where he finds many funerary monuments, also identified as poignant architectural works the epitaphs of which describe the tragedy of lovers separated by death. Scared by

a vision of hell and overtaken by anguish, Poliphilo returns to the coast to find Polia, just in time to board Cupid's ship. It is no coincidence that Cupid plays the role of navigator and that Love becomes Tecton, the mythical carpenter, shipbuilder, and pilot, the Homeric ancestor of the architect. Cupid's wings become the sails of the ship,

another archaic theme associated with the role of the architect in the myth of Dedalus and Icarus, as father and son attempt to escape from Crete and the architect is credited with the invention of wings/sails (see in this connection my article "The Myth of Dedalus," *AA Files* 10 [1985]).

On the other side of the water, on the island of love, Polia and Poliphilo are finally together, but not before having been blindfolded by Cupid. The possibility of meaningful architecture depends upon a realization that visible form and language refer to something other, recognized only when the dominant sense of sight (and Renaissance perspective) is mediated

by the body's primary synaesthetic (tactile) understanding. At the privileged place, the center of centers, the two lovers witness an ultimate ritual of love, now performed by the immortal gods themselves (the tragic story of Venus and Adonis), and endure another delay . . . Polia's version of the story is then heard. At the end of the narrative, however, Poliphilo wakes up from his dream alone yet complete in the presence of an architecture

that evokes the memory of fulfillment, the final recognition of the mystery of depth, the wholeness that, however "weak," grounds us as purposeful beings in the universe.

The dominant male voice of *Hypnerotomachia* raises questions, despite the hero's enlightened choices. This aspect is particularly critical in the second part of the text, where the voice of Polia is heard yet still in the tone of the male architect. The very notion of eroticism that grounds architectural meaning in *Hypneroto-*

machia, therefore, could still be translated as a delay of fulfillment and as a strife for ultimate completion. Such absolute fulfillment is almost made possible today by the accomplishments of technology, encouraging the architect to continue producing buildings through the implementation of a purely instrumental will-to-power. While Polia's voice is restrained and practically reduced to silence in the Renaissance work, in our technological world we should seek to magnify the resonance of our consciousness's feminine dimension. Thus we might be able to recognize the recollection of love over the absence of fulfillment as a ground of meaning, leading to a changing attitude toward the world that may deconstruct instrumentality and allow us to articulate action more as acceptance than as negation, and to posit care and compassion as a primary attitude to engage in the poetic making of architectural work.

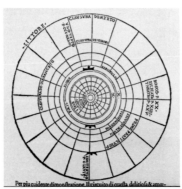

Hypnerotomachia Poliphili was never intended as a work of high literature. Its themes were common in the Middle Ages and in the works of the early Renaissance Italian poets. Clearly, the main concern of Colonna was architectural and alchemical, a concern for the disclosure of a symbolic order in the world of human action. Yet the language is highly imaginative; Maurizio Calvesi has even claimed that it is an invention in its own right. Indeed, the language is an idiosyncratic vernacular Italian with much Latin syntax and vocabulary. The erotic content is blunt and often full of cliches, with abundant specialized architectural and botanical technical terms. It is a strange dialect, constructed yet "popular." Predating the inception of the novel (before Rabelais and Cervantes) and the normalization of prose in European languages, the language of *Hypnerotomachia* displays a texture prophetic of our present quest to reconcile personal creation and a political common ground in art and literature, suggesting a potential collapse of the difference between poetic forms and the languge of popular culture.

As one might expect, many aspects of this work speak more specifically of the temporal and spatial structure of the Renaissance world. Yet it is precisely the historical distance between that world and ours that allows us to grasp our own position and to appreciate options for present architectural practice. The linear narrative of *Hypnerotomachia*, for example, ultimately refers to the grand narrative of an ontotheological history, syncretically reconciled with the cyclical time of cosmology and thus no longer to be taken for granted as a disclosure of our measure of time. As we know from contemporary film and literature, such a measure demands the collapse of cyclical and linear time to become the chronicle of a pause, a spatial narrative of one instant. Our dream voyage could not possibly be a liturgy of initiation between nature (the dark forest) and culture (love/architecture) but must rather be a trip in and through technology, the substance of our world. Today the dark forest is no longer a threatening and disorienting place; technology is its equivalent, representing precisely that which we cannot control yet also a place of potential meaning once we recognize its mysterious origin (depth, not trickery) and our ability to deconstruct its language in an operation of acceptance, twisting, and eventual healing.

The woodcut images of *Hypnerotomachia Poliphili* represent the loci of classical architecture visited by the hero. The text provides minute descriptions of the monuments, including the colors and textures of materials and iconography of these buildings, usually referring to the Roman goddesses Fortuna and Venus and furthering the propitiation of human destiny through love, harmony, and fertility. In this way the classical loci were intended to function as models for a superior fifteenth-century architecture. In addition Poliphilo is often fascinated by the enigmatic presence of hieroglyphs inscribed in buildings and fragments, the meaning of which is analogous to that of architecture. In the case of these discoveries, Poliphilo deciphers and renders the images in language yet seems to acknowledge that the ultimate meaning of such evocative figures must remain hidden. Thus he is prepared to accept the ambiguity of architectural meaning, one recognized as inhabiting the surface of the image yet resistant to clarification in language.

Despite the lessons derived from the fact that models carry ethical over and above aesthetic or formal values, and from Poliphilo's understanding of meaning as both present and ultimately unnamable, the relationship between text and image in *Hypnerotomachia* cannot simply be extrapolated to meet our own situation. Today the crisis of architectural representation demands that we no longer take for granted the reductive use of images in architecture. In our world of simulations it is irrelevant to consult *Progressive Architecture*. No forms of representation that lead the architect to make "pictures" of preconceived buildings are fruitful, regardless of the models' contents. A critical awareness of the cultural (and particularly scientistic) implications of conventional tools of representation as we use them is directly connected to our potential to create an architecture both more personal (and thus "original") and more eloquent in its social dimension, contributing to a richer world that can speak about the human condition and its mysteries (see, in this connection, my "Architectural Representation beyond Perspectivism," *Perspecta* 27 [1992]).

Because the Renaissance duality of architecture and nature has been obliterated by technology, it is possible for artists to transcend perspective representation through its own devices and thus reveal a mysterious new cinematographic depth in a technological architecture, supporting the hope that the dangerous enframing of which Heidegger speaks might be deconstructed. Perhaps one day soon it will become possible to collapse the difference between technological and aesthetic culture, and with it the difference between rationalism and irrationalism that has sustained and frustrated modernity since at least the early nineteenth century.

With regard to the dominant descriptive and explicitly directed nature of language in *Hypnerotomachia*, we may also wonder about the appropriate relationship between words and architecture in our own time, particularly in the wake of Jean-Jacques Lequeu, Arthur Rimbaud, surrealism, and, of course, James Joyce and the new literature. Rather than abandon the possibility of an architectural meaning of presence in despair of a deconstructive leveling off of equivalent significations and loss of originals, one that eventually leads to an architecture-as-writing (or cyberspace!), perhaps we could start by imagining that in this postmodern world, as in Poliphilo's Renaissance, a significant architecture (with very few exceptions) is yet to be built. Our orientation in examining possible models, however, must be ahistorical rather than look backward to the sources of a single authentic architecture and forward to "progress" as a dialectic of styles. Our search must cut across the old Renaissance categories of the fine arts and the now irrelevant distinctions (from the point of view of an articulation of meaning) between painting, sculpture, architecture, and film. It is an issue of values rather than aesthetics. The majority of large-scale building in the last two hundred years has been determined by the requirements of economics or technology or at best results from misguided formalism. This built world, regardless of its form, is articulated by the prosaic language of technology. In the gaps between metaphoric naming (poetic language) and the world of action, however, particularly in the realm of theoretical projects, we may be able to retrieve a meaningful silence capable of transcending the old duality of being and nonbeing and with it an immanent architectural meaning flowing from the work as we read it in the vivid present of our embodied experience.

Pondering *Hypnerotomachia* reveals how difficult it is for us to assume that, inhabiting as we do geometric time and a scientific geography, we may still arrive "somewhere." Once reality, and particularly the classical landscape as the site of architecture, is stripped of its specific mythological content, the classical loci manipulated by postmodern style architects as fashionable forms appear devoid of value. Yet we must ask if there still is a dream unaffected by modern Cartesian space that can possibly lead us "somewhere." Toward the place of our architecture? Today, in the homogeneous space of the modern, scientific world, we move efficiently yet go nowhere, and objects remain constant beings seemingly unaffected by the motion of becoming and the archaic notion of place. Nevertheless, most of us have had the experience of visiting works of architecture from the last two hundred years that fill us with wonder. What is the nature of these works? This architecture, more often than not, appears uncomfortable in the postindustrial world, oddly poetic like Le Corbusier's La Tourette, Sigurd Lewerentz's Klippan church, or Antonio Gaudí's Casa Batlló, or else it exists in the form of theoretical projects like Piranesi's Carceri or John Hejduk's Masques, works that regardless of medium or size address the basic (traditional) questions of symbolic order and thus implicitly question the possibility of their existence as mere simulacra or comfortably efficient buildings in the city. From the user/ spectator, these works (with their narrative programs) demand a self-transformation leading to a different relationship between embodied consciousness and the world, an attitude of devotion, re-creation, and release toward the works, distinct from the conventional modes of aesthetic or scientific contemplation (disinterested), or instrumental manipulation (willful), that have characterized Western culture to date.

We learn much from *Hypnerotomachia Poliphili* as soon as we reject any homogenizing reading and posit a perceptual faith, accepting that there is meaning, however weak, in the original. The essential intention to articulate a possible ethical position through a narrative that acknowledges important models for the practice of architecture is still valid. This is so particularly in view of the current philosophic understanding of truth—shared by Heidegger, Hans-Georg Gadamer, and Gianni Vattimo—as set into work by art, and of a diagnosis of the postmodern condition in which the only alternative to the strong Being of traditional religion

and science seems to be the weak truth that shines forth through recollection of historical works. Also important is the basic phenomenological lesson of *Hypnerotomachia* connecting architectural meaning to embodied experience through discourse rather than simply accepting meaning as an effect of exclusively mental or intellectual processes liable to be dismissed as a logical impossibility in the age of immanent reason.

Most philosophers in the continental tradition have long understood the futility of attempting to address ethical problems through a framework of categories, as if morality could be "weighed." This limitation is still not fully grasped in the practice of architecture or scholarship. The articulation of literary narratives beyond explanatory frameworks that have been exhausted in the context of the Western logocentric tradition seems to be our only alternative, particularly in accounting for a serious reading of Nietzsche's realization, from the absence of a transcendent framework of values, the death of God.

Alternatives to a denial of architecture as "presencing" meaning, inferred from the writings of Jacques Derrida, and to the reduction of architecture to simulation (Jean Baudrillard) have been put forward in hermeneutic ontology and phenomenology, particularly in the late writings of both Heidegger and Maurice Merleau-Ponty, in the works of Paul Ricoeur, and in recent interpretations within the same tradition by David Michael Levin, Vattimo, and Richard Kearney. While acknowledging the end of history in the sense of a single narrative secularized since the seventeenth century in the myth of scientific progress, and thus also the necessity to deconstruct the logocentric metaphysical tradition with its notion of abolute being and truth, Kearney and Levin support the distinction between Descartes's *ego cogito* and the embodied, imagining self. Accepting this controversial distinction, it becomes possible to put forward an alternative to both an escapist and ultimately nostalgic critique of technology (often offered by post-modern style architects) and to a noncritical embracing of simulation.

Heidegger offers three key notions when he asks us to be aware of the dangers of technology and its enframing but warns us that attempting a nostalgic escape into tradition poses an even greater danger. These strategies should qualify the architect's understanding of creativity and his or her relationship to technology as articulated in any new narratives. In the language of philosophy the suggested attitudes can be summarized as an openness to the mystery of the origins of technology, a release (*Gelassenheit*) from the things that make up our world, and a quest to deconstruct the language of science and technology (*Verwindung*). Heidegger uses *Verwindung* to name the need to "overcome" technology outside the dialectic linear history of progress. The term, according to Vattimo, calls for an overcoming but also for an acceptance, a healing and a twisting of the technological language that constitutes our very being. Heidegger's request for "letting things be," on the other hand, articulates a different relationship between embodied consciousness and the world, one that transcends the dualistic, instrumental formulations of being and the logocentric will-to-power found in Nietzsche and early Heidegger. *Gelassenheit* implies a self-transformation that recognizes, through phenomenology, the potential ground of meaning in the prereflective engagement of embodied consciousness in the world. It brings about perception as it could be, beyond the reduction of reality to a world picture (perspective).

Phenomenology has shown the importance of retrieving the body as the locus of meaning, deconstructing Descartes's objectified, mechanistic body and biology's organic body to posit instead a network of intentionality, the intertwining of self and world. Merleau-Ponty speaks of the flesh as an "element" (like the traditional fire, earth, air, and water): being as becoming but without the danger of nihilism or the absolute relativization of meaning, maintaining the density of consciousness as a vivid present outside the Christian-technological project of history with its future orientation and its obsession with actualizing utopia. The creative and political dimensions of architecture are unattainable without recognizing this radical ground of meaning, unnamable perhaps as it is always culturally differentiated in language and historically specific, yet a ground that must be acknowledged as intersubjective and transhistorical. Meaning is never given in architecture through democratic consensus or through rational or functional models. The individual imagination of the architect with its capacity to construe history as it might have been and imagine a possible future remains the only true alternative, one that must be implemented in the act of making.

In order to contemplate the potential architecture of the future as a *poiesis* that is not solipsistic, this self-transformation evoked by phenomenology is indispensable and leads to a recognition through personal experience of the body as the site of meaning, to which the work of art and architecture speak in the medium of the erotic. Erotic knowledge is never experienced by the mind alone. It always occurs in the world; it is of the flesh. It is knowledge of things by the individual body and is also a knowledge of beauty, which is the whole. Erotic knowledge is a paradigm of "truth as unveiling," the Heideggerian *aletheia*, as opposed to the objectifying "truth as correspondence" inherited from Plato by Western science and metaphysics. It is a disclosure of Being, one that is never given once and for all but speaks of the presence of lighting, of the horizon that makes "things" possible.

It is perhaps interesting to remember that Plato, in his characteristic liminal position in the history of philosophy, could himself be read as articulating this Heideggerian concept of truth (quite in opposition to his better-known articulation of truth, in the myth of the cave as a light that excludes all shadows) when he insists that *agathon* (the sun) makes truth visible but is never to be beheld directly: truth and goodness are therefore not objects of contemplation, as in science, but of experience . . . except perhaps at dawn, a time that may even today be the most propitious for the retrieval of poetic discourse . . . .

The strategies that we may derive for architecture from hermeneutic ontology and phenomenology thus seem to have been partially prefigured by *Hypnerotomachia Poliphili*. Indeed, an understanding of the architect's potential as a creative artist whose imagination is not reduced to the function of either romantic production ex nihilo, or classical reproduction of a transcendent order seems crucial today. This strategy is the most appropriate on which to found an ethical practice of architecture capable of avoiding both solipsism and nostalgia in a world where images, simulations that are merely reflections of reflections, have acquired the status of reality. In this context the realizations of phenomenology concerning our capacity to perceive differently become instruments to deconstruct the technological common ground without abandoning the possibility of speaking a shared language and making, eventually, a truly eloquent future architecture.

"You should know that Polyphilo dreamed about being in a threatening dark forest and narrates the myriad things he saw, a veritable strife for the manifold love of all, which is the meaning of his name in the title. With elegant style he tells of many postmodern marvels deserving of a place in the memory theater of the future, architectural monuments encountered in his search for Polya, his beloved."

His dream takes the form of a trip through scientific geography, one that occupies three paradigmatic spaces; the private space of the hero's bedroom, the public space of airports, and the space of the airplane, beyond a conventional categorization that now seems inoperative. These spaces are only modulations of the technological continuum, of a single quantitative universal entity, our "intersubjective" reality, at odds with the mythical landscape of places that constituted the ground of classical or traditional architecture. The technological trip par excellence, air travel, occurs as a revolution of the globe, the totality of our finite space, at approximately sixty degrees north latitude, during twenty-four hours of measured time. The technological trip is deconstructed through the paradigmatic human dream, the dream of flight, which underscores all architecture present and past still devoted to reconciling man, the vertical creature, with gravity. Polyphilo travels westward through the homogeneous space of our scientific universe; he is constantly in motion but arrives nowhere. He is always in the same place yet visits magical architectural objects pregnant with meaning, works that constantly question the assumption of a universal, geometric space as the place of human existence. His time is therefore always the present, catching up with the time of his departure, the simultaneity of simulacra, yet it is always sunrise, a privileged time of day that propitiates the fictional articulation of human temporality and that may allow for a return of mythopoetic narratives, even at the end of history.

The modern dream of Polyphilo is a dream of flight, with its vertical motion, one still capable of going somewhere. This motion of the poetic imagination allows the modern hero to "inhabit" the diverse works and "deobjectify" them, extracting a philosophical and ethical lesson for the architect of the future.

Alberto Pérez-Gómez

Suddenly, I found myself submerged in a vague and incomprehensible penumbra . . .

A frightening discovery! It was warm. From somewhere around me there emerged a dim, turquoise light. Something perhaps existed out of the reach of my sight, something thoroughly different and challenging to be found beyond the limits of my prison, on the other side of the primordial egg.

For the first time I experienced curiosity, but coupled with an immense fear of the unknown. After all, my previous state in non-being seemed perfect and I had no unsatisfied needs.

But on that occasion my will did not matter. An infinite and inexplicable impulse made my body shake and tremble. Amidst violent convulsions I had to stretch, possessed by energetic movements that were always beyond my control.

My muscles became tense. The power of the force acting upon my body was so great that I lost all sensation. I forced my eyes to close. Over my narrow horizon a violent storm was raging. A resplendent flash of light pierced my body and imprinted in my heart the fullest range of colour. A continuous clamor took hold of me, followed by a deafening, sharp crash.

The intense flavour of fresh air. Pleasure. And pain. And my day had dawned.

Entry from Frances Coco Lonna's personal diary, Lerwick, Shetland Islands, 21 December 1944

AFTER A LONG, dark night arrives the moment we have been waiting for, the moment when our familiar old luminary hesitates between life and death, almost imperceptibly, corroding with its orange breath our mathematical certainties about the future and our false historical values. The golden warmth thaws our logical prisons and loosens our grip on the numerical conception of time. Twenty-four milliseconds become a lifetime. And our body remembers with excruciating clarity its almost forgotten and most ancient impulses, all that we have lost or have willingly given up. The final moment that is the awaited hour of the day! The appointed time beyond history! At least once . . . Perhaps only once.

My room is empty. It has been like this for at least two hundred years. We all now wait alone. Yet this glaring void still laments a loss, an undefinable loss that can no longer be cast in the fashion of a classical tragedy. For it is evidently our radical solitude that makes it possible to dream, to compose poems about absence in the presence of life, to attempt writing in the present a chronicle of the gap.

I must transcribe the epiphany of this elusive time of day when one can stare the solar disk directly in the face, when the spawning luminary stands suspended at our height, two finger widths above the horizon: a lapse at the edge of dreams, lasting an eternal instant . . .

The unending centuries of our nightmarish insomnia have suddenly vanished. The mechanical ticking has stopped. We now confront the space within a pause, the span of an interval for universal transference. This is the propitious time for all human creation, when we become united with the golden nucleus of coruscation that both implacably consumes our life and jettisons existence toward infinity.

The order is clear on the map, at sixty degrees north latitude, revealed on the walls of the room that dissolve into a web of lines. Like the electronic footprints of missile trajectories, these tracings seem to suggest an opening toward infinite nothingness, in sets of overlapping and successive projections.

A warm morning brume envelops my naked body. The window frames a uniform flat blue, indicating that winter has arrived. Anise and silver and the smell of dust, aged between the covers of my books. *Is this all that endures? A hollow groin or a sharp groin between two shallow vaults.* Wandering through the million pages that I am, I sink into the softness of the pillow, inhabiting the interval between dream and reverie, while a void in my entrails reflects my beloved's absence, the imminent doom brought about by the absence of knowledge and a proliferation of electromagnetic impulses.

The unveiled young woman that used to cast the greatest shadow or the greatest light on our dreams has less substance than a ghost, barely a translucent and faint mnemonic projection. The breasts of the moon, the anise of our breath and the flower of her thighs can only be possessed as indistinct magnetic impressions. *I fear that authentic wisdom, the enlightenment that results from the generative union in procreation, may no longer be attainable. In the democratic, genderless universe of genetic simulation and electronic space, sexual love appears as a hedonistic, inconsequential, and absolutely finite consumption of energy. The inveterate purity and incorruptibility of sex at its source, the faculty to reproduce our own image, has not endured as a simple reality. Gone forever are the times when one's instinct for sexual pleasure remained virginal even when one's sex was not intact. Forever?*

Within the sombre spiraling structures of my mind, the logic that mimics genetic molecular systems gives way to the pounding seven syllables of a Spanish verse, a rhythm of sadness and despair. The flat blue sky liquifies and pours into my body, ravishing the orthogonal connections of an incapacitated intellect. The moon shines no longer, yet the orange particles that were once scintillating filaments over the soft skin vibrate with intensity. *Caught between the awareness of my personal mortality and the realization of cultural apocalypse, I am overwhelmed by a dazzling sensation of warmth, frenzied by an obsessive longing.*

FALLING INTO A DEEPER slumber . . . A flow of sleep and linen obliterates the limits between body and world. *I love this linen that stretches and rumples, coming down on me like sand when I play dead, enfolding me in sleep.* The construction materials of our dwelling place are the physical incarnations of love: earth and milk, excreta and semen, children and angels. There is a demolished house in the palimpsest of the only remaining wall of my room: fragments of loosely attached wallpaper, the rust-stained furrow of the toilet drain, layers of peeling paint like annular time rings in the trunks of trees, black and smudgy outlets for the distribution of gases and liquids, ugly stains of sweat, stale breath, urine and the sultriness from the bed of a lover.

Yet I yearn for more. For places that might be thoroughly inhabited and populated with imagery and desire, unlike the obsolete constructions that occupy the inhospitable grid of our city at the moment of awakening. An anguished realization of universal homelessness! My wistful disposition has received no satisfaction from the romantic nostalgia of historical sites or from the mute, unyielding structures product of economic, political, and technocratic necessity. Our mortal children must soon populate the third millennium, beyond tyranny and anarchy.

The pounding rhythm again distorts the fragile logic of thought. *The measured passage of time!* I fall further into deep sleep, and as I fall I keep myself from falling.

There are many diverse kinds of sleep, manifold dimensions of dreams and modalities of unconsciousness. If the body fell asleep completely and suddenly every night, dropping into the same total unconscious state, we would have to undergo the

4

experience of death constantly. The limbs, the organs and the multiple systems of our body, in fact, sleep in diverse thresholds at different times. This accounts for the diversity of our dreams and for their ability to reveal a perfectly coherent reality.

Indeed, I have in my possession a magical idol, an icon that will protect me, a veritable personal key to unravel the disorder of the world. This chart, like that on the wall, is presumably a mapping of the city, the region, or the universe, and it is so deeply engraved inside me that I cannot ever lose it. The key, which also keeps the appropriate time, shall on every occasion enable me to escape from danger. *The path, however, is long and painful to follow, and it may suddenly end at the sea.* As I run, my body becomes lighter, my legs expand, and, unexpectedly, I fly. All the muscles of my body transform into immensely responsive steering instruments.

The city appears strangely familiar from above, extending all around me to the circular limit of the skyline. I traverse wide streets and perspective boulevards planted with trees. *One has to be very careful to avoid becoming entangled in the branches of large oaks, but today my control is impeccable.* I direct my flight sensing the distance between my palms and the ground, experienced through the tension of my stomach muscles. My mass is a dynamic force distended along the vertical and horizontal axes, literally pouring out from my solar plexus and my fontanel, piercing and demolishing the wind at the front of my head. *On other occasions I have floated and drifted haphazardly, but not today.* Freed from the determinism of gravity I can break loose, flying close to the earth without fear and saving all obstacles, forever escaping from the burden of desire until the end of time.

I know my native city very well. A mere insinuation or wish should take me to any destination, but as I enter a roundabout my speed becomes disconcerting. I turn into a dead-end street and feel doomed by my mistake. *My pursuers will now surely catch up with me.* I descend, landing over a structure with large concrete overhanging roofs that look like the sheds of a transportation terminal. On the inside, the building is even more disorienting. The ceilings are very low and the external walls are glass plates. A dark shadow looms, severing a cable, and an alarm rings. I exit back onto a terrace where, surprisingly, I come face to face with the sea, crashing at the bottom of a cliff. *Extremely dizzy, scared, and delirious, I don't know what to do with the inexhaustible power that so poignantly discloses the present enigma, which evidently is the Truth. I am trapped, with nowhere to go; overtaken by a frustrating recollection of the pale experiences in our world of everyday life, dull by contrast with the intimate boundlessness of flight. Yet an omnipresent anguish stops me from flying over the sea! A confident and forceful projection into the horizon is in all likelihood the only true option, but my will is not strong enough.* I glance at the map and make my way back to the city, where I expect to be absolutely secure and in charge of my compulsion . . . The dream takes hold more and more profoundly, lasting the duration of crepuscular time.

5

I NOW WALK firmly bound to the earth. *The sun is bright, but an intense gloom, my own regret or perhaps a somber expectation, unveils a premonition of the sharp shadow of a tower projected on an ensanguined pavement.* Shining with metaphysical radiance, the city resonates harmoniously. Every stone is an offering to transcend human mortality. This is no longer the city of my childhood, but it could certainly be the original abode of humanity. My heart begs to sing in praise of a vision of hope.

The old capital, founded upon fratricidal blood like Sodom or Rome, is ostensibly an arena of joy and fulfillment. A shimmering sunlight that envelops and inebriates the scene bursts into a thousand sparks following the motions of birds on the liquid fractures of ashlar fountains and on the gleaming surfaces of classical ornament and sculptures. This city is criss-crossed by a complex web of hollow alleyways. Tight humid spaces are intercepted by innumerable bridges and flying buttresses that act like a shroud of lacework, woven by masons to stop souls from too easily escaping into the light blue sky. Stone and brick, ascending and descending paths. Sweet air. White and green marble and earthy masonry: texture of ice in death and suppleness of skin in love.

Strolling along the alleyways, the order of the city is manifested as potentially mystic and erotic. Invisible murmurs speak of divine revelation and evil threats, proclaiming a litany of inveterate cosmological dualities. The streets appear strangely abandoned. This is unquestionably a genuine city of the past, but filled with the color and brilliance of the present, simultaneously dead and ethereal. Green and grey windows suggest syncopated rhythms; vibrant, yellow-pink foliage hangs from the balconies amidst bright discordant tapestries clothing an ancient medieval ritual, or intimate cotton and lace garments, soiled by blood, seek solar purification.

Under our feet the city of stone transmutes into pure music. The tempo of a promenade trailing the irregular topography of the streets is the exhilarating beat of rapturous touch and essential expectation. Limbs and senses engage in an enduring embrace with every detail and every corner, culminating in a dramatic public space of pubic configuration.

The plan of the square may be that of the Virgin's cape or perhaps, more plainly, the *V* of the Virgin with the vanishing point on top but not at the horizon. The buildings surrounding the square are of regular height with deep, mysterious arcades and small, shadowy Gothic windows clustered in groups of three. On the sloping clay tile pavement, triangular sectors are defined by dotted lines of weathered gray stone that meet at the point, vanishing, under the smokestacks.

In the square the abode of the past is revealed as a magical apparition, empty but eternal. An eloquent testimonial to the order that can be gleaned in the history of man, the sediment of honest religiosity. Here stands the majestic tower I suspected since my arrival at the gate, deploying its unique and explicit anthropomorphic verticality. No other tower can be seen in this city, where man is obviously bound to the earth.

The voice of the solitary tower is conspicuously silent. *Its conical instrument cast of metal and fire has probably been long moved to a museum, demonstrating a lamentable ignorance of the efficacy of bells as a liberating vehicle of flight.* The piercing harmonic percussion that had granted man access to the ethereal regions of the heavens is now seemingly denied to him.

In the hope of quenching my increasing thirst I approach an indefinite flat trapezoidal object, toward which points the free hand of the statue at the center of the square. There was once a source of water between the shadow and the paving, but it is now frozen. The bright, reflective aquatic crystals fit together in harmonic correspondence, creating a family of lines, angles, and projections of original complexity and unfathomable depth; certainly beautiful to behold but quiescent and tasteless. My thirst obviously prevails.

Around the sides of the central monument a sequence of bas-reliefs depicts a ritual that might possibly take place on the urban stage. A group of young men and women is represented holding hands and dancing in a circle, participating in some sort of collective celebration. *Perhaps it is the commemoration of some special day, or simply a festive gathering under the sun, of a party of discolored northerners escaping from the perpetual darkness of winter.* It is possible to imagine the repetitive and obsessive beat of hand clapping and bongos that prepares the participants for the sacrifice. Treading upon the red paving stones of the urban stage, men and women move their bodies sensually. All are clad in tight, worn-out blue jeans plainly revealing thin, beautifully tanned male torsos and erect female nipples under colorful elastic blouses. They leap gracefully to staggering heights and, when I examine the relief very carefully, some of them can actually be seen to fly.

On the next panel nine girls chosen from the group are seen in distinct, carefully choreographed positions, adopting innumerable gestures. They appear to dance around the low masonry posts that mark the perimeter of the square, corresponding to each of the nine sectors of the fan-shaped pavement.

In the final bas-relief, the nine beautiful adolescents sit naked on the meticulous curve formed for this purpose along the confines of the square. Their hands appear to be tied behind the posts while their thighs are held within heavy bronze rings, forcing their legs open, hard and tense. Their delicate features, shaded by their placidly closed eyes and mysterious smiles, contrast with the brutal metal paws that grasp the rings, emerging from flaming volutes embedded firmly in the floor.

Under the enigmatic bas-reliefs, a few cryptic etymological elucidations serve as clues to decipher and reconstruct the ritual. On five separate tablets are given alternative, opposite, and complementary meanings of words that reveal the ambiguous ground of existence.

7

DWELL,
to inhabit, to continue in existence after others are taken or
removed;
to be stunned or laid astray;
to raise amid clouds.

SACRIFICE,
that which is offered to deity as an act of propitiation or
homage;
that which allows man to dwell;
that which is simultaneously sacred and polluted.

TEMPLE,
the altar of the sacrifice, itself a perpetual offering;
a place for contemplation;
synonymous with architecture, the stylobate or pedestal of the
statue.

NUMEN,
from nuo, to make a sign, like the architecture of the temple;
sacred revelation;
divine will.

DIVINATION,
the priestly revelation of divine will;
muse, or the science of the poet;
the task of man.

ON THE FOURTH SIDE of the monument, one last panel contains a poem that can only be rendered in free verse from the original Italian:

Clouds of calcareous crystal,
dreams of smelted rock.
The dark desert extends to the horizon.
Damsel of gauze and porcelain,
sweet wine of palpitating pubis.
The luminous ocean overflows beyond her lips,
Waiting.

AS I LIFT my eyes from the inscriptions and face the flattened perspective, the oracular presence of the empty space becomes still more vibrant. In every resplendent particle of air we can sense the existence of the horrible. We breathe it in with the greatest gift, which is transparent but hardens and crystallizes inside our bodies, precipitating and taking on sharp geometric forms, like pointed irregular stars cramming the gaps between our organs. *There is always a new virus, natural or manmade, reprojecting the origin of life. More deadly and terrifying than all of the operating theaters, torture chambers and madhouses!* The lingering cry of the sacrificial victims now fills the space. Thousands of people of all nationalities sing and drink. They may be partaking of the event in a renewed openness to being, or perhaps on the contrary desecrating time by their loss of memory and drifting forever into nothingness.

Their perfectly triangular pubes are facing the erect tower, in line with the inlaid radii that meet at the point of infinity in a nonperspective world, at the source of sensual delight from which the rays of the Virgin's halo had also emerged. A red cloud that could be the sublimated blood of the sacrifice rolls along the converging lines and congeals as a subtle vermilion fluid at the focus of the square. At that point, where the celestial makes contact with the subterranean and infinite pleasure embraces absolute death, from that fissure rises the tower. But the tower is now circular and stands even more still than before. I turn my gaze upward, trusting to find the initial of the Virgin drawn by the needles of the clock. The tower is in fact a chimney. *Perhaps a crematorium.* The flue, which would normally be invisible to perspective, can be seen as a black hole filled with a dark red billowy smoke, the gore of the sunset staining the sky once the silken belly of the deity was ripped open. *The day-ity?*

Ignoring other mysterious objects in the square such as containers loaded with broken classical figures and shattered stained glass, I follow a dotted line that takes me to the plinth of the statue. The pedestal has the proportions of a bed, the dimensions of a coffin. On one rectangular face a bas-relief represents a translucent flattened inverted pyramid of brick, stone, or flesh. The horizontal upper side of the triangle seems to contain and become a crimson flower in bloom. Its pointed petals extend the diverging edges of the pyramid. One palm length to the right, there is a representation of a fine crystal wine glass. Its curved sweeping lines, like those of tulip, contain an opaque red liquid, presumably a claret.

On the other side of the pedestal a lock of auburn hair barely touches the pink aureole of the reflection of a low, veiled sun. Under the emblem a concise inscription reads: "If I could succeed in bringing the occiput to the pubis." What is likely to be the source of the strange hieroglyph is disclosed at the lower right-hand corner: "Med. Jrn. IV, 164, 1800."

I walk slowly around the monumental podium, discovering multiple coincidences and reciprocities among the many words and images in this charmed circle. *This spiraling repetition of events must be an insinuation to unravel a mystery. I am desperate and immensely thirsty. An obsessive idea: the plinth must conceal a place of love. It is perhaps feasible to penetrate the solid architecture and populate it with tropes, finding fulfillment at the center of the traditional city. The heart and kernel should naturally constitute the location for human dwelling.* A few verses inscribed on the lower right-hand corner of the pedestal's north face even speak of astronomers making poetry, of music and loving care, of the enigma of clocks, flags, and shadows.

The dense, diaphanous parallelepiped doesn't yield to my yearning, however. The unfamiliar presence of reality and the luminosity of objects have obviously prevailed, making the thought of living in this city a seductive possibility. Sweet odors of decay, multiple footprints and overlays transform it into a veritable palimpsest of the past, projecting an illusion of safety. *A terrible delusion!*

The platform keeps on reflecting my own figure, hermetic to formal manipulation and ubiquitously revolving upon itself and in my mind. Instead of shattering into particles of cosmos, it denies access to the fruit that has been promised at its center. *The navel is a perspicuous concept whose privileged spatial qualities are easy enough to understand but that appears to be utterly unreachable when sought within this traditional city with its classical monuments.*

Suddenly, but not surprisingly, the sharply delineated shadow of the statue becomes manifest and pervasive. *In all probability, the effigy is a doctor honored for the supreme discovery in the field of biotechnology.* Previously full of sunshine, the square is transformed into an ominously overcast precinct. The outline of the shadow of man takes over the city, a permanent shadow that sinks heavily into all the materials it touches. His indelible mark impregnates and corrodes every atom of matter, making the orifices of buildings seem faded by comparison.

On the surface of the pedestal is now an image of my beloved Polya, for whom my heart has been longing. The firm contours of her body appear distorted. The immense and amorphous right leg, pressed against the glaze of the plane, seems to lose its rigidity. Her head and left elbow are cast upward, while the left leg, slightly apart, accentuates the inviting hard line of the pelvic bone. Burning with desire, my mouth touches the icy parallelepiped and senses an elastic vortex of insubstantial crystal projecting itself from her navel and surrounding me. Captured by the reflection on the surface, my vision continues for an instant, but my body is numb. The flesh is prevented from contact by the enveloping void. All my senses, except for vision, have been suspended and frozen in a different time.

In love with Polya's waist and impeccably white buttocks, I intensely desire to strike her flank rhythmically. Her clearly delineated vagina appears with utter objectivity, as if rendered with the purest black line on a luminous surface, inviting a digital penetration performed with the care and precision of a surgical intervention. *I can discern in my mind every shift of direction of my middle finger, every position, and the progress of the operation as a function of mathematical time and quantifiable pleasure. It is as if I were watching through a gridded magnifying glass in slow motion. Is this frustrating spectacle, a purely optical knowledge of thresholds, the model of any future wisdom?*

The metaphysical clarity finally deteriorates into a blinding fragmentation of curvilinear virginal flesh, signaling the last second of the first hour of unfulfilled desire. *A very short hour. The reflections bear in on me and make me lose track of myself. I must have sat on a bed in a mirror . . .* I turn, spin around, and collapse on the bed. Within my dream I fall asleep and dream another dream. A drop of sweat runs down between my ribs, marking the passing of the first meridian on the map.

THE GLAZED REFLECTION now includes the rising sun and myself and, behind the monumental vaporized double pane of glass, the airplanes, sailboats, and distant office towers of the city. *Although I have become part of this reality without apparent difficulty, a great sense of loss weighs heavily on my spirit. Mathematically it is easy to explain what has happened as the leakage and collapse of one dimension. But it seems impossible to substantiate this suspicion through empirical demonstration.* On my lap a book of Spanish poetry lies open. Perhaps not surprisingly, the poem measures time, evoking in verses of seven syllables the obsolete city of our past. It is entitled "Reflections":

> The night has been demolished.
> Behind the window,
> a fiery darkness
> of timeless microliths:
> castrated bells.
>
> Clappers resounding
> a litany of hours
> while the maiden sleeps.
>
> In the old, vacant city
> the stone will never bloom.
> Only the tower stands.
>
> Erect, but never touching
> hands that don't hold,
> coarse silk stained
> by the bleeding of dreams.
>
> The iris of the night
> does not witness the night.
>
> The body as white as snow,
> is soft no longer, cold;
> the mouth of amber, cold.
>
> The night has been demolished,
> but the desert prevails.

2:35:32 I have been sweating profusely, probably long before entering this comfortable maze of polished steel and glass, littered with padded ergonomic furniture. The universal neon light eliminates all impermanent shadows and with them all trace of time, increasing the disorienting quality of this space. The people sitting around me appear to wait. They are expressionless and void, utterly consumed by the glare that pervades the terminal building. My fellow transients, of the most diverse ethnic origins and nationalities, become homogenized facing the large television screen in one corner or disappear behind their newspapers. *Innumerable facsimiles of the same newspaper!* Meaningless manifold scripts under one identical universal image of a smoking mushroom.

2:35:33 I must have been sleeping for many hours. My limbs are in desperate need of some exercise and I decide to walk. *Around, as usual.* On the other side of the wide, carpeted ambulatory are a number of undifferentiated doors, presumably leading to toilets, security offices, bars, and more plush waiting rooms for executive and first-class passengers. The impeccable structure could be anywhere in the world. *Its location must be along the sixty degrees north parallel though, according to my geometric apparatus.* It is, in fact, nowhere: at the absolutely precise place determined by the statistical analysis of air traffic flow. *A location chosen at random, like our personal birth from the primordial chiasm?*

2:35:34 The perfectly adequate air-conditioned environment services the body and creates myriad delusions for the mind. A grid of corridors is marked with clearly legible, color-coded signs. Rational and normalized patterns link up aspects of life that have always found their appropriate places in the traditional city, establishing relationships adequate to their inherent tensions and meanings. The complex orthogonal network assigns homogeneous coordinates to disparate groups of shops, some exclusive and others that seem to reappear at every turn, administrative offices for private enterprise and government agencies, restaurants, a luxury hotel, an interdenominational chapel, and a morgue behind a curtain. The circulation system thus hides all that might be irrational or controversial. A numbing effect results from the exact fit between the building and human life as a purely material, serviceable process. Booths promoting star wars, declaring that Jesus saves, and endorsing nuclear energy and the simultaneous termination of Jane Fonda may be the sole plainly visible points of articulation where the contradictory side of reality infiltrates the terminal.

2:35:35 Resembling a powerful drug, the system qua building is manifestly capable of neutralizing erotic and criminal impulses, allowing only the material debris of sexuality, robbery, and murder to exist. *The time and place of humanity are definitely dislocated by this structure that obliterates the inveterate spatiality and temporality of the body. Here there must be no discernible change or decay between birth and death but rather an electronic time that is neither linear nor cyclical.* There is also no apparent differentiation among the sectors of the structure evidently occupying the front, back, and sides of my body. All points are located in a mute, absolute geometric space, neatly and cleverly subdivided by a superior planning program of prodigious organizational power. The environment provides information in the form of digital signs and recorded signals speaking directly to the mind. The bodily senses are still suspended: smell, touch, and sight are not addressed, except as receptors of codified data.

2:35:36 Over my head a set of multiple blinking monitors immediately engages my attention. They evidence an impeccable logical control over the complex network of speeding vehicles. Even delays and cancellations are displayed on the screens as premeditated acts, causing no discomfort. Elsewhere the metallic glitter of insignia on the uniforms of the service personnel adds significantly to the overwhelming glare. Their luminous aura appears curiously appropriate to the shining aircraft and communications equipment with which these men and women interface in order to construe ubiquitous universal space. Also notable are the intense, impossible colors of many glossy images advertising comic destinations where the contemporary traveler might become immortal.

2:35:37 I wander aimlessly, like the hundreds of people whose paths we cross, without looking or sharing. Objectively, each individual operates with the expediency and precision of one who knows exactly the purpose of his actions. All motions, however, are oblivious to the profound meaning of gesture and devoid of compassion. In this troublesome enclosure, the sun glowing brightly and the feeling of a restless heart facing the enigma of love are barely possible memories. Interrogating sporadic mechanical gazes, identical in men and women and all cast upon a horizon hidden away by perspective, I obtain frightfully redundant answers: loneliness, a silent cry, corroding marrow, impenetrability of visceral space, frustrated passion, and eternal death. *Not even a slight acknowledgment of the possibility of metempsychosis!*

2:35:38 A significant area in the center of the ample hall, marked by a lowered ceiling, is crowded with pinball machines and video games. The characteristic noise of the particle beam weapons reverberates throughout the glass and steel structure and covers all other sounds. A perpetual war is being waged against enemy spaceships, bringing about the unimaginable destruction of multiple planets and universes. On each corner of this central cluster are cubicles of clear plexiglass rented out for propaganda purposes to technocratic organizations that gamble on the future of the world. On one of the cabinets, whose entrance is framed by two cylinders of plastic pink marble and a broken pediment, is a small blue cardboard sign over the counter. The notice, written in an ornamented postmodern script, reads:

15

Travel Insurance

Loss of a limb, eye, or tooth	**$100,000**
Loss of two limbs	**$1,000,000**
Loss of life	**$10,000,000**

2:35:39 A man dressed in black is selling a sharp metallic object to a client. The merchant is patently a self-made man. His neoconservative bowler hat and tie betray his exemplary stable personality and faith in the system. He had taken the instrument out of a display case under the ominous sign. The transparent case, whose proportions recall those of a pedestal, contains numerous similar elongated and spherical souvenirs that explode in symphonies of opalescent fulgurations. The knife is accompanied by a certificate of authenticity that, according to the merchant, guarantees its Japanese origin. The bright light over the booth illuminates an inscription embedded in the certificate like a watermark. The single sentence reads:

The most wonderful thing about life is its uncertainty.

2:35:40 Faced with this sudden revelation of oracular insecurity, the traveler must fully accept the tragicomic truth of his status. Indeed, in my right hand I hold a small suitcase made of opaque artificial leather, dark in color and completely unoriginal in design. *In the past many bulky trunks full of crucial valuables were left behind. A recurring nightmare: the vehicle would always stop with ill-fated consequences. Searching for the lost valise, the driver (or the captain) would lose his life. I would then painfully continue on my own, running uphill, to find only a smaller bag with an empty banana peel on top . . .*

2:35:41 *It is now crucial to care exclusively for indispensable things, all packed in my important piece of luggage whose measurements strictly comply with the specifications for carry-on baggage.* My little case hopefully comprises a personal order of salvation, perhaps the secret of the lost dimension. In any event, it is all that one can hold at once without letting it fall out of perception, and this might prove to be crucial for the success of my quest. The uncertain contents: the intrinsic collection of things that is our reality at hand, not a simulated surrogate of electronically produced stimuli. *Happily modern man, although uprooted and condemned to perpetual exile, is empowered to carry his home around, with him and in him, rejecting the fallacies of necessary consumption. The reported sightings of box men in Japanese airports and bus terminals are on the increase . . .*

2:35:42 On the other side the anarchist's image is reflected in the mirror behind the counter of the souvenir shop. His undertaking to deconstruct dead institutional frameworks turns into a substantial personal threat in a world kept permanently at peace by the balance between nuclear super-powers. The stranger might, indeed, place a translucent sphere filled with plastic explosives in my unattended suitcase. *This cumbersome terrorist menace places added demands on our constant vigilance and responsible character. There may be no other way to obliterate the hostile world of the present that I also abhor. Traveling naked is not yet feasible.*

2:35:43 My suitcase, with its particular collection of personal memories, would likely develop into a profoundly touching work of art at a propitious moment upon reaching a certain destination, but it could also simply vanish with the cosmos, destroyed by the threatening nihilism of the same personal will. *The order of the real: a radical recreation of the ground or a forcible destruction of obsolete institutions. Are there other plausible alternatives or a more appropriate place for the implementation of either viable future than the regimented and homo-geneous space of air travel? This consummate fragment of utopia is evidently open to the expectations of universal brotherhood and also to instant international de-stabilization. Given the present circumstances of society and ecumenic culture, either alternative might be suitable if not equally felicitous. Fate alone will decide. But in this crotch of consciousness I also recollect the words of a wise ancient Greek who said "Character is fate." Treading along the borderline, full of hope we must proceed.*

2:35:44 A large advertisement in the form of a giant, back-lit transparency entices with blissful promises travelers willing to enter the cafeteria. It depicts an oversized glass of milk and a young girl covered in silvery lace holding a cello. She smiles and leans slightly toward the instrument, stand-ing on a field of grass that surely has been spray-painted chlorophyll green. *A tame unicorn may not be far behind her, at the very center of the oasis. I remember my thirst, but my body has forgotten the sensation of dryness. T-h-i-r-s-t has been reduced to the substance of its six dot-matrix letters, a perfectly understandable and typical concept.*

2:35:45 Prey of an increasing anguish, I long to discover a way out of this dark forest. In search of the exit, I continue walking through endless anon-ymous corridors, aisles, and gates that indicate entrances to numerous cities and regions of the world. Identical screens over each gate exhibit names from the table of contents of an atlas. The names have been positioned at random or possibly through a complex, indiscernible ordering pattern. Often a flickering light signifies an invitation to pass through the marked door, ostensibly offering the possibility of abandoning this utopia and actually arriving in some other place.

17

2:35:46 I intersect the airport's land transportation concourse, where no food or drink are permitted, and finally, after listening carefully to the half-intelligible recorded instructions, follow a metallic echo to gate 27, the last possible exit to the west.

2:35:47 The gate is shadowy and half-hidden at this hour of the day but otherwise identical to the rest. I sit and wait. After an indefinite lapse of time the morning mist finally lifts: a hazy film is removed from my eyes. The hackneyed nature of this space is indeed its first recognizable quality. *A space where I have never been before.* Standard window details, curved plastic moldings, brushed-metal streamlined fixtures and cylindrical air-conditioning vents contribute nothing to the definition of this uncertain place. *The same bothersome glare? Not merely incoming light: radiation. An intense psychological malaise, due perhaps to a lack of effective personal control over my thoughts and actions, is now utterly explicit.* We are back in the space of perennial waiting, the paradigmatic abode of the traveler. *After so much struggle there seems to be no other intersubjective space as we come to the end of the millennium. No place for dwelling?* In the reflection on the large pane of glass, in front of the aircraft and the distant office towers, the two-dimensional grid materializes as the exclusive preexisting framework in which to conceive of our well-serviced bodies and their technological support systems.

2:35:48 My soft chair is provided with a personal TV monitor showing a continuous tape of suggestive scenes and impressive men and women in a display of normative heroic accomplishments. In staccato succession: an electronic rainbow with colors never seen under the sun, a computer-generated fusiform structure flying through two goal posts and over a network of numbered lines on a green field, punctuated by the effigies of supermen with very thick necks . . . the noise of sirens, crashing cars, and falling bodies; splinters of glass exploding in slow motion, a manicured hand shooting a bare-chested man, and a red, viscous liquid spouting violently over impeccable and perfectly ironed clothes . . . very long, tanned exercising legs, shapely wet orifices, and sensuous smiles; overdeveloped male torsos and muscular arms, sweating bodies longing for liquid fulfillment, drunk or injected, lust framed by scanty pastel underwear or brightly colored swimsuits . . . a cry for universal repentance and admonitions of a forthcoming apocalypse, an old woman sewing the crotch of a torn white lace intimate garment, part of a soiled wedding dress lying beside her, kneeling men and women, manicured hands raised overhead containing the invisible power framed by the camera, healing grinning prostitutes with false eyelashes and other paid participants, panoramic views of the Artificial Paradise resort from the Helicopter of God . . . These and other similar clips are interrupted by insistent advertisements enticing the passenger to invest money and commit his or her very being in one of these voyeuristic delights. *There is no choice between simulations of power, eroticism, and mysticism. All pornography. The delusion of presence and involvement match in my memory the distillation of modern man's experience of the city, regardless of its geographic coordinates. Are the only actual possibilities for love masturbation or abstinence?*

2:35:49 A sharp spasm under the cerebellum seems to sever my head. The absolute brightness and total transparency of the environment again reveals the order of imminent doom. *A dialectic of such clarity is utterly unbearable. Gasping for air, I realize that I am breathing millions of nitrogen, oxygen, and rare gas molecules: the same fear of lethal crystallization that I have recently experienced in the vacant square!*

2:35:50 A glance at my suitcase allows me to recover my composure. In a haze I walk across the aisle to reach the water fountain. I press the metal button and drench my mouth with an indescribable liquid, a solvent that starts to wash away the six letters imprinted on the inside of my forehead. The substance is clear and sparkling, but it seems to rise rather than drop into my stomach.

2:35:51 *Evidently the source of fresh water is unattainable. Most likely, the wanderer in the forest, full of anguish and thirst, would fail when seeking to appease his tormented heart. Guided by the harmonious sound of trickling water, he would reach for the blue crystal of reflected moonshine, only to discover in the mirror a pitch black sky, studded with undrinkable stars. This must be the tragic and unavoidable reality of the modern forest in which we are lost, indeed, not unlike the old city where all baptisteries, fonts, and piscinas were either dry or nonfunctional . . .*

2:35:52 A guttural, electronic voice abruptly interrupts all reflections suspended outside of dreamspace. *The nymph Echo herself.* It's the time of departure. The flight out of gate 27 is now boarding. *A threshold at last. A potential transgression and disclosure. This is the exit that we have been seeking!* Recovering some of my lost drive, I manage to suppress my thirst and avoid falling further into the abyss. Suitcase in hand, I cross the corridor and plunge decidedly into the expanded retractable tube, which hopefully will fail to extend the space of terminal ubiquity.

2:35:53 *Unfortunately all fears are founded.* The airway, indeed, is not a placenta, and the disheartening revelation of an infinite threshold leading nowhere becomes distressingly explicit as soon as we leave the boarding bridge behind and the bellows deflates. With a pneumatic sigh rises the tide of latent despair. I am imprisoned within a tight cylindrical enclosure of character analogous to the terminal, striking indeed for its unfettered potential mobility in time and space but extremely restrictive for real bodily motions. *The uninhabitable interiority of a line, the entrails of infinity.* I slowly make my way toward a seat. *Surely the deplorable absence of love is manifested in the persistent modern tragedy of unfulfilled thresholds, in the interminable time of departure. This must be the actual subject matter of the dream, a chronicle of a delay!*

19

2:35:54   I choose a location by the window, near the wings. In my ears
I sense the sharp, muted groan of the life breath as the door is locked and
the ancestral time and place are excluded from the cabin. The pressure is
adjusted, and electronic bells signal the imminent liberation of the horizon.

After storing my small case where it can be reached, I fasten my seat belt
and examine the publication in the pocket of the seat in front of me. The
middle pages are devoted to a map with the North Pole as a geometric
center. The whole globe is thus unfolded into a circular spider web with
the twenty-four meridians distinctly shown. This map is probably very
useful for plotting aeronautical routes following great circle courses. It has
the advantage of allowing one to directly measure distances from the North
Pole along the meridians. Employing a special scale of infinitely variable
curvature, it is also possible to use the chart to calculate accurate flight
times with reference to the grid of circular parallels. *The spherical surveying
instrument seems surprisingly familiar: a tracing of my wall, the charted route
deeply imprinted, the multifarious key that I possess.*

This device is one among many other useless experimental gadgets that
are advertised, following articles in which their importance is allegedly
demonstrated. "In Search of a Definition of Life: Spiral and Living Matter,"
"Diverse Calculations Concerning God, Some of Which are Evidently
False," "Will the Genesis of the Universe ever be Photographed?", "Some
Synthetic Observations Concerning the Aerodynamic Properties of Addition," and "Perspective of a Representation of God" are some of the titles
presented in the publication.

Sometime later the seat on my right is occupied by a slim, solemn-looking
gentleman. His eyes are of a piercing light blue under a wide, mystical
forehead. As soon as he is comfortably installed, he opens a book and
resumes his reading. Almost unwillingly, I become captivated by the text
of which I manage to discern a few fragments . . . man calls illusion what
in truth is the most expressive of realities. Illusion is a mask for nonbeing
. . . but man cannot escape into nonbeing because nonbeing cannot be cast
into words, it is ultimately unknowable . . . willfully accept being imprisoned in illusion . . . this is our single true hope . . . in a world where the
loser invariably wins . . . where abjection is always exaltation . . . impris-
onment must be equated with freedom. Submit to the world of illusion in
order to attain true mastery over the world of reality . . .

*Uncannily appropriate meditations! Calderon's "Life is a Dream?" The purpose
of my day?* Soon the plane accelerates into its twenty-four-second threshold
between life and death, bestriding the crepuscular time of choice. The
familiar bell signals that we are airborne and that the primary emergency
systems have been disconnected . . . 2:35:30 . . .

AN ODOR OF FORCED, pressurized oxygen and burning tobacco immediately saturates the cabin. I tumble into a state of abandon that almost
leads me to renounce existence. In a fit of erotomania I am seized by an
uncontrollable vertigo, once more at the edge of the balcony. In the gloomy
depths of the ravine, beyond the window pane, the Atlantic Ocean crashes
violently against the rocks. The shadow lurking behind me is soon
approaching. *But now it is clear that I cannot go back to the city of our childhood.
I have no option but to continue flying, projecting my imagination toward the
horizon of the future. The danger of explosive decompression is obviously real, but
the promising rewards of flight are immense as well.*

For a moment I can feel once again my humid torso against the pillow
that embraces my sleep and caresses my face. I can also sense the cool
sheets touching my sensitive feet, the soft bed against my knees, and the
concavity between my legs—the memory of pleasure and pain. I fall back
into sleep, plunging into an even deeper order of dreams.

21

SWEET DREAM of flight! I float upon the void, toward the fore of the vessel, a still, dark, and indeterminate space. I glide without disturbing the perfectly continuous whole, becoming intensely aware of my breath as the only perceptible source of motion. *The source of life? This realization conveys a sense of self-fulfillment: I must be entering the Third Sector at thirty degrees west, the time for the awakening of creatures from hibernation. This is the point that stabilizes the position of heaven and earth. The positive and negative poles of the electromagnetic wave revolve in a cycle, ever returning to their point of departure, unfailingly succeeding one another. It is here that the great period begins and ends, with myriad recurrent things that die and pass away, yet again revive and once more come into being.* I remain and traverse in a blissful suspension in this ceaseless and incomplete space. Time collapses without interruption; without any action being taken, all things arrive at their completion.

In this ship that penetrates heaven all is utterly mysterious. The ethereal womb of the earth remains immaculate, concealing even its most predictable operations. The vessel has water levels for leveling and plumb lines for setting things straight, but all instruments remain in a curious state of disuse, unmonitored by the idle woman and the two men in uniform. The vessel has obviously reached its most efficient speed and cruising altitude and now works in deep stillness. It seems that our route was set, together with our destiny, by an invisible order of electromagnetic waves embedded in the elaborate circuitry of the navigation instruments. This architecture has no form yet, like the most impalpable of featureless essences, brings about change and, hopefully, perfection.

At this point of entry, the point of birth, the shape of the sky appears lofty and concave, resembling the membrane of a hen's egg: *the cockpit.* The edges of heaven, like those of an open umbrella, meet the surface of the

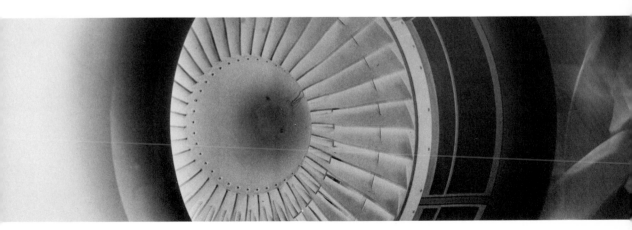

perimetric ocean and float on a primeval breathlike vapor. *My own emanation?* Under this celestial canopy hovers a flat, quadrangular object, its surface glossy like the sea. Below its shiny limit tiny cracks capture the light from three indistinct sources, or from the unfolding reflections of the morning sun, revealing a web of lines more numerous than the convolutions of the human brain. When I concentrate upon the object, both the center of the heavens and the center of the earth appear elevated, while the outer regions seem low.

This intriguing device is surely the object of my search. Is it the brain controlling the vessel? Although three-dimensional and of a size such that it could be carried by a man with his arms stretched laterally, the navigation console displays only one horizontal, rectangular face of ambiguous proportions, either totally flat or infinitely deep. Its enigmatic surface invites a downward glance and suggests penetration through its multiple layers of transparency and opaqueness, while its permanently frontal presentation reveals that it must be traversed from east to west, from right to left, still bounded by its short sides.

The world of the object adds the elements of wood and metal and their modern alchemical plastic congealments to the metaphoric earth, water, and fire. To inhabit this world we have to renounce our conception of the antipodes and the inveterate image of the sky as solid and crystalline. The heavens are probably void here, and air does not exist as an independent element. In a place like this a distant vision of things is likely to be at least as unclouded and plain as a close examination of objects.

When the plan is frontal, walls are the hinges of continuity rather than edges of a never-ending dialectic. Change is unceasing; from the intimate corners of the soul to the boundless limits of the universe, the qualities of these spaces are as mutable as the luminaries and even my life breath: calm breeze, fresh wind, or gusty whirlwind, inhaling or exhaling, quietly sighing and blowing or violently moaning and heaving. The very same wall that may disappear entirely when submerged in the morning mist can seem as substantial as a mountain under the sun. Figure and

ground become equivocal on the surface of the object: an infinite variety of possible situations belonging to one inextricable and nameless continuum. They are linked only by the fluid pace of our experience, woven into a tapestry of manifold, shifting scenes with a single and imperceptible thread.

The closer I approach the unfathomable plane, the more enticing its intricate order. It oscillates constantly under my gaze, refusing most resolutely to be fixed at a given distance in perspective space. *A truly spellbinding effect! What hand outlined these crystalline depths? The painstaking effort demanded by such excellent craftsmanship is admirable. Polya may be absent from the infinite prismatic reaches, but surely the scrutiny and contemplation of this place will take me closer to her. I shift my gaze and I am filled with her joy and her love. I look again and hear only a gentle brook.*

While marveling at these wonderful effects and searching for a threshold, a short and menacing bearded figure abruptly materializes behind the object. *The omnipresent menace! Is it a dark shadow by the balcony or the bat of immense greenish wings over my bed?* In a bureaucratic voice he demands a logical explanation of this phenomenon and ridicules as meaningless this Thing because its infinitude cannot be explained in the realm of perspectival "common sense." This construction cannot be quantified or classified, it serves no ideological purpose and cannot be translated into a tool of production or some sociological artifact. I utter some incongruous words about the primacy of desire in a world forgetful of mortality, about evocative places made with loving care and the frustrating impenetrability of the city of our childhood . . .

This man wears his intelligence like his uniform, from which it is obvious that he has had the technical training to qualify as a member of the crew. He is, however, only capable of perceiving the millimetric outer crust of phenomena, the layer that collects dust. Perhaps a late twentieth-century flight engineer, he seems to be concerned with the representation of a reduced reality as seen from below, with the accurate diminishing heights and distances as they appear to a man standing on level ground. He is unable to comprehend that the moment has come for the fusion

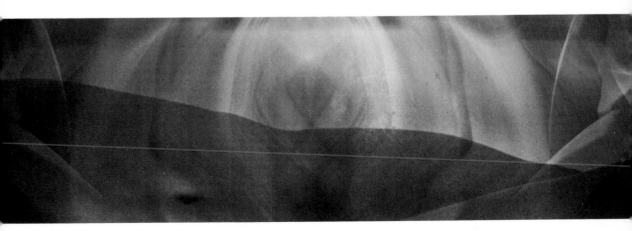

of presence and representation. Since ancient times it has been well known that, to represent the reality of a large object like a mountain, it is insufficient to look up at it from a fixed point and reproduce its frozen profile. Rather, the representation must include the wealth of the mountain's multitudinous slopes and profiles, condensed into one essential vision that will also recreate the reality of what goes on in the valleys and gorges, in the lanes and courtyards with their dwellings and houses, and in the even more invisible dreams of the inhabitants.

Despite his declared interest in the order of the world and all the evidence of history, the engineer remains unconvinced. *He cannot comprehend how the clarity and cloudiness of reality has to be grasped in the permanent fluctuation of a distant view, which necessarily brings about the revelation of that which is truly at hand: light, shade, the visible, and the invisible. Maybe the real difference between his world and mine is in our concept of air.*

I blow at him, and he disappears.

I continue my exploration relieved. I attempt to enter at the single threshold that perhaps can be exited as well: the earth or chessboard, the only perfect square on the plane, an absolutely black and possibly bottomless shaft. The square, not surprisingly, is the closest figure to the short, right-hand side of the rectangular plane. On the left is a gentle sloping face that creates the illusion of exiting toward the west, a ramp of sorts that reaches the limits of the object. *This is surely a delusion though, given that the architecture must be penetrated and exited frontally, along the vertical axis.*

As I start my descent into the plane, a digital message in light appears on the mirror surface:

One should have a knowledge of the historical background; one should enter the garden in a peaceful and receptive mood; one should use one's observations to note the plan and pattern of the garden, for the different parts have not been arbitrarily assembled but carefully

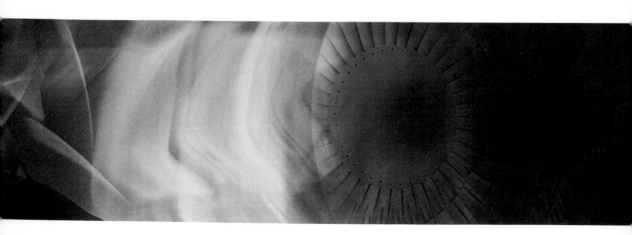

weighed against each other like pairs of inscribed tablets . . . And when one has thoroughly comprehended the tangible forms of objects, one should endeavor to attain an inner communion with the soul of the garden and try to understand the mysterious forces governing the landscape and its coherence.

Slowly penetrating the crystalline membrane of the earth . . . *I fearfully realize that the crisis of the city is analogous to the demise of the garden. Paradise is long lost! Thrilled I am by the prospect of forests and streams, mist and haze, but I know full well that their profound meaning is accessible solely as a memory implanted in my body. It is only thus, recreated by the words of my poetic imagination, that I will ever merge with this sacred and indelible order.*

Without leaving the vessel I can inhabit the streams and ravines of a completely rectilinear landscape. The place is permeated by a faint and indescribable music that could have been the cries of animals and birds or a music of the same pitch played with an inexhaustible variety of timbres. Although I gain admittance through the abysmal shaft as planned, the interstitial space of the surface layers traps me with my own reflection. My own fractured image is lost within the multiplicity and simultaneity of scales and in the illimitable distance of the transparent silken walls.

Light glitters and dazzles the eyes, while my feet struggle to remember the geometric order in the experience of multiple platforms. Walking leads nowhere, and the sensations are always diverse. I encounter reflections and counter reflections of familiar forms such as temples, towers, and pyramids at every turn; all monuments invariably sink into the ground. The order of the foliage is equally the order of the processional plane, where my feet slip on the shifting base level. The sky plunges into pits while translucent earth rises diagonally, capturing the reflection of clouds along the horizon.

After a hundred paces I recover myself in the black square, which has turned utterly white. *Ice has optical characteristics that allow it to appear either absolutely black or totally white under changing light conditions, but the temperature is pleasant . . . There is obviously a mystery to this capricious and unyielding gateway that must be extensively pondered.*

Examining the shifting dimensions of the square, I catch sight of a strange instrument located at the center. *It is surely a measuring rod.* This ivory contraption is irregularly marked and its long part is attached to a circular mechanism, itself subdivided into twenty-four sectors of fifteen degrees. *Perhaps this apparatus holds the key to the generation of the inscrutable order of the garden and to the geometries of the planes!* The platforms are obstinately bounded by orthogonal lines, parallel to the square, and by oblique lines that apparently conform to the twenty-four geographic directions. *They must also relate to the order of my journey . . .*

The never-ending music, the disposition of the place, and my respiration are intimately related. *When breath is in motion sound comes forth, and when sound comes forth the breath of the world is broken. The breath of life ensues from sound, and vice versa. The unfathomable technical processes needed to construct this work are, in all likelihood, the secret of its harmony.* According to the second inscription, now visible on the polished exterior, the breath of the earth ascending above and the breath of heaven descending from the height, gather and suffuse in music:

Their drumming is in the shock and rumble of thunder; their excited beating of wings is in wind and rain; their shifting round is in the four seasons; their warming is in the sun and the moon. Thus the hundred species procreate and flourish.

The breath of the earth also creates the geological order. Stone is its kernel and bone. In large masses it forms rocks and cliffs, in small particles it constitutes sand

and dust. Its seminal essence is transmuted into gold and jade. As can be seen in petrifying herbs, trees, and animals, its changes are manifold. The architect allowed for the breath of the earth to rise through the surface, for it made all things in this world pure and wise. Sky and earth are inverted in the garden because rain, dew, and frost proceed from the earth and do not precipitate from the heavens as vulgar belief would have it. A third legend written on the glistening surface reads:

The wind is the life breath of heaven, and rain is the life breath of the earth. Wind blows in accord with the seasons and rain falls in response to wind. We can say that the life breath of the heavens tumbles down and the life breath of the earth goes upward.

With her life breath the architect has made a place in resonance with the life breath and movements of nature and also with my very own . . . deep breath marking the absolutely vertical axis between the divine eye and the pubis, rising and sinking, excited and expectant. My breath keeps pace!

Distance shifts. I face again an object that occupies a central position at the fore of the vessel, at the point where the course of the future is resolved. The object both invites a projection of my body and refuses entry to my physical person. *I am simultaneously voyeur and participant. An abstract order becomes absolutely evident. It manifestly precludes its representation in a conventional artistic medium, but the object remains profoundly enigmatic, welcoming an unlimited multiplicity of readings at various scales.*

The shiny horizontal plane fuses the objective and subjective, evoking our present state of being, our optimistic acceptance of the void. (A vacuum permanently surrounds us . . .) Constituted at the edge of the mirror's surface, the plane reflects and accepts my presence and the electronic letters that allow me to name it. What exists beyond the utterly flat exterior is a layered space ranging from zero to infinite

29

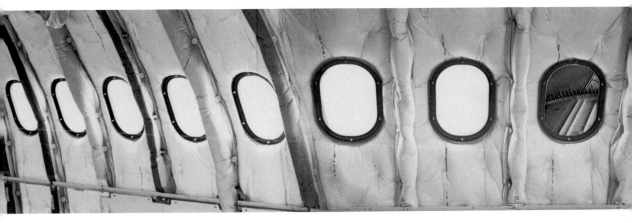

depth, an incomplete order that unknowingly holds the reflection unintentionally cast by the observer. It is an order that begins and stays at the point of contact between the unnamable as the source of the universe and the namable as the originator of all things. I am reminded of the man with piercing blue eyes . . . truth becomes fiction when the fiction is true . . .

The magnetic forces that determine our trajectory have also shaped the topographical features of the geomantic landscape. The fourth inscription reads:

> **How the mysterious geodetic influences are distributed according to the contours.**

The object now discloses its essence as a physiographic chart in which the boundaries of every square inch correspond to the celestial divisions on high. The relation between the phenomena of the heavens and the physical features of the earth can be clearly seen in the construction. The jigsaw map reveals the order of immortality by means of exaggerated topographical relief. A fifth inscription appears on the lustrous surface:

> **In the tomb chamber, the hundred water courses . . . together with the great sea were imitated by means of flowing mercury, which machines made flow and circulate. The celestial bodies were all represented above; the geography of the earth was depicted below.**

The order disclosed by the object is a map of the earth or of a city whose decaying walls have been retraced at slightly different angles, following the most recent instructions of the geomantic diviners. It is also a talismanic image that ensures our safe journey through the plotted lands, surely the embodiment of fortune,

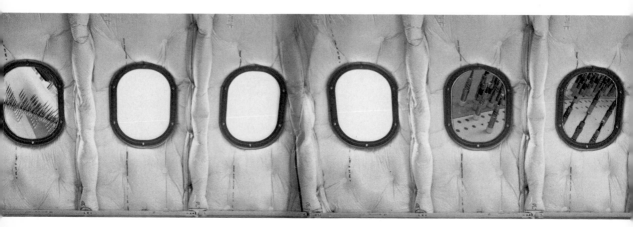

subjected to the whim of the magnetic fields, showing the way of the **aimant,** *of the aimer or needle, toward my beloved.*

Placed in the realm of reality without mediation, the object represents precisely the state of its deployment, its becoming at the point of contact between truth and illusion, frame and view. The configuration of the strata of space happens as a projection of the frontal order onto the ground and cutting into the depth. Its horizontal elevation dissolves the distinct characteristics of nature and artifice. The vertical elements (except for my presence) become indiscernible and constitute a homogeneous and nonhierarchical crowding of phenomena transformed into recumbent projections of rectilinear planes with orthogonal and diagonal edges.

Within this world experience conveys a perennial sense of endlessness and pointlessness. Is this symbol opposite to the labyrinth, a prophecy of the order to come? In this space there can be no disorientation, because there is no orientation, no beginning or conclusion! This is not the primordial idea of an architecture concretized in rituals as the labyrinth was for the traditional city and its institutions; this object is the architecture itself or perhaps some higher revelation of the order of the real through form, an artifact as yet unnamed!

The gateway invites my attention. At this angle the square is visibly incandescent, offering the purest and most dazzling reflection on the plane. A type of instrument, it is composed of two superimposed plates, the lower one square and the upper one round. The latter revolves on a central pivot and is engraved with the twenty-four compass points. In the center of the circle is embedded a series of brightly glowing crystals, arranged like an elongated spoon. These shining stars are linked by means of sharp incisions that form accurate lines on the surface.

At this moment the attractive woman in uniform places the lodestone spoon on the earth plate. Like a cock over a belfry, moving in the direction of the wind, the spoon hesitates and spins, revealing the lineaments of destiny. *Tracing our route?* She had been keeping the long, streamlined

31

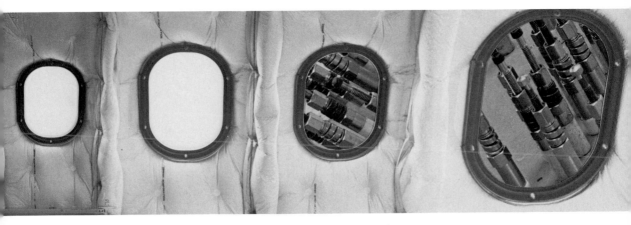

pointer on her lap all this time, waiting for the propitious moment to deploy it. Her colleagues, frozen gestures on mechanical devices, also appear to have been participating in some kind of ritual. The square now plainly resembles a chessboard! The men in uniform take turns tossing on the checkered slab undefinable objects of circular and longitudinal shape. When two of these pieces become attached to one another, the game stops and the position of the pieces is carefully recorded. The sixth message reads:

The lodestone animates chessmen. The blood of the cock is rubbed with needle iron and pounded to mix. Then, when the lodestone chessmen are set up on the board, they will move themselves and bump against each other.

The square unveils the essential quality of the mirror surface in its purest form, the nature of the empty site. The mind, like a mirror free of dust, focuses more clearly in front of a looking glass. Facing their concave and convex mirrors, the three crew members vanish. The liquid crystal instrument panels expose merely their viscera and other opaque and private parts. On the glossy surface of the object the seventh inscription reveals that these are variations of a special kind of mirror:

There are certain "light-penetration mirrors" with inscribed characters of an indecipherable ancient style. If such a mirror is exposed to the sunshine, although the characters are on the back, they pass through and are reflected on the wall of a room, where they can be read most distinctly. Their principle is really inexplicable; even the faintest lines become conspicuously visible.

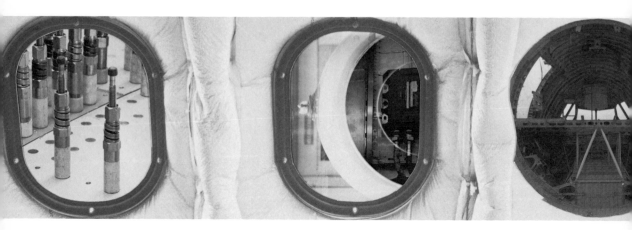

Caught anew in the reflection, I irrupt into the square. The measuring or surveying instrument is now functioning as a sundial. What should be noted is obviously the length of the shadow and not its direction, but the thin black stripe appears emphatically projected close to the character indicating forty-five degrees west. *The course is set, but I must hurry.* I stride across the square, now paved with a pattern of inlaid T, L, and O outlines, arranged conforming to central asymmetries.

When I step out of the square, its quality as a dual mirror becomes repeatedly noticeable. It is the epitome of black and white, always fluctuating between the two extremes in a perpetual cycle. Other colors are conspicuously absent. *The mirror can either receive and recreate the brilliant fire of the sun or collect and crystallize the radiant water from the moon.*

I walk at a steady pace in the hope of discovering more, but the complete lack of hierarchy is dizzying. *Is it really possible to descend as I climb or to resent in my heart the effort of climbing as I descend? Is vertigo the result of true knowledge?* I strive to follow a northwesterly course, guided only by the melody of the ringing stone, the drum, and the other six instruments that intensify and fade as I face their respective cardinal positions in my rambling path.

I arrive at what seems to be a single-room building with concentric draftproof walls. Fragrant smells of spices carried by the vapors of the cooking pot draw me in. This is the sole space in the garden where colors are vibrantly present. Bright orange silk curtains form a tent over twenty-four pitch pipes used for the detention of universal emanations. *The cockpit where I had evidently arrived?* Everything is set erect! *This must be the place* . . . A chamber to await the coming of the cosmic life breaths, one for every fifteen-degree sector on the map.

The eighth inscription finally discloses the name of the maker:

Chhi. Manufactured in the People's Republic of China.

On an altar veiled with a pearly silk tablecloth is an object, a vase perhaps, demonstrating the paradox of squaring the circle! While its base and opening are circular, the urn is essentially a square prism, about three times as tall as it is wide. Made of some kind of translucent stone or artificial material, it is covered by a lid that in profile resembles a nubile breast. Four inscriptions are engraved on the rectangular faces of the object:

I

There was something undefined yet complete in itself, before heaven and earth. Silent and boundless, standing alone without change yet pervading all without fail. It may be regarded as the Mother of the World.

II

The Valley Spirit never dies. It is named the Mysterious Feminine; and the doorway of the Mysterious Feminine is the base from which heaven and earth sprang. It is always there within us; draw upon it as you will, it never runs dry.

III

He who knows the Male yet cleaves to the Female becomes like a ravine, receiving all things under heaven. And being such a ravine, he permanently knows a power that he never calls on in vain.

IIII

The highest good is like that of water. Water quenches our thirst; it is in the womb and is the mirror of meditation. The goodness of water is that it benefits the myriad creatures, yet itself does not wrangle but is content with the places that all men disdain.

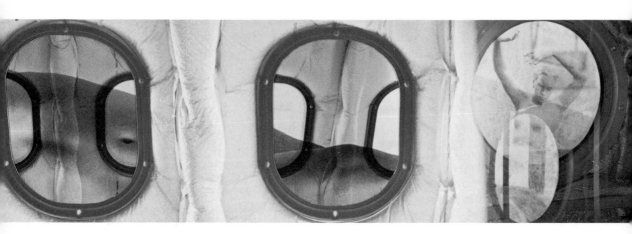

I lift the mysterious lid and discover that what appeared to be a nipple is in fact part of another longitudinal object contained in the jar. This smaller piece, molded out of clay, is unmistakably phallic. *Perhaps a viewing tube for stargazing?* I remove the cover, which is actually a ring penetrated tightly by the conic top of the tube. Under the concave ring is one further inscription that reads:

I

The highest good is like that of fire. Fire makes us warm, it is in the viscera and in the generative organs and is the heat of meditation. The goodness of fire is that it benefits the myriad creatures and, although it often wrangles, is content at the center of the world.

The stargazing tube comprises in itself another annulus, fused with its cylindrical body. It is a projection of the lid on the vertical plane, inscribed with the diagrams of constellations. I fondle the construction, carefully examining the delicate and complex tracings cut into its surface. Running my finger along the smooth interior of the roundel I am overwhelmed by an exorbitant pleasure, probably arising from the knowledge of fate. Through the androgynous object I now stare at the diaphanous silken curtain that brings back my longing. *The indistinct image of my beloved Polya is imprinted on every crease and undulation of my body.*

The lights shining from the surrounding walls are disposed in such a way that the shadow of a beautiful girl can be distinctly seen in the distance. I cannot approach her, but I can see that she is reclining at the edge of a narrow, adjustable bed or chair and is somehow strapped down and comfortably immobilized. It is now evident that the skirt of her uniform is slit up the side in the Chinese fashion. She might even be barefoot. Her right leg is visible to the thigh, emerging from the slit skirt, while her left foot is firmly set on a slightly higher platform. She is holding a black metal appa-

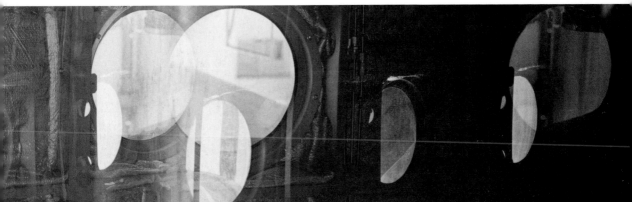

ratus with two knobs and three adjustable vertical and horizontal circles marked with white numbers. Intently looking upward through the sighting device, she is obviously plotting our course according to the stars. *A useless, archaic practice in the age of Doppler navigation?*

The ivory silk of the curtain creases following her motions, betraying the sensuous features of her body while she transcribes her findings onto a large piece of graph paper. I am amazed by the intimate connection between the orthogonal navigational chart, which shows only symbols, names, and coordinates on a grid, and the relief map disclosing the delicate skin, the rounded firm hip and the soft slope of the loins. Both realities fuse into one as our fate is inscribed.

The glare of the curtain becomes unbearable, while the fragrant smoke from the incense clock slowly dissipates into the life breath and finally stops. For an instant back in the square, I envisage the pavement as a precise black-and-white grid, identical to a chessboard. Imprisoned in the interval of mirrors, I can understand the continuity between the world of sea and land and the world of infinity. The last legend is displayed on the reflective exterior of the object:

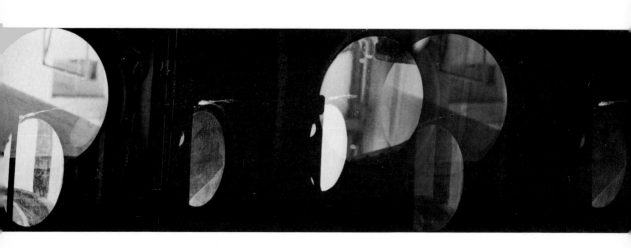

Thereupon I left and resumed my wandering,
To the wide world's end. We came to the Gate of Gold,
Racing the rushing wind to the Spring of Purity;
Bestriding the Pole of Division, I looked back behind me.
Traversing the four dimensions,
Roving the six directions of space,
high in the aurora's cracks and fissures
I passed and, far below, in the bottomless pit.
In sheer depths, the earth above was invisible,
in the vastness of the heights, the sky could not be seen.
When I looked, my startled eyes saw nothing,
when I listened, no sound met my bewildered ear.
Thus, transcending inaction, I attained the great clarity,
and entered the precincts of the Great Beginning.

37

Just now the square on the plane becomes pitch black and fractures, giving way under my feet. *Clear air turbulence?* My body turns into a vortex of night and falls into a fathomless pit. Blackout.

STUPOR AND PLEASURE, east and west, objects and their shadows dissolve into the three times and the six directions of the prevailing darkness. For some time I twirl with faint cognition, clinging always to the square trap door. *Enduring . . .* Soon the violent waves lose their force and their energy dissipates into the horizon. Suspended between ascent and descent, I have a glimmering premonition of a new threshold.

Between east and west! I am still in the gloomy cockpit, somewhere over a primordial sea. I can't feel the floor, but the sense of falling stops. *The atmospheric loneliness of this place reminds me of my devotion in the metallic reverberation of my every palpitation and sigh. I burn lasciviously as I recall that my soul dwells in the object of my immoderate desire. Perhaps I hear some music, very, very far in the distance . . . The touch of love? Intertwining motions of supple limbs or the harmony of the order as yet unnamed? The offspring of architecture?*

The music invokes a stark image from the glaring depths of consciousness: the translucent skin of a liberated angel reflecting a lurid light, pale yet inconceivably white. *The pigment of crushed snow crystals under the moon? Ultraviolet glow?* I can see through the angel's diaphanous body stocking and even under her skin. Luminescent subtle matter that becomes denser and more opaque at the ubiquitous center, between navel and penetralia.

An electric surge activates the control panel. Traced on the liquid display screen that must also be part of the vessel's guidance system are three coincidental images: inscribed in a circle and merging with each other are a triangular sector of pizza and its powdery taste of chalk kneaded with tears, the triangular plan of the piazza, and the triangular shadow of the tower's pyramidal termination, at the very bottom of the vertical shaft. The joint between the angel's wings and her omoplates has been finally resolved: black and white triangles, all with their points down.

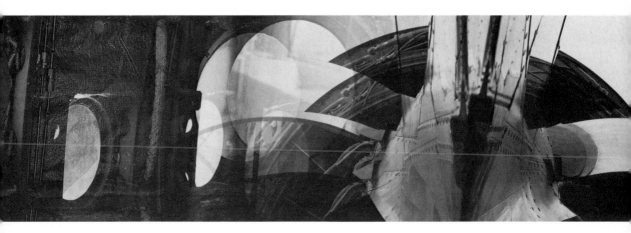

The angel of the star-shaped ideal city that now presents itself on the screen perhaps regained her virginal wings the previous night and is about to embark on an easterly course. *In the opposite direction but always coming back?* The suffocating heat and shade of the terminal building close in on me, with its incomprehensible letters presumed to convey crucial information for the travelers wishing to cross the gateway. *The same aluminum capsule? The place of essential loneliness is always a traveling compartment . . .*

In a fit of anxiety I catch a glimpse of a descending stair that perhaps can be entered. The cabin partition is obviously the shaft wall, lined with tombstones: two or three bodies per window, along the fuselage! The vessel always occupies the same place, its link with the ground severed. *According to the schedule, the ordeal of separation and departure should only have taken a moment but (as is usual with love?) this instant (and not orgasm) lasts longer. From fall to atonement, we wait. A full day, in the hope of ultimate detachment?*

The beautiful angel (she has enormous, glowing eyes and classical features) impassively pulls the door away. The gateway is unobstructed but I lose my balance. *In the whirling fog I remember my suspended fall through the wondrous square gate of the mirror structure.* The pitch intensifies. There is probably no murkier shadow than the darkness enveloping a vertical drop, capable of absorbing even the shrill cry emitted by imploding viscera. In the absolute darkness of the void I plummet through the cemetery toward the vanishing point of the fan-shaped square, but not for long. Immediately through the tower's vertical shadow I reach the light and irrupt into the immaculate triangular pubis with its promise of delights.

Between the objects and their shadows! I finally come to rest at the point where in the past the now invisible tower and its shadow met, where the sacrificial blood was collected and pleasure and pain converged. Caught anew in the interstitial space, I descend into the plan through the point of negative infinity, the vertex angle of the isosceles triangle. The precise geometric configuration appears clearly only when I enter from above, revealing a sort of urban stage. *This rare overview ensues from the extraordi-*

narily accurate overlap of the visible and the invisible: light and shade, freedom and necessity, life and death, open and enclosed space. A coincidence of dualities manifest through the diaphanous surface plane.

Once inhabiting the transparent plane of the stage, however, the simultaneous order might be revealed only through the particular pieces that barely insinuate the possible connections. It is evident that the invisible platform is the interspace of playacting occupied by the vessel, the plane of existence between freedom and necessity. This novel stage could replace the antiquated Palmanova but might also entail a new mode of experience. In this city of the future, the totality would no longer be represented as such but merely glimpsed through the fragments.

Facing the flickering screen, I cannot forget that on entering Palmanova from the heavens I could discern the visible geometric order that revealed the invisible and immutable hierarchy of the cosmos. Once within the walls though, men cannot abandon their bodies to exist in the pure intellectual joy of the immutable. The star-shaped city is really a bleak and inhospitable reality, an imposition of meaningless and arbitrary geometries that have since characterized our dreary urban life. In all likelihood, the angel of eroticism dislocated her wings on the very same day that the foundation stone was laid!

A new city is now possible in the gap where I have fallen, between the objects and their shadows, a city equally suspended between east and west. To gain admittance one must renounce all attachment to objects live or inanimate and become a thing among others. The organic body and its mechanical sensations are to be abandoned. As real substantial shadows, capable of objective description, we can relate the incidents on the plane of the stage with their local shadows. The latter are no longer cast on the surface as usual (this is of course impossible due to the very nature of the airplane) but appear as coincidental, as three-dimensional events under the plane. The hopeful enigma of reality can now materialize as the shadow of a shadow, like the infinite reflection on the variegated face of the earth, logged in the memory of my travel.

41

At the entry point my shadow becomes a line projected radially and lengthwise during the greater part of this hour. *Bounded by the two sides of the triangle, it will eventually merge with the picture plane: the screen, the window, or the section of a proscenium arch . . .* Things normally considered as insignificant are thus disclosed as having a meaning in themselves and through their relationships to other things. *The meaningful space of human drama is regained at the expense of denying full access to the temporal body and deferring physical penetration. The experiencing shadow does not exist materially in a fixed dimension, and the object of its experience, the walls and fragments on the plane, exist only insofar as they constitute a three-dimensional drawing. This reality, effectively hovering between the conventional three dimensions of obsolete geometry, is defined by hard and precise limits in absolutely frozen time. It is accompanied by immutable letters, which are the ideal medium for representing the characters in the play: the shadow of God's burning desire.*

The triangular plan of the stage is squared by two perpendicular furrows, one to the short side of the proscenium and the other to the edge on the elevation of freedom, along our trajectory. The two orthogonal slits do not intersect at an axis mundi. They are rather the grooves of destiny on the airplane of existence, indeed a transparent plate, effectively plotting the possible stage motions of the characters. The virtual motions of the plane, the essential motions above the plane, and the impossible motions beneath the plane are contained within the triangular frame, but their connections can only be established metaphorically. *The whole is obviously invisible from within. When we are disembodied, the horizontal and vertical realms must be experienced successively rather than simultaneously.* My shadow continues to be slowly projected from the point of negative infinity toward the east, in the direction of the shadow dweller's room.

Above on the right, the thin, lathery starched veil of the sky; below on the left, the massive, cavernous plaster curtain of the earth: the backdrop. Amid the yellow and mauve walls placed along the grooves of destiny the tower disintegrates. The hoops of the round have difficulty staying on the

tower once its masonry core is corroded by the flatulent space of the chimney flue. Some rings rise and others sink in the waters of the lagoon, renewing the perpetual vow of marriage between the city of the land, the sea, and the heavens. The upright axis of the gyroscope flounders, but like everything else its motion frozen in position is linked with the underworld.

The round now comes to light as the reflection of itself. The carefully crafted piece of wood in the form of a truncated cone is evidently the reflection on the canal of the conical termination of the chimneys. The smoke that always rose in adulation of the gods is directed downward. An inscription appears on the screen:

Fate is character(s).

This whole apparatus is a monument dedicated to ambiguous gods, singing its praise to phallic pleasures and vaginal pains, to the unhappiness of life and death. A second legend on the opposite side of the screen now reads:

Hymns and phallic songs would be obscene if they were not in honor of light. And light, through which we go into a trance and speak in tongues and for whom we beat the drum, do we realize that it is consubstantial with darkness?

In its reflection the round takes the shape of a hollow, pressurized helmet, the head of a double-faced man. *Is this the alternating circle of time? The sinusoidal electromagnetic waves with their positive and negative poles that keep revolving in cycles?* The helmet can be entered through a single cross-shaped opening for seeing and breathing. This deep incision produces a sharp lamenting sound when penetrated by the wind. The cry of the absent spectator can still be heard however, transformed by the shadow into a

permanent gloaming, illuminating the entrails of the holder of the lost tower.

Lacking an external surface, the vacant body is accurately modeled on the inside, like a cast of the space that only surgeons know. The tissue and organs of the colossus are made of some plastic substance that reproduces their most objective, awesome, and repulsive characteristics. *This is, indeed, the first vision of the temple.* The liquids, although vitrified, seem to possess their authentic textures and colors. There was no apparent disease in this body! In every organ a broken, small iridescent disk reminds the visitor of the old afflictions related to each part of the body and their scientific cure. Prominent are the biochemical codes that reveal functional paths between each organ and the brain and that allow for effective psychosomatic healing. This is the body produced by genetic engineers, physiologically perfect and, so they believe, potentially eternal.

The rightful position of manifold anatomical details can be easily recognized, until I arrive at the location of the heart: the space of the genitals. *Containing the lost tower, this compartment appears to avoid Cartesian determination. The space of the heart seems to overlap the space of the genitals and neither can be differentiated from the space of the mind.* Amid disorienting coordinates I find a silvery disk, still intact. *A cure for the sickness that fills the ubiquitous space of modern man may never be found. Is this the inveterate plague that periodically comes back in different terrifying forms and at no time can be eradicated? Maybe the old psychosomaticlovesickness!*

Introduced in the appropriate slot, the indestructible record describes a disease that had caused social and moral collapse. In monotone an electronic voice reads:

> Although related to a particular virus, its precise origin remains unknown . . . In the early days many respectable doctors and pathologists believed that contagion by simple contact was possible, but all documented

instances of the illness to date have been associated with different forms of physical and bodily transgression . . . When afflicted with this disease, the body's immune system falls apart. The symptoms are extremely varied. Before any explicit physiological or psychological discomfort is felt, the skin is covered with red blemishes, which the victim suddenly notices as they turn dark purple. Immediately the victim's head begins to boil, and the brain expands to occupy the interstitial spaces in the cranium. The forehead becomes unbearably heavy while the muscles are seized by an uncontrollable fatigue, until the body finally collapses. Every cell is driven toward annihilation. The innermost organs, particularly those of the digestive tract, strive to turn their internal surfaces inside out, exploding and gushing through every orifice and fissure. The victim's pulse slows at times almost completely, condensing bodily fluids, and at others races madly after the boiling fever. Soon the rotting organic matter searches for an outlet, resembling lava on the verge of eruption. Horrible blisters break through the skin like air bubbles, and the flesh becomes crystalline and brittle before decomposing on contact with the atmosphere. In most cases the disease ends in death. The few patients who recover are invariably subject to unbearable erotic frenzy, which leads them to extreme criminal or demiurgic acts . . . Surprisingly, the corpses of plague victims show no lesions when opened. Death seems to take place as an alchemical transmutation. All bodily fluids appear shiny like polymers. The gall bladder is filled with a black,

45

viscous liquid so dense as to suggest a new form of matter altogether. The blood in the veins and arteries is also black and viscid while the pus is hard as stone. There is neither loss nor destruction of inner tissue. The inside of the body may be preserved for eternity in all its (im)perfection!

Leaving the disk behind, I exit the polymerized colossus through the helmet's cruciform opening. From a distance the round resembles a medieval defensive weapon or a funeral monument made of riveted mat plaster.

Not far away stands a dazzling metal sphere. *The oracular circle?* Its silvery shine reflects every instrument and thing around it, except where my shadow is cast over its surface. *Happily there is no trace in the reflection of the familiar objects in my suitcase.* Despite its ponderous appearance, the leaden sphere is perfectly still, in seeming defiance of gravity. The sun does not roll along the line of least resistance. *This is in all likelihood why the sphere remains irrationally immobile on the inclined plane.* On the screen two concentric circular legends read:

The beginning of a circle is also its end.

The same road goes both up and down.

When I stare at the exterior crust of the low, mercurial sun, a series of consecutive spherical hieroglyphs are incised in my mind. *It is not difficult to decipher their meaning:*

> *The astropoets are joyous . . . The day is radiant, the stage full of sun*
>
> *. . . Overleaning the veranda . . . Music and love. The woman*
>
> *toobeautiful . . . Dying for her velveteye . . . The painting of an*
>
> *enormous red chimney . . . Object of the poet's adoration . . . Revisiting*
>
> *the night offspring and cadavers . . . The river carrying extombs . . .*
>
> *Who wants to live again? Promises are more beautiful . . . Windful*
>
> *flags hover the square . . . As long as the clock does not stop . . .*
>
> *Premonition of arrival . . . The minstrel smiles . . . In the crepuscular*
>
> *stage he writes loveletters while the stone warrior sleeps.*

The spherical place full of sun appears also as a tube of light, projecting its circular section vertically over and under the vessel's instrument panel. Symmetrical to the sphere and at the same distance from the proscenium frame, in the center of a square described by the perpendicular grooves of destiny on the stage platform, is the bright room of the shadow dweller. *Is this merely a reflection of the pilot's realm?* Entering the tube of light, a luminous gallery within the plaster curtain, I abandon the surface of the sphere and penetrate the sectional zone.

DESCENDING INTO the pedestal of shadows is like infiltrating a large

animal devoid of viscera. The inner world, the underworld, is visibly empty. Akin to a cave, it is traversed by the single tube of light that becomes fainter at greater depth. The mineral curtain, which could be the interior lining of the sacred cow's saddlecloth, has three deep square openings and is flood-lit from below, increasing its effect as a backdrop. *Is it also the lining of the box of shadows or the internal space of the cargo compartment? Is it the house for the mortal remains of humanity? Probably not, because the box of shadows is lying vacant at the bottom, with its tapered lid hanging aloft.*

One of the openings in the plaster backcloth, the closest to the lighted gallery, is for the shadow dweller to look out into the magnificent tomb. *The sky itself?* This opening may also allow the voyeur beyond the proscenium window to catch a glimpse of the shadow dweller in order to unravel destiny through her gestures and movements. The other two openings are in fact picture frames for the nonexistent faces of a man and a woman. The outline of these frames is repeated as a rectangle in bas-relief engraved on the appropriate end of the suspended lid. At the entry point, the locus of negative infinity now distant forty centimeters, is a perfect image of the absent cadaver: a nude hermaphrodite. This hyperreal statue is immobile yet strangely animated, manufactured with new and unidentified synthetic materials and uncharted techniques. Its skin, devoid of hair, white and smooth like porcelain, covers a body both youthfully muscular and round. The small buttocks and firm breasts are bare, while the enigmatic genitals hide and protect one another, merging into the hieroglyph of love and knowledge, a secret symbol of absolute oneness.

There are four inscriptions, one on each face of the empty box of shadows (the picture frame of the absent cadaver). On the long sides the two legends read:

I would remain naked if the beast had not covered me.
Search and you will find.
Leave me.

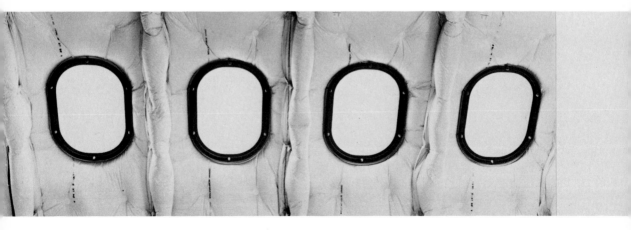

Whoever you are, take this treasure.
But I admonish you, take the head,
don't touch the body.

The short sides of the opaque, translucent plastic casket also bear cryptic inscriptions:

All men think.

Nakedness always conveys the impression of total newness.

Caught between the inner edge of the sectional zone and the outer edge of the realm of shadows, I am astounded by the suggestive spectacle. In a surge of reflective consciousness I lament my inability to understand thoroughly . . . Logically, for the future? Simply stand under the present . . .

49

BACK AT THE POINT of departure I am again suspended between ascent and descent, crossing a threshold without any assurance. Time seemingly regains its normal course. The scholar with piercing blue eyes who had been sitting at my right is now reading an ancient treatise on monsters and marvels! From his open book I read that true hermaphrodites are those who have both sets of sexual organs well formed and are able to use them in reproduction . . . and that ancient and modern laws oblige hermaphrodites to choose which sex organs they wish to use and that they are forbidden on pain of death to enjoy any but those chosen . . . on account of the misfortunes that could result from tampering with the duality of nature and using both to become one . . . for some of them have indeed abused their situation with the result that, through mutual and reciprocal use, they take their pleasure first with one set of sex organs and then with the other . . . *Incredible! Could this be the order of the future?*

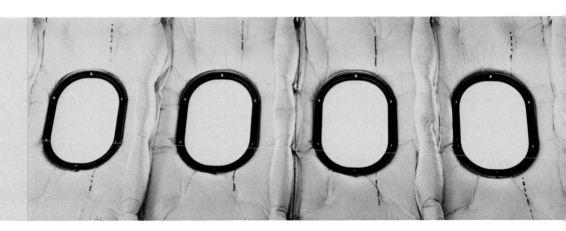

Between ascent and descent lies a path, but so far away! Now the triangular plan is revealed as a pyramid in section that inscribes a spherical cenotaph. The section is that of a truncated cone as well, similar to the disintegrating tower. This gigantic monument is deployed simultaneously over and under the airplane of existence and only in the sectional zone, beyond the proscenium window. While the top half of the sphere recreates the vault of heaven, it is utterly dismal, contained by the void and mass of the external conical volume. There are no stars in this empty universe, and the sky itself has an ominous, almost liquid quality pouring in through an invisible oculus. The lower half of the sphere discloses the cataclysmic qualities of the earth, the veritable womb of humanity. One object disrupts the perfect sphere of this innermost space: the box of shadows, occupying (*as since time immemorial!*) the lowest central position.

The cenotaph can only be entered through its section, which reveals the order of its architecture, the immediate presentation of the old order of nature. Directing my experience at will, up or down along the vertical axis, it is easy to ascertain the reciprocity of ascension through the oculus and descent through the picture frame of the box of shadows. In both cases, as I pass through the sectional limits of the sphere, the square plan of the gateway unfolds, reminding me that I am still caught outside the threshold. As I rise and sink, the square footprint is simply projected, creating either a tower or a shaft as our path.

Following the downward spiral, the slumping masonry pit around me is transformed into a vertical cemetery of abysmal depth. Blistered corpses lie perpendicular to the wall, floating in earth or on water. Only a small, shallow square in bas-relief circumscribing the crown of the head marks the position of each body. *Pressurized windows? Picture frames? The materials lining the walls of this most intimate of spaces were once used by mankind to build a very tall tower to reach the heavens and steal from the gods the secret of immortality* . . . Close to the bottom the wedding ring has dissolved, like atomic aftershock, into a series of perpetual concentric circles on the surface

of the water. Its shadow, black and permanent, never shifts with the position of the sun.

Reciprocally, around the mounting staircase the apparition of the immense tower is reified in steel. A tubular grid of empty picture frames, like ready rods now exposed, receives only the applause of silence. *The secret reinforcement of a missile silo open to the view?* The absent spectator in this apocalyptic public space can only collect carbon bits that dissolve to the touch. Scorched canvas remains where once the conical chimneys and pink facades, the holy men floating through the air or walking on the canal, the charming barefoot young girls sitting on marble cubes playing lutes, and countless undersized albino dogs with brazen eyes were immortalized in the painterly depths of geometric perspective. All is gray, and near the summit there is no trace even of metaphysical color. The angel of the annunciation was solarized when the immaculate impregnation yielded its fruit and the virgin conceived. *Man could thereafter pretend to be god . . . Why did she ever consent?*

The top and bottom of this vertical path constitute extremities: a quadrangular pyramid lies at the terminus. This geometric solid, however, is no longer truncated like the round and the cenotaph. Its lines truly meet at infinity: a pyramid of the brightest burning light, a pyramid of somber and permanent shadow.

A space and time of coincidence! The end of unbearable solitude? Perhaps the ultimate and clearest symbol of the fate of humanity . . . An internal physiological adjustment, maybe a change in my sleeping position or a bit of clear-air turbulence, expels me to the outer edge of the sectional plane. *The experience of flight? Between ascent and descent, space is not yet accessible.* Confronted with my pliable reflection in the window, I am forced in frustration to accept again the role of spectator, but on the public's side of the proscenium frame.

51

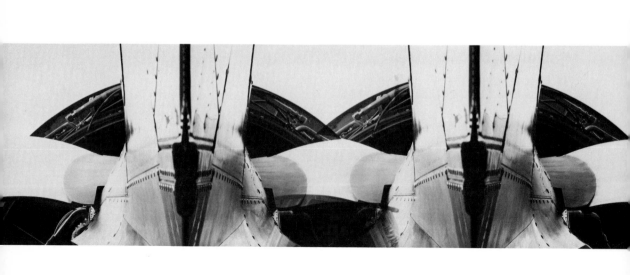

THE STAGE, perhaps the same aerial landscape, is now singularly exposed to the sense of sight (the dominant vision of knowledge for a fixed spectator), and from the outer edge of the sectional plane the triangular perspective stage is manifest as a projection on the proscenium window. It has become an ambiguous, perfectly flat but intensely vibrant three-dimensional painting. Color values, hitherto unimportant, are incisive and violent. Every hue speaks its own unmediated emotion.

The hovering lid of the box of shadows is like the uninhabitable line dividing the spectator from the stage. This line, which is also the diagonal of the square gateway not yet traversed, can only be part of our experience in death. Perhaps this is indeed the mystery of architecture, always one step ahead of humanity and denying the possibility of full inhabitation . . . The box for man's ashes is now revealed as a frame onto a bottomless depth.

This prospect, capturing the edge of the world as it approaches the transverse axis of human sight, is as close as one can come to a presentation of order in the failing distance of post-perspective time. Again it remains futile to attempt a projection of my whole body, with its fixed organic proportions, into the work. Always the same place? This three-dimensional painting subverts the natural continuum of perception. No more little men walking along axes! It is, instead, absolutely present as a deobjectified order that creates its own site and does not exist by virtue of its location in Cartesian space.

From this new vantage point the rediscovery of theater as the ground of order scintillates. The city of tomorrow appears again as a possible theater of negative infinity that excludes trivial action and posits man as one object among others, recapturing the city's role as the seat of truly participatory drama.

The stage reveals, above and below, the interplay between the realms of freedom and necessity. The characters remind us that we are not free and that, indeed, the sky can still fall on our heads! Reduced to their geometric essence, the dramatis personae turn into pure frozen gestures that communicate a superior idea of poetry, an immediate apprehension of order and the value of life. Without superfluous mediation, the range of gestures and techniques unveils the truth of reality: the core of the urban stage is the void of our hearts. *To stand under the absence of gods may be the first sign of hope! The play demonstrates the alienation of man from the world and its objects.*

The cast of characters discloses the presence of architecture's being, even though its existence in our contemporary cities may have to be questioned. Or is it, in fact, the as yet unnamed order of the future? The play is deployed along the unfathomable line that is the space of encounter, the line of mortality that both separates and weds light and shade. The reciprocity of the public and the private, of freedom and necessity, is manifested in this interval, in the dimension of space within a line. Along this line that hyphenates the spectator and the stage extends the arch of eroticism. Otherwise invisible, it bridges the intimacy of the room with its unlit corners and the public square full of sun and abrupt shadows. This hinge is the line of the steam locomotive that has always unrolled on its track the ultimate identity of the cemetery and the public square: the city of the dead and the city of the living.

From this new point of vision, my confused memory identifies the structure of the theater with the section of the cenotaph, and this with the androgynous stargazing tube that I had found inside the jar, under the lid in the form of a nubile breast. Once again I am overcome by a supreme desire to possess my beloved Polya, probably awaiting me behind a door, at this very line of erotic encounter.

Between the plane of the proscenium frame and the upper and lower curtains of cloth and plaster that constitute the backdrop the characters represent an immobile love scene, the original copulation of the sky and the earth. Still actions:

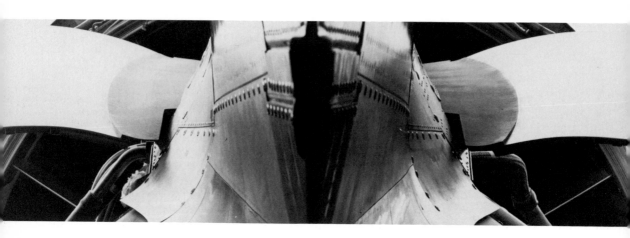

Frame 1   The sky's light conducted by several translucent ducts penetrates deep into the darkness of the earth's womb, which holds in its midst the box of shadows.

Frame 2   The yellow wall dissolves all colors as it drifts toward the higher mauve wall with its long diagonal slit.

Frame 3   The solvent of colors and the divider of colors would melt into gray air if the surfaces of the walls were to even barely touch.

Frame 4   The wind, supported by an armature of wire, fertilizes every orifice and generates a cloud of wrinkled, starched cloth.

55

Frame 5   The chimney explodes in ecstasy, ejaculating its rings into the sky and projecting its roots into mother earth, while the perspective arcade conveys a presentiment of genital shallowness.

Frame 6   The limpid sphere of metallic light and the somber round of wooden shadow close this mute love dialogue without tears, where each copulating character is unanimously and unitarily two.

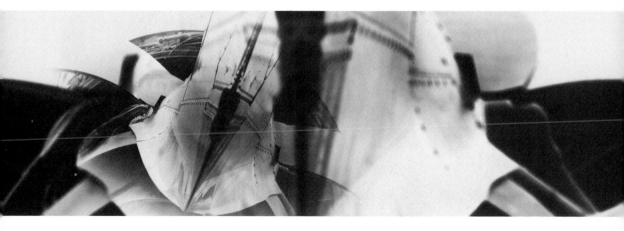

ONCE I HAVE made sure that the shadow dweller is absent, I decide to abandon the frontal position and move around the triangular object. It occurs to me that no human being can hide between the folds of the curtain; nevertheless, my yearning to inhabit this wonderful place prevails. Wishing that it might develop into the real order of existence, I circumambulate this curious impossibility, attempting a fuller appropriation of the stage.

On the right side Freedom's long elevation displays itself as autonomous from anything under the plane. Even though the characters must be the same gesturing subjects that I observed before, from this angle they reveal a totally different order. Probably built by liberated men and women and resting confidently upon seemingly solid but invisible foundations, they appear eternal. Here, the characters copulate alone or in trinities, performing obscene circus acts. *It is evident that all true freedom is dark and infallibly identified with sexual liberation that is also obscure, although I do not yet know precisely why* . . .

In the complex circuits of multiple intercourse the characters become fragmented. Excluding the idea and the feeling of birth and death, the combinations on the stage of freedom are reduced to hedonism and torture. The salon is heated to an unusual temperature and illuminated by chandeliers. All present are naked: storytellers, wives, little girls, little boys, elders, friends . . . Everyone is sprawled on the floor and, after the example of animals, each character changes, commingles, entwines, and couples incestuously, adulterously, sodomistically . . . The company gives itself over to every excess and every debauchery that can warm the mind . . .

Parts of the leaning colossus, previously hidden under the round, now resemble fragments of a marionette that has lost its anthropomorphic features. The cords linking it with the puppeteer, whose presence one can infer behind the fabric cloud in elevation, have snapped and hang haphazardly from the stage wire armature. The purpose of the whole articulated wooden machine is to set in oscillating motion a handlike skeletal structure that surrounds and glides over a very long, cylindrical object. The mari-

onette transfigures into one of those strange men depicted in Venetian narratives, dressed in wax, with noses as long as sausages and eyes of glass. *Just as these birdlike doctors with their double sandals failed to be protected from the Black Death, the mechanization of love fails in its quest for infinite efficiency in pleasure and leads to the contemporary disease of fragmentation, the tragedy of absolute unfulfillment in the pervasive simulation of eternal cryogenic life.*

An intense pulsation takes hold of the glimmering sphere as I try to focus on its surface. The coruscation of the sun filling the urban square gives way to a series of revolving images of which the most dominant is the pigeon of San Marco. *Will the explosive device grow to deconstruct the simulacra in the old city and substitute a novel order? (I must always keep my suitcase within sight.)*

From the sphere emanates a golden fog that settles like dust on lofty winged lions, on the infested and ill-smelling reflections of gothic and classical palazzi, and on the beautiful, naked blond cherub who ran around the ducal palace colonnade followed by his parents in the hot summer afternoon. The pigeon swallows the cacophonic music of a wasted romantic age that, without form and melody, sets a rhythm for coffee consumption on the square. Visiting the gilded paradise in the Byzantine basilica, the lateral spherical V-shaped gap of the German tourist's dress, the symmetrical front and back of which are held together by a line from the center of the neck to the center of the hip (ignoring the thickness of the body), coincides with the inverted perspective depth of the mosaic representations on the apse.

A nostalgic collage of spherical projections reflecting an order that, in fact, no longer exists? Such was the order of reality at a time in history when war and destruction were also possible as truly human acts. In the old urban arena, before killing an enemy one had to stare at the white of his eyes. The city of San Marco, scarred by countless passions and desires, seems movingly alive in its boundless obscurity but is in fact a stately corpse animated by a spurious life in a pacified nuclear world.

The field of stone contracts and dilates, becoming narrow and open as it

57

is transmuted into light and shadow. This thinning cinematographic theater reveals a labyrinth of hope and disillusion. Ebb and flow of emotion. Oscillating distortions. *The palpitating image of the beloved stripped bare? The enigma of the city as a stage of erotic encounter?*

The streets are completely empty except for the tourists, inconsequential voyeurs. On the deserted red square the pigeon lies dead. It probably ate of the pulsating sphere and the order of the old city exploded in its entrails. Now the pigeon is growing, its turgid body swells until it fills the center of the square. The rest of the city loses its glorious coloring and is obliterated.

No one lives in Venice anymore. In all likelihood its facades are only preserved along the canal from the train station to San Marco. The remaining parts of the one-time glorious maritime capital have deteriorated and become inaccessible, most islands being underwater. When tourists arrive, after having been counted by the authorities, they are expected to pay for admission and take a boat from the station to the square. The boats now surely run on rails fixed to the bottom of the canal, alternating vaporettos and gondolas, while the whole system and its typical characteristics, the murkiness of the water, its artificial stench, etc., are controlled by men in white robes who operate electronic instrument panels located in an invisible bunker behind some facade.

Now the tourists are visiting the pigeon, squeezing in through its mouth! Inside they find realistic simulations of old Venetian institutions and experiences. Placed in appropriate settings, in obscene juxtaposition, illustrious Venetian citizens of all ages perform the actions for which they became famous. These are the beautiful corpses of the last Venetians preserved for posterity and injected with Raymond Roussel's life serum.

Comfortably seated on mechanical winged lions, the visitors first witness how the old campanile, with its gilded spire lit with fire to serve as a beacon for the Maritime Republic fleet, crumbles to the ground on July 14, 1902 at 10:00 A.M. The reconstructed tower is built downward as a cemetery. Trans-

parent walls expose a lattice of cubicles where live cadavers forever await death.

Every so often the mechanical winged lions stop, allowing the visitors to step out into postcard stage sets to have their pictures taken. Behind the cardboard facades that accurately duplicate the originals the tourists can stay in comfortable hotel rooms with showers and cable television, personal rations of shampoo and liquid soap, evening mints and smoke detectors. Visitors can sample perfectly safe varieties of Venetian food cooked with artificial ingredients (it is said that the Black Death caused the city's final demise) and buy exact reproductions of all of the art treasures ever produced in Venice. All items can be ordered by telephone from catalogues placed in each room. And, for a modest sum, tourists can acquire splendid Venetian men and women for the purposes of crime and sexual intercourse! *The cadavers of plague victims suffered no internal disfiguration . . .*

If visitors are short of time or must continue their journeys, the mechanical lions can take them on a tour of selected cubicles: the Red Priest stares at a young orphan girl's legs as he improvises a section of "Lauda Jerusalem" on the harpsichord . . . Pantalone now appears as a Venetian bourgeois in a play by Goldoni . . . the cicisbeo casts his gaze upon the canal while the noble woman in his care touches herself . . . Francesco Foscari becomes extraordinarily thin in order to be doge for thirty-four years . . . the heroic Carlo Zeno recalls in jail how he personally tested the passability of a ford by wading through water up to his neck . . . a prostitute seduces a masked gentleman at Cafe Florian . . . the true cross miraculously floats over the Grand Canal . . . the nuns of three convents compete for the honor of supplying a mistress to the newly arrived papal nuncio . . . hundreds of master craftsmen leave for home passing under the archway of the Arsenal . . . Vitale II Michiel is assassinated by the populace at the doorway of San Zacaria . . . pigs and cows squeal as they are slaughtered in the Rialto market . . . the masked noblewoman holds the long nose of the doctor with both hands . . .

Then the tourists are excreted through the pigeon's anus. Numb and comfortable, the simulated droppings continue to accrue, covering and asphyxiating the world . . .

The sphere stops vibrating, and I must continue my journey around the triangular stage.

ON THE LEFT SIDE Necessity's long elevation also resembles an autonomous order. Here the order of creation is exclusively uncovered. A starched curtain perpetually hides the order of culture. The single absolute verity of our finite existence is represented by the coffinlike box of shadows that rests in front of the plaster curtain. *This is the reality that grounds and reveals the true and the false but remains thoroughly incomprehensible apart from the realm of freedom, where human experience makes death in life possible.*

Suddenly an asphyxiating darkness permeates the air: the unmistakable smell of fear. *A stranger at the airport may have placed an explosive translucent sphere in my suitcase. This is a distinct possibility now that plastic explosives can pass undetected and are ten times more powerful . . .*

Suspended between ascent and descent, back at the point of negative infinity, my excitement in anticipation of crossing a threshold is exacerbated. The same familiar landscape materializes under a bizarre obfuscation. Everything seems in question. In the space of the stage where I have been before, all known characters appear new and unfamiliar, reconstituted in an alien structure. *Perhaps now, once and for all, it will be possible to penetrate the mirage of endless reflections, the theater within a theater, to arrive at the essential locus of fulfillment.*

"Ooo-oo-oooom." A humming fills the space. *Omnipresence? The fifth hour must certainly last longer, still at the outer edge of the sectional plane . . . Or am I?*

The hitherto invisible gateway looms ahead. On previous occasions I had

the sensation of falling through its square geometry, but I have never fully traversed the vertical threshold plane. Now is an opportunity to admire the genius behind this amazing work. *I must undertake a careful examination of the dimensions and execution of this piece celebrating the entrance into a more promising realm, where I will hopefully find Polya and attain pleasure in her company.*

First I measure the gateway to ascertain if the magic of proportional relationships, evidently present, can be determined with mathematical precision and thus be prescribed for the future. I notice square frames made of matte black metallic substance incrusted on the front sides of two dark, luminescent cubes flanking the base of the opening. *These unusual modules, subdivided along their edges into accurate units of length, are presumably surveying devices.* As soon as I extract one (and not without effort), from its groove on the gateway, an unexpected magnetic field forces me to hold it horizontally. *Puzzling effect . . . The entry must be square in plan, measuring sixteen square modules, and a perfect cube in elevation.*

In my perception though, the obviously immeasurable gateway takes the form of a square-and-a-half in elevation, or four square modules in width by six in height, a total of twenty-four. *The facade has only disclosed its true shape after a metabletic transformation!* Also, as I turn the metal square from a horizontal to a vertical position, the sides of the device, which might be used for measuring height, immediately become elongated, making the apparatus utterly useless except as an equalizing instrument.

The gateway's builder has clearly understood the importance of a geometry embedded in perception, in the rhythms of breathing and copulation, in the qualitative distinctions between horizontal and vertical directions and measurements. His is the poetry of the craftsman and the dancer, whose works attain significance as frozen projections of the body image onto the plane of life. The congruence and precision of the extraordinary gateway respond to rules antithetical to mathematical recipes. They divulge instead the primordial and ever-ambiguous order of perception. These

61

rules are surely the basis of the crucial invisible harmony and are ethical and philosophical in nature, demanding that the architect be good, reserved, sweet, patient, curious, and wise.

Every detail of the construction is congruent with other parts and with the whole; nothing is fragmented, accidental, or preconceived without reference to a total outlook. Is this again possible? Also an infinite vision? The design is manifestly a product of discoveries made by the sight of fingers. Not the hands of workmen solely concerned for well-being, but wise extensions of feeling guided through poetic making by an interest in Being. This is, perhaps, the fundamental secret behind the gateway's eloquent order.

As I advance toward the structure, it appears increasingly as a mere flat elevation on the inside plane of the proscenium window. Ambiguously, however, it also seems to have real volume, suggesting a central octagonal tower inscribed in a square plan. The gateway thus exists as the synthesis of path and place, itself the theater, emphatically marking the threshold through a deep, keyhole-shaped opening flanked by the two cubes.

The structure is devoid of ornament except for two variegated, transparent figures that could well be congealed refractions. These idols reach the third cubic module in perpendicular length and are located on top of the matte black bases. A central stair climbs to the height of one cubic module and leads to the scissure of the threshold. Only the octagonal drum protrudes above the line that determines the height of the cube in elevation and raises its peak to the final height of six modules.

Unexpectedly, a grid of remarkably precise lines of light appears. A reticular cage, constructed with impalpable incandescent particles, demonstrates the accurate dimensional correspondences among the gateway's parts. Placed on the summit of the pointed roof, a spherical finial is the single element that conspicuously lies outside of the luminous scaffold.

In the center of the squares hovering laser numbers appear sequentially, designating the twenty-four sectors of the threshold that will have to be traversed before completing my journey. The enumeration starts from the bottom left-hand corner and proceeds to the right, concluding in the top

row with module 24. It becomes clear that the gateway is also a temple of divination, a clock for determining the appropriate time for human action. *The secret of squaring is analogous to that which allows man to seek harmony with the order of creation! This harmony is love, and love is epitomized in music. The builder's metier is analogous to that of the composer of melodies.* Regardless of the luminous elucidation of proportional correlations, the presence of being is overwhelming in the ineffable melody emanating from the construction.

As the numbers disappear, one by one, groups of electronic words that remain legible until all of the digits have vanished appear within each square:

1	**hands as sextant, eyes as compass, sex as rudder**
2	**a letter unanswered**
3	**masturbation of the soul**
4	**eyes as sextant, sex as compass, mouth as rudder**
5	**passageway between thoughts and feeling**
6	**hugging and squeezing a corpse**
7	**the idea and the feeling of death twisted together**
8	**dwelling of thoughts and feeling**
9	**stiffens all over like a banana**
10	**the eye is transfigured and the mouth develops a halo**
11	**the spinal column becomes a finger caressing the brain from within**
12	**dimples all over like a pomegranate**
13	**intellectual heroes and sentimental cowards**
14	**the return to nature's womb**
15	**the shortest form of forgetfulness**
16	**sentimental heroes and intellectual cowards**

63

17   the pupils of the eye protrude
18   a degeneration of the road to infinity
19   the inversion of death, the reversion of birth, and the
          annihilation of time and space
20   the whites of the eye protrude

21   boredom complicates character
22   the first stage of afterlife
23   all our senses bunching around the stem of time
24   boredom simplifies moods

21	22	23	24
17	18	19	20
13	14	15	16
9	10	11	12
5	6	7	8
1	2	3	4

For an instant the message can be read in its entirety, from top to bottom. Soon after, the cage of light disappears.

THE GATEWAY now stands out in all its uncanny materiality, conveying absolute concreteness such as gravity alone can never produce in our conventional world. *Like the feeling of two bodies entwined in one of those rare and fluid moments of enduring ecstasy?* The vaginal scissure and the octagonal prepuce have now merged into a single hieroglyph . . . This structure presents in the universe of physical immediacy all places of synaesthetic recollection and anticipation. Its corporeality becomes, indeed, the most powerful reflection of our bodies, of their diurnal frontality, rationality and emotion, flesh and memory, desires and imagination. *It is obvious that the architect has chosen his range of material values very carefully, with restraint and clarity. Paradoxically though, none of the materials used here is identifiable. They are thoroughly artificial and without precedent, possessing new colors and textures, while referring to the earth and sky, fire and water. Metaphorically they are at one with nature, but not born of it.*

The materials also betray a mastery of sophisticated manufacturing processes, far more advanced than anything I've seen to date and consequently difficult to describe. *Uncharted and often untested techniques capable of producing miraculous effects, such as the flight of man?* They are the personal secrets of a demiurge with profound alchemical knowledge, procedures that stem from the act of making itself and might perhaps be passed down to the initiates. *These processes are glaringly different from common technology. They have no other objective than the attainment of meaning through the revelation of the fragility of human existence and are therefore perfectly useless for simulating an order by means of efficient domination and control of nature.*

In profound contrast to the architecture built by the past, this amazing gateway rising from rivers of fire and water, bathed in a strange ashen light of tempered climates and set amid a clearing of moonshine and azure shadows, suggests a meaning contradictory to its materiality: *Nothing is solid.*

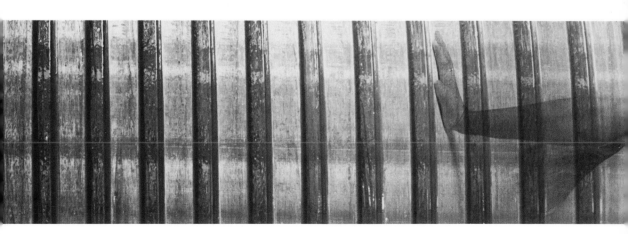

The greater the conflagration bursting from the ground through numerous crevices between the cubes and the stairs, the more abundant the emission of milky water ejaculating from the keyhole orifice and pouring down the steps. The fertilizing liquid is constantly deposited in both transparent flanking cubes, always full, while the overflowing water is gently conducted by symmetrical V-shaped troughs to fuse with the flames and in so doing beget a mist. This is the evanescent veil of breath, the substance of the structure's meticulous immateriality.

Delightful images emerge from the exquisite, undefinable materials and marvelous craftsmanship that make the gateway possible. Figures move infinitely in apparently abstract patterns. The quality of plumed and incandescent wings: flesh tones purer than those of alabaster, reds more intense than those produced by the crystallization of rose petals! Most striking, the colors are pristine and uncontaminated, unveiling the unnamable essence of the respective materials, rather than betraying superficial or added qualities. These substantial colors, which effectively construct the tableau, are animated by an internal light, like the pigments of life itself.

The cubes flanking the stairs are, in contrast, oppressively bleak: the most explicit presentation of nothingness as the ultimate absorptive mass, grinding being to a halt. This total, essential blackness conveys a stillness that differs sharply not only from other material colors but even from the darkness of the deep shadow behind the keyhole opening. Indeed, the blackness of embodied experience there is somber yet vibrant, stirred by invisible winds and by a few corpuscles of live sunlight that radiate within its depths.

Examining the cubes carefully one can find, besides the grooves for the modular squares, invisible inscriptions that can only be read by touch. The black letters on the left cube refer to the spherical finial on the roof:

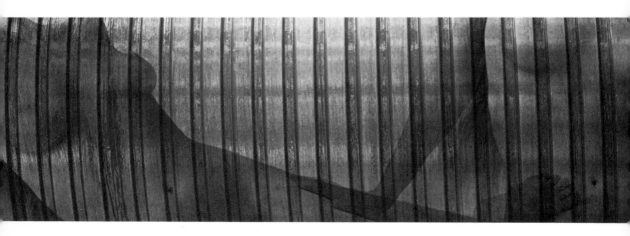

The brain is shaped by lovemaking into a spherical rump, so absolutely smooth that it must remain immobile. The act of love transmits to our nerves and tissues the sensation of total roundness: the image of God.

The inscription on the right cube is more extensive:

God the Mind, being both male and female and existing as life and light, by a word gave birth to a second God, the Demiurge, which then being a God of breath and fire, made the cosmic order of the perceptible world, and its rule was called DESTINY . . . Next Mind, the Father of all beings, engendered Man like himself and loved him and gave him all that had been produced; for the man was beautiful, reproducing his Father's image, since God was amorous of His own image. When man saw creation, he wanted to produce something himself; and the Father gave him permission . . . Then God broke the bond that united all things, and male and female were separated in both man and animals. At once God said "Increase and multiply and let beings with intellect recognize themselves as immortal; and let them know that the cause of death is love.

67

Polychromatic totems stand on top of each cube. The interweaving figures of both idols shift kaleidoscopically with each view. On the left an enrap-

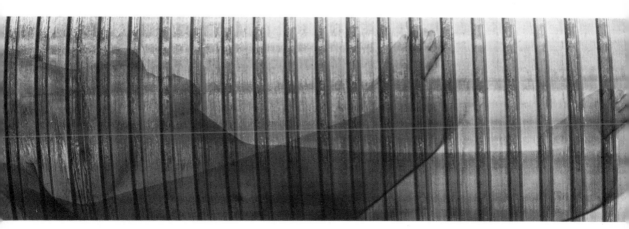

tured eagle with open wings abducts a young child, clutching its shirt in order not to hurt the delicate pink flesh with its claws. The child, naked from the navel down, is resting its feet on the bird's large tail. The plumage around the eagle's beak stands on end, and its violently throbbing tongue betrays an uncontrollable voluptuousness. Voluptuousness Herself sits on a throne with Vatican insignia. The head of a pelican emerges from a deep purple religious habit. The throne metamorphoses into a tree in which the shapely and remarkably smooth legs of the young woman are transmuted as a result of the failure of love. Her drapery suggests and partly unveils her virginal body, the breasts fully visible with nipples as diamonds, her golden hair floating until it fades into light and mist.

The vertical narrative of the luminous totem on the right is equally difficult to describe. A black panther casts a sensuous gaze upon a rapturous man whose head is distended backward, both hands firmly grasping the horns of a bull's head that emerge from his lower body and his sex. The cross of the bull's horns is presiding over a ceremony in which the mystical novice's head is shaven and the pleasure-yielding orifices of her body spiritually sealed for eternity. The young gnostic woman, removed from the world, introspectively attains perennial ecstasy. Her breasts are overflowing with milk. She is holding a lighted torch downward in her right hand and an extinguished torch upward in her left, her golden hair likewise floating until it fades into light and mist.

The androgynous tower-gateway now reveals itself as the paradigmatic mouth, a structure otherwise devoid of ornament. The central stair and the lips around the keyhole are of the whitest possible skin tone, conveying a blinding erotic iridescence to the threshold. The octagonal tower itself seems to have been built with siding consisting of parallel stripes of blue, surpassing in spirituality the clearest of noon skies. The technique for constructing the pyramidal roof probably entails the application of a secret amalgam of graphite particles, shimmering with internal humidity: an effect befitting man's natural lasciviousness! This quality complements stunningly the natural feminine lubricity, evidenced by the trickling liquid that con-

stantly renders the steps slippery. The spherical finial has been constructed with two diametrically opposed materials: one half is made of the brightest of exploding silvers, the other of the darkest of imploding obsidians.

I could admire endlessly the grandiose structure, the exactness of relationships, and the inexhaustible but evanescent diversity of texture and color. The gateway pays tribute to the complementarity in love of fire and water, of sun and earth, of the maker's intellect and his erotic disposition. *This vision of a potential new order is overwhelming, a joyful sign of hope for a venerable time to come.* My sight remains adrift, floundering on the surface of objects. *I am in a frenzy; my mind overflows with amazement.*

Pleasure now excessive. I fix my intermittent stare on the various details of the glimmering fissure. Dominated by blind wantonness, mouth gaping, I yearn to satisfy the desire of my gaze and fill myself. *O architecture! A mere reflection in the waters of remembrance? The memories of your future in the company of my cherished Polya abound!*

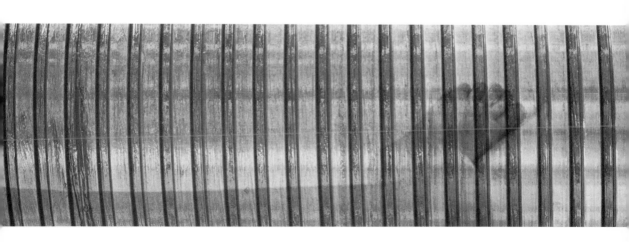

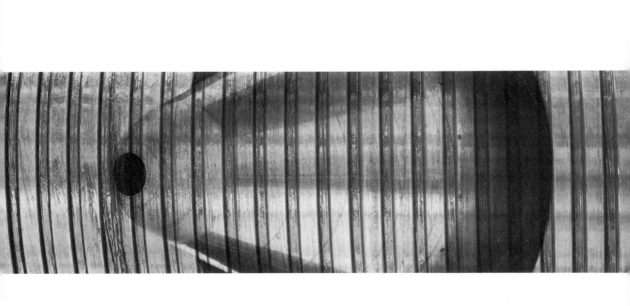

THE HYPNOTIC AURA of the gateway is sufficient to annul my anxieties and obliterate my most recent memories, even those of impending doom and chaos! I cannot believe that such flawless work was created by either mortals or immortals. The careful presence of the thinking hand! While the gateway's size, symmetry, elegance, and precision of craftsmanship and execution all appear as astounding qualities of the Divine, its unnatural materiality far surpasses any imaginable examples of existing or potential products of technological manipulation, genetic or otherwise.

I stand back to examine the collage of fragments and debris on the stage. *I cannot help but lament the immense pleasure and meaning that these ruins of a future order might yield to our thinking bodies if they were complete and accessible in their temporal and spatial fullness. The final realization of the concrete poem of reason . . .* But here and now I fix my eyes on the keyhole . . . *Perhaps beyond the threshold I may find the venerable altar of Venus and Eros, Astarte and Kama; the origin of the mysterious fire, the bow and the arrows, or simply the beautiful naked woman with her iridescent skin, floating in defiance of gravity behind the gauze curtain, her absence from my side excruciatingly painful.*

I remove my shoes and socks and proceed up the steps, feeling intimately refreshed at the contact of my feet with the cascading sheath of life water. On the threshold the blond cherub who leapt onto the spherical projection through the shallow colonnade rises above my head enshrouded in a still mist. He turns and describes a spiraling motion, flaunting his round, porcelain buttocks, until he eventually melts into the very substance of the hymen.

Without hesitation I now penetrate the membrane. *Through the glimmering fissure or one more illusory threshold?* There is no violence. The quasi-cylindrical passageway unfolds as a reality of simultaneity: at once enormous and

tight, cimmerian and luminous, polished and bristling, humid and hot. One space swarms in the other space, like little stars and sparks or the tinsel embedded in the panels of extruded plastic. As far as I can tell, amid scattered shadows, I am fully inside. *This could, at last, be the vessel of love.*

Along the sides of the tunnel, at a distance impossible to estimate, plaques or screens of a black, glazed material are inscribed with amber electronic characters. There may be one per passenger. My movements are precisely reflected in every monitor as I advance into the passageway. Confronted with my image from the front and back, my body is confounded. This multi-vantage-point cinematic representation of myself is related to my motions in congruent and reciprocal binary relationships of such complexity that, for a moment, perhaps close to a full hour, I am convinced that this deceptive phantom is my real body and soul!

I AM CAUGHT in a peculiar state between consciousness and delusion. My disorientation is exacerbated by the immaculate cleanliness of the pavement and ceiling, totally free of organic matter, and by the heterogeneous maze of conduits, circulations, and connectors, both visible and hidden, necessary to service the sleek screens, their central artificial intelligence, and other assorted outlets and ventilation grills.

A vibrant frieze of frozen electronic mosaics runs on a line along the sides of the passageway. It depicts vast arrays of bodily fragments garbed and framed to enhance lascivious feelings. This symphony of games and feasts is linked thematically by simple, interweaving melodies and sharp, evocative rhythms and by the uniform quality of high definition video colors.

The scenes in succession: men and women holding hands and eating mushrooms through a slot in their huge simulated buttock-heads, which are in fact thin, helmetlike, satin headpieces that conceal their real faces and make them look like insects . . . a large sphere with the texture of a

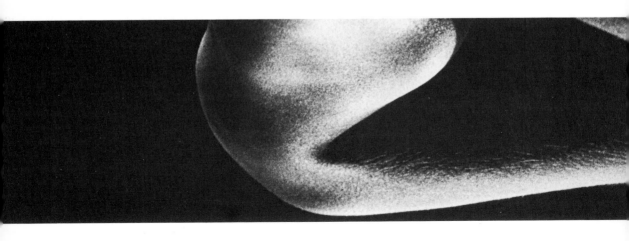

blown-up human skin balloon rolling along the horizon of a gray landscape, its valve shaped like a nipple and placed exactly at the center. In the foreground twin sisters with bulging pants and exposed navels dance frantically, their arms around each other's shoulders . . . the sun, also a shining nipple, excretes droplets while setting behind the mountains. Among them the volcano's contour is, frankly, pubic, its top capped with a sprinkling of tiny hairs . . .

Next along the frieze, lying back on the branches of a cork tree that has been immodestly stripped, poses a young woman whom I recognize. She has truly metaphysical features. Her skin is intensely white but not transparent, and her jeans are held in place by a breast protector and suspenders of the same material. Someone has stopped drawing the foliage and buildings, and from the perspective emerge thousands of yellow butterflies. At the vortex's center appears first a sad, profoundly erotic gaze and then a vagina that opens up like a rose on the colorful carpet: a soft, undefinable body the immense flexibility of which allows for unimaginable contortions, moving as if guided by the peristaltic undulations of a mollusc. Near the end of the frieze a slim woman dressed in a black lace chemise and a short, tight red skirt, dances with a bare-chested man. Their gestures are so sensuous that the considerable gap between them is obliterated by an energy differential approaching infinity. She leans back once, twice perhaps, onto the idle right hand that barely touches the humid threshold and a cornucopia of flowers and fruit.

Contrasting with the flatness of the images on the frieze, two parallel myths in the form of three-dimensional colored light reliefs fill the internal surface of the cylindrical vault. Each hologram is animated by autonomous movements of a nonmechanical nature, and the stories are deployed, like a continuous exhibit of tableaux vivants, along the full thickness of the keyhole:

73

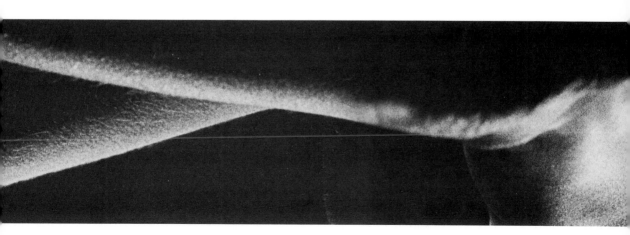

ON THE LEFT

Pasiphae, the pulchritudinous queen, crouches naked within a wood and leather cow, her knees and elbows resting on the beast's hind and front legs. The machine is revealed as a cutaway axonometric showing the queen leaning forward while a lascivious bull in the distance focuses his gaze on the bovine genitals, seeking unwittingly illicit intercourse.

King Minos takes a hike and crosses the line between the bull and the mechanical cow. NOTHING happens.

74

The bull and the queen make love. Their offspring is the monstrous Minotaur, a product of both adultery and hierogamy. He is placed in the labyrinth, then slain with the help of Dedalus.

Dedalus builds wings for him and for his son Icarus. Intoxicated with power and love, Icarus flies too close to the sun, the wax holding his wings melts, and he falls to his death. Torn with grief, Dedalus offers his own wings as a sacrifice in the temple of Apollo.

ON THE RIGHT

Virginie, the beautiful flight attendant in uniform, adopts a shameless pose, her voluptuous painted face uplifted. The machine, a sort of crenelated platinum crown pointing downward and lined with crystalline semiconductors, is disclosed as a set of labyrinthine technical diagrams of an electromagnetic device. In the distance the stark naked supermale exhibits his permanent erection. He is wired to the crown while strapped to a chair and is about as intent on his purpose as a cadaver.

The pilot places his hands in the space between the electrified magnetic poles of the powerful love-inducing machine. NOTHING happens.

The supermale and the machine to inspire love fuse in convulsive paroxysms while the pilot and flight attendant attain voyeuristic orgasms. As it may have been mathematically projected, the seductive machine is seduced and subsequently falls in love with the man. The red-hot crown collapses into the supermale's skull. Their offspring: the coagulated translucent water or explosive tears of molten glass flowing down his cheeks. The labyrinth of twisted molecules from the life water wielded by Dedalus is transformed into a new generation of better and more splendid men and women.

Dedalus grafts wings onto his new genetic breed. Inebriated with power and nihilism, the bionic birdmen and women fly and copulate eternally behind the clouds. Torn with grief, Dedalus amputates his wings and longs to recover his mortality.

75

I WALK, walk, and walk. An immeasurable distance! Perhaps only two or three paces or the length from the tip of my middle finger to the palm of my hand, but I come to the end of the threshold. Beyond the gateway's thickness all seems enveloped by grim and uninviting shades of gray. The contrast is extreme between this image of darkness and the colorful electronic icons that line the tunnel of the keyhole orifice. The heavy surrounding walls seal all apertures, visible and invisible. Despite the fact that ears can certainly hear deeper than the eyes can see, a chill silence prevails.

Afraid to continue on this course, I decide for a moment to retrace my route and make my way back. Suddenly I face the lacerated opening I crossed a moment ago. I am struck by a startling combination of unusual noises and a repetitive, very soft high-pitched music that comes from the direction of the ruins. *An acoustic carving of space?* The noise is probably the result of substantial transformations undergone by the architecture in the preceding sectors. Built upon a liquid melody of sustained and merging electronic notes, the strange music weaves threads of crystalline percussive sounds without resolution. In all likelihood the sonority emanates from the transmutation of artificial materials as they decay and coalesce into one another, unexpectedly becoming biomorphic, visibly living tissue.

Behind the folds of the bloody, ruptured hymen, gigantic, amorphous Dragon abruptly appears, emitting a strident song while constantly modifying its shape, obstinately remaining in a permanent state of flux. This ever-changing manifestation of life may be impossible to depict. No appropriate speech can be invoked to stabilize and ground its horrific reality. *The monster is utterly present, eluding our appropriation while it alludes to a superior order and therefore, in a sense, must endure beyond words. This is how it has always been yet we still feel compelled to describe it.*

The Dragon's most striking characteristic is that it is simultaneously animal and human. *Are there perhaps no more autonomous orders?* Its frightening lack of form makes its essence wholly transparent, fluctuating between a

structure of bones and a structure of flesh: vertebrae, elephant's tusks, human skulls, panther's teeth, bull's horns, serpent's skin, panther's eyes, human buttocks, flaccid and firm breasts, female genitalia, the trunk of an elephant, and testicles hanging under an armpit. All polarities are reconciled in this embodiment of the self-fecundating Mother Earth, the womb and the grave of man whose roots, penetrating the cubic ground, are about to metamorphose into a serpent.

This formidable apparition astonishes me beyond all bounds. The monster will surely advance toward me and I shall perish—in a terror that resembles ecstasy—asphyxiated by its sooty but intensely seductive deadly breath: the primal aroma of corporeal excretions!

I turn my back on the Dragon and run, plunging once more into the gloomy, disorienting tunnel. The meandering gallery makes it impossible to fix one's mental location. I hasten, in panic, as if drawn forward by an unavoidable force. Corridors and apertures repeat themselves and open into one another in countless unfoldings, while the passageway yielding to my body in motion is the only true one, mysteriously contradicting my perception. *The thread of Ariadne would be of no use to unravel this order! My own anguish makes the path increasingly narrow and somber. Primordial suffering or original sin?* Through the tension in my legs, I sense at first that the tunnel is descending, the light growing fainter and the Dragon's utterings can no longer be heard. Beyond a certain point, however, the slope of the ground can no longer be determined. There is no more vertical motion. Darkness descends upon me as if it were a viscous, mercurial fluid, excommunicating all light. Not even a trace of dimness from the entrance! I can hardly distinguish my hands as they grope for obstacles in this cavernous pit. The laden air is almost impossible to breath! *The unlit expanse where the distinction between inhalation and exhalation is obliterated? Pitch black.*

Perhaps the somber waters of chaos that predate all eternity presently surround me. A subterranean wind! Neither gentle words nor harmony in the voice of the earth. No sacred river, no sunless sea. I am paralyzed in dread. My muscles stiffen like those of a corpse, and in its immobility my body recedes

from consciousness.

Am I, in fact, inside Dedalus's labyrinth, the primordial symbol of cultural order? Have I finally found the concrete materialization of the human condition, the dwelling of being—lost? Or the long corridor of the vessel that is the space of being, where life glides, perpetually growing in height and excavating in depth? Have I perhaps escaped the Dragon of Light simply to plunge into its very entrails? I seem to be embraced by intestinal coils and bats' wings, as if journeying through a digestive tract from the mouth to the anus. This structure probably constitutes the foundations of the marvelous architecture that I have formerly visited! The gutter and the cosmos? An astounding revelation of universal isomorphism, yet I still yearn to return . . . Perhaps the Dragon will vanish and I will be safe . . . Vain hope!

It is obviously impossible to return to the origins. Clearly the Dragon has become consubstantial with darkness, and I must continue on my path through its serpentine body in order to discover a new luminosity of being. I have entered the womb of the mother and cling to her in fear, wishing to be regenerated as her child. Perhaps my blood now joins the plasma of the serpent and in these gutters that spiral into the depths of the earth spills through its crevices searching for the sacred, the primitive geological veins that coagulated at the embryonic tremblings of chaos. Hopefully I can be reborn into the second great cycle of history and possess a vitality from having assimilated the mother within myself . . .

Despite these hopes I feel exposed and helpless. *Traveling naked on an empty stomach? In a state of tension as if all were extended, inflated, and subjected to compression. My own tension, alone, in the immensity that is now inside. Nothing outside, all inside.* Again the unexpected visit of the short, shaggy flight engineer who always requires exclusively functional explanations! *This must be a bad omen, prophetic of an ill-fated destiny. The engineer's spell of rationality falls upon me, forecasting even greater suffering and anguish.*

At once the dismal dungeon takes the semblance of an inescapable prison. My strength fails even further, and I fall into a gulf of exasperation. Still

immobilized, I vehemently desire my own death. *An inhabitable order of volumes composed under the light may never again be feasible! Logic is outdriven by an unsurmountable despair.*

I am deeply saddened by the thought of forfeiting the fruits of my devotion. My inner desire, however, is intensified by this prospect of ultimate detachment . . . The short bearded man vanishes into vertical, slightly disjointed slivers as soon as I invoke the name of Polya and the echo of my breath reverberates in the funereal vaults. *I am not prepared to let my body rot in these infected and ill-smelling entrails! If I can only avoid touching the breasts of the goddess as I walk, I may narrowly escape being buried alive.*

As I remember, the labyrinth is surely the foundation of the concrete poetry of reason, the other side of architecture, where I must seek my beloved. Indeed, the straight corridor is at once hard and soft, flesh and stone, like the city itself. One instant I tread between two walls of petrified sponge and frosty crystallized foam layered with sharp and dangerous edges, stepping over hardened bubbles of chlorine. The next moment I glide on a stream of molten metal and opalescent veins, now barely warm. A smooth surface that vibrates with inner life and guides my progress along protracted curves where to distinguish between slow and fast motion is senseless. *This is possibly the very realm of inverted perspective in which distant objects are clear and pristine while those closer in are dark and invisible. The labyrinthine sphere that I may have finally become!*

Excited by this elucidation of the enveloping chasm, I recover some strength and slowly continue my pursuit along the passageway. The shadow may soon infiltrate our pores and exude a humid heat. *Perhaps the serpentine digestion of the serpent? Sensation itself: the first ascent.*

THIS PRISON, which for mankind represents the necessity of unbuildable architectural invention, is revealed to my introspective vision in the

form of thirty consecutive frames, a series of incrustations formed over and within me. My life boils in every successive image of objects and thoughts. Each frame explodes into darkness in front of my eyes when I attempt to penetrate the spaces by stepping into them. In every instance the baroque mist lifts and the distant spaces and events acquire an uncanny metaphysical clarity. In the foreground the chaotic obfuscation of the tunnel scatters backward, flattening the perspective spaces into impenetrable planes. Unlike the Dragon, the views offered through the frames are not fluid; they simply present an initial and an altered state. A realization of parallax? After the explosion has taken place it is possible to detect how the transformation has affected the initial state by squinting.

The literal iron bars and the represented human prisoners that limit and fill the original dungeons vanish after the explosions. In the first frame, behind the arch that was previously a barred opening, the prison becomes more real as it attains infinite dimensions. An implausible set of colossal steps that are not a representation but rather appear to be constructed on the flat plane provide the limitless boundary. What remains is an unbuildable, utterly precise, and novel architecture that conveys depth through endless stairs and balustrades that can only be fathomed by a disembodied gaze. Escaping from this utopia by reducing it to precedents in the form of conventional fixed scales or perspective points of effluence is obviously impossible.

In several successive frames prisoners of stone are pulled apart and fused into posts, like fragments of an order at last oblivious of gravity. There follow paradoxical intersections of wooden bridges and masonry pillars that would occupy the same space if they represented building in three dimensions, cumbersome circular piers surrounded by sweeping stairs and crowned by radial galleries and bridges that go nowhere, and centrifugal towers placed under the spell of inexplicable forces that transcend the logic of statics to attain truly bewildering effects. An improbable architecture maybe, but real nonetheless, revealing the unutterable poetic truths of construction. The imprecise and faint imitations of nature in the background of the literal prisons are replaced by a maze of hallucinogenic stairs, vaults,

and buttresses that recede into negative infinity. In consecutive frames are a colossal, wheel-shaped skylight magically held in midair, a gateway that opens into the massive center of a stone pier, and an assortment of Gothic towers collaged over pitched roofs. These rest successively on top of brick vaulting, slender Corinthian columns, granite prisoners, effigies of heroes, and implements of torture. In all frames the sky itself is ubiquitous but vacant and unreachable, appearing low under the grills or beyond upright webs of masonry and beams.

All fragments of the disintegrated wood and stone buildings are held together by chains of rope or by their own transmutations into smoke. The views exemplify a new tectonic that only operates on a plane, in a nonspecific dimensional universe that demands invention over imitation. *This fragile order posits the primacy of the poetic imagination and thus imprisons modern humanity with its antithetical values.*

The architecture becomes a self-generating machine, terminally incomplete, building on its own ruins. The prison buildings, originally represented as fixed containers of sorrow, turn to be the act of building the prison. The prison as an institution is no longer present. *Is it no longer possible? Has man failed in his attempt to dictate the laws of morality by reason alone? Are we back to acknowledging the ineffable reality of an incomprehensible divine justice? The spiraling order in history and its unavoidable repetition?*

In one of the frames a distant forum is obliterated by a silhouetted screen of assorted devices for torture and impalement. The wooden stage-set machinery replaces all architecture deployed in the domain of perspective, the traditional theater of the world. In the final transformed view pulleys move incoherent building fragments, juxtaposing evocative pieces of concrete poetry, the residues of history. The large mechanical devices are the order itself not conspicuous in the product of their action. *While conceptualizing buildings as machines eventually led to the demise of meaning in the city of my memory, rational devaluation is violently transcended by this exploded identi-*

fication. The instruments of torture are also manifestations of architecture as a verb, once and for all replacing the obsolete noun and positing poetic destruction in place of technological building.

I take one more step . . .

AFTER AN UNFATHOMABLE period in the depths I am aroused by a dazzling altar. *My earlier perceptions in the mysterious labyrinth must have occurred without external light!* I move toward the brighter chamber; in the distance I can see a beam of sunlight. The darkness of death is indeed consubstantial with the blindness of rebirth, the penumbra inside the egg. *What happiness! What pleasure!* My heart, close to annihilation and devoid of love, recovers its composure. The hope of finding Polya once more dictates my quest.

The center of the chamber is occupied by a horizontal slab of human proportions that seems to hover in the dim space. Around it, still deeper in shadow, lurk two or three vertical manly figures with indistinct features. *I am reminded by pedestals and sarcophagi and also recall travel insurance counters in airports . . .* The figures resemble statues of men with green smocks holding syringes and other surgical instruments. From one side on the table are four thick pieces of cord and a white silk scarf, surrounding the blood-stained ligaments of the angel's body. From the other side the tangential point between zero and infinity is occupied by the angles of a fragmented cosmos on the horizon.

Angels and angles? The first of two complementary disclosures suggests that the labyrinth may be perceived differently if entered from the exit. Perhaps sometime before a woman had pursued a quest similar to mine but in reverse and had degenerated into a man after she had either offered herself or was forced to lie on the sacrificial table in the central chamber where I presently stand. According to ancient wisdom, women can easily degenerate into men because they have as much

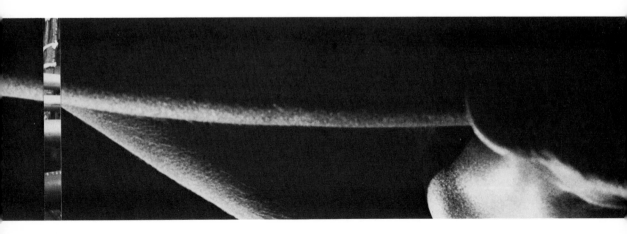

hidden within the body as men have exposed outside. Young pubescent girls were often observed to expel what was concealed within, and this was deemed to be Nature's way to perfection . . . The reciprocal degeneration is only possible by a human act, castration. In the distance nature is disclosed as a human conception. *Art is the true human nature, our only means to grasp the essence of Creation . . .*

The central position of the operating table as a seat of oneness, of the purely spiritual and unceasing orgasm of androgyny, is both corroborated and denied by a second revelation. On the slab's other long side an artist's drafting table or seat of creation is surmounted by a mirror that reflects the promised land, whence the ray of sunlight emanates. *This is truly the vision of a new world.*

I can see what is with certainty and realize that, if necessary, I will create whatever does not exist. For some time I have felt the void but have been unwilling to hurl myself into it. I believed I was refusing the world; I now recognize that I was refusing the void. For I know this world does not exist and I know how it does not exist. Until now my suffering has consisted in rejecting the void without understanding that the void is already within me. The sharp angles and sterilized geometries of the reflected landscape remind me that the Dragon will never be killed. Doom and salvation! At present, though, hope must prevail as an order has arisen from the chaos. The goddess was probably swallowed by Python, waiting for us at the center, and her navel is now in the endless serpent's body. I am obviously not dead but feel that I have been separated from existing being. Procreative love may no longer be possible, but there must be something else. Writing always in the past cannot be the only option . . .

I leave the altar behind and continue toward the light. It seems to recede into the far distance . . . Quite unexpectedly, convulsions shake my body. Exerting a superhuman effort with my legs and arms, I emerge upward through a tight orifice.

Again the omnipresent humming that accompanies distended time: "Ooo-oo-ooom . . ."

I HAVE ARRIVED at a delightful place, an artificial paradise where the norm may be to maximize pleasure. *A different place?* The prospect of a new adventure obliterates all memories of monstrosity, for the overwhelming menace with its poisonous, radioactive breath will never be seen here! Perhaps the levitating cherub was a good omen. The spiral line of his ascension, deconstructed and transformed into the geometry of the womb and the vagina from which I have emerged. I walk away.

Already well beyond the membrane, prey to excitement, overcome by the guilt of transgression . . . *I fear that this intrusion into a forbidden place may have severe repercussions. Again the same sin, now clearly unoriginal? It is also impossible to go back.* The threshold is totally invisible, having become homogeneous with the geometry of the whole: *a final mimetic act. In any case, it is better to accept my fate and die here if necessary than to return and perish in the blinding obscurity of reason.*

This region is surely not a place fit for mortals but one inhabited by divine essences. Without protection the body would probably freeze instantly and turn inside out under the force of the pressure differential. Danger overwhelms in this vessel, and all previous redoubtable encounters recede. The apocalyptic vision of the Dragon abides, the embodiment of genetic manipulation—not an illusion but the permanent dark side of the wondrous order of the future. Right here, behind the plastic panels, under the floor, in the chapel beyond the rear pressure bulkhead, where the ominous orange "black boxes" are kept . . . *Ultimately I am joyful for having escaped into another luminous manifestation, possibly beyond the thin eyelids of my sleeping body. The seemingly happy world we now share.*

This place is, indeed, the ultimate materialization of precision, the applied

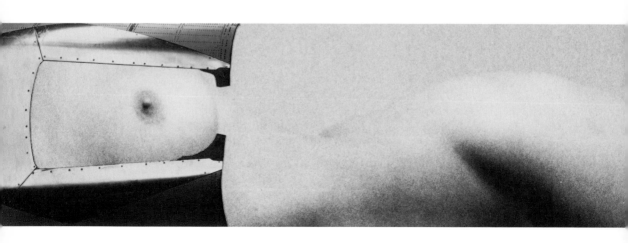

poetics of mathematics. There is no trace of nature other than the fertile presence of humanity and its physical and psychic excrescences. Sharp angles of graphite and crystal, curved metal and plastic, all perfectly still or moving at a relative speed of 939 kilometers per hour.

The man with piercing blue eyes has been scrutinizing a set of blueprints that map the absolute passage of time. Another time is also being measured within my suitcase by a pulsating sphere sympathetic to my heartbeat. The space between life and death was recently reduced to an infinitely small interval during twenty-four seconds of acceleration along the horizon. We are now airborne, and for the duration of the flight a certain time shall not advance . . . the threat of nothingness subsides. *Will this continue round the clock?* In the vessel all is arranged by consummate control and systematization.

The man to my right lowers his table and jots in his notebook:

The most important historical instrument of transcendence has always been mathematics because it generates its own development regardless of whether what is developed can be reconciled with the rest of the reality . . .

In any case, creation ex nihilo is impossible for a race of mere mortals whose destiny it is to embrace the void . . .

In the visionary drawings of the city that cannot yet be built the geometric density illustrates how tortuous and irrational such a reconciliation could be and how close is the enigma of the labyrinth to the dream of transcendence.

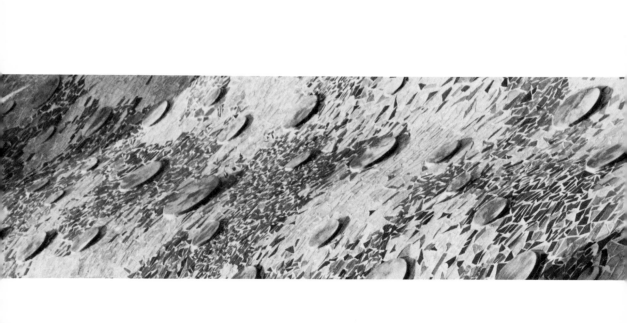

A DELECTABLE, ambiguous, and ultimately impenetrable landscape captures my gaze and obliterates consciousness. I experience the central drawing in a deceptively linear sequential progression of fourteen frames. *A mysterious cycle?* The tracings, perhaps primitive marks or electronic footprints, have a markedly horizontal bias. If this is not a musical score, it is most probable that the series is one of two. The progression contracts in one direction and expands in the other, drawing out through precise black lines on a white field the intrinsic qualities of landscape from the air: the richness of land and sea, city and country; the complex tapestry of the world of man. In extreme contrast with the horizontal landscape, we travel along the primordial gap that manifests the essence of verticality in unison with the sky.

On the other side of the invisible vertical plane, beyond the aircraft's window, the opening through which I escaped the labyrinth is unrecognizable. Magna Mater now irradiates a glaring green light. All is covered with a lush, immensely varied foliage. *This is the pubic growth that befell homo sapiens when the horizontal axis between mouth and anus became vertical and the cosmic eye was transformed into the pineal gland.* All architectural ruins surely lie behind the house of the rising sun on the far side of the generative mountain, at the center of the drawing, under the perspective arch.

The region between the earth and the sky resulting from the original separation is the semen of time, the nocturnal mist or chaos deposited in each of seven recesses. The misty breath of ever-existing time generates birth and death and the senses of all living things, one for each day of the week. This is also an unlit, windy gap, a slime of lines separated into

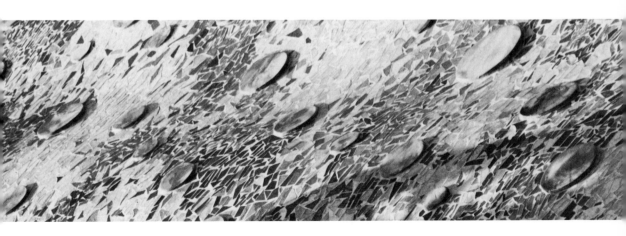

vertical sky and horizontal earth, the world of man and the ground of his geometric order, both constituting the boundaries of the realm of light.

This bewildering landscape reveals the first stage of universal differentiation through its pure horizontality. In a westerly direction, suspended outside of time, the sky lasciviously longs to penetrate the earth, and concupiscence takes hold of the globe to achieve this union. Rain falls from the heights and impregnates the earth, from which springs forth life for all mankind.

In the second drawing, slightly more contracted than the first as we advance toward the horizon, is a bridge of ancient proportions. It straddles a very somber residue of primal water, the darkest ocean in a landscape constructed with the thinnest of elemental lines. At the plane of the earth, where man stands upright and contemplates the sky, the bridge reflects a symmetry of coincidental distances. The dimension extending from the firmament to the earth's surface is identical to that between the land's crust and its foundations.

This vision of a throbbing ocean of primordial slime tempts one to rejoin the One through death. Only my intractable desire to find Polya prevents me from giving up the struggle of differentiation. Pausing on the bridge, I hear a message of thunder, a rhythmic sound celebrating the radical uncertainty of human life in the presence of a created order. *This hieroglyph decoded recommends that patience be exercised in our quest to embellish and purify life and that pleasure should be enjoyed slowly and parsimoniously.* The earth, which emerges from an indefinite expanse of primeval water is, in its manifold diversity, a construction of the same lineaments. A black gulf transfigures into the diaphanous, life-giving veins that nourish nature.

The third recess extends across the square window plane like the two previous ones. Its proportions, however, are greatly elongated. This tracing is three times more compressed than the first, occupying only about one-thirtieth of the square's vertical dimension. In this landscape of thick, accurate lines, it becomes clear that all things are composed of air and night,

and that the primordial water must have begotten all of the gods. This evolution was surely violent! From a veranda suspended over the surface: a powerful oblique line rooted in the earth and cantilevered into the heavens. I witness the shining tunic tear and the silvery egg shatter. An abstract spout of turbulent water: a dotted angle. Stemming from the earthbound cloud it swallows the phallus of him who has first jumped into the air. A salty aftertaste, intimately corrosive, fills my mouth with its simultaneous associations of revulsion and pleasure, life and death: *the bodily excretions resulting from the act of castration. The original verb for ordering and legitimate human creation?*

In the next recess of the landscape I encounter the maximum differentiation of being. All aspects of the cosmos are at last manifest: the orders of topography, plants, animals, and men. On the dance floor there are traces of ritual and sacrifice, the human acts of mimesis and catharsis that emulate divine creation. Through an enhanced sense of touch I come to know that the pores of the skin are the way or passage for the creation of water from human action. *When matter began to be arranged, there came into being a kind of way or passage, and after the way a limit or goal. The way is like a beginning or origin, whereas the limit is like an end. With the advent of man, these became the beginning and end of all things, and the totality of things acquired a nature similar to that of ink lines . . . Man is the craftsman-architect, the way or* pore *is the drawing; the beginning and the end are birth and death.*

The fifth recess is on the other side of the sequence, closer to death and rebirth. The proportions of the horizontal slit are forty to one. Water is condensed anew. On the left, the dense, crystallized primal water; on the right, the many rivers and springs of the world. *I had almost forgotten my intense thirst during the last few hours! My urge to drink turns into an obsessive craving.* In the center a masonry quay provides a point of repose. I stand quietly between the two inaccessible waters and revel in the smell of human seed, the hot and ethereal breath disclosed as the origin of fire, wind, and water.

89

I also become aware again of the plastic plane that seals the square windows of the aircraft. The landscape approaching the horizon is, in conclusion, a purely visual reality; a georama deployed in full under the moon. From my comfortable seat I can now see the sun as a hollow bowl overwhelmed by fire and surmounted by a mushroom cloud. Below, the whole earth boils and an unquenchable flame pervades the great expanse. The darting gleam of thunderbolt and lightning would blind even the most brazen men. Chaos smolders in the fire while the broad heavens and the earth are drawn together once more. The sparse lines, the elements' permanent shadows, are inscribed forever on the dazzling page as the visible universe approaches its disappearance.

The seventh recess is the thinnest manifestation of the landscape, before it lapses into a single evanescent line. *The horizon, the final occultation (incest and rape, absolute death) cannot be spoken about but it can be rotated ninety degrees and transformed, by erotic desire perhaps, into a potential axis mundi of hope!*

I CAN HEAR the gurgle of the sap rising. The lineament is transmuted into a winged oak, the trunk and branches of which support the sky while remaining rooted in the earth. Closing the cycle, the new structure is not simply a pillar, a person, or a linden, trained in the classical manner. Its vertical symmetry is reinforced by the striking similarity and reciprocity of its roots and branches! *Up is down?* The structure also takes on the physiognomy of a fragmented skeleton prepared to become the site for the creator's labors of love. *It will eventually gather our terrestrial life and the blue sky, allowing vertical motion.*

Before I can possess Polya, I must weave a fabric of elemental lines in my imagination, a tapestry epitomizing the essence of the earth's variegated surface. The old custom required that one lay it over the branches of the great anthropomorphic tree prior to taking a wife . . . I have searched the walls of my room for a

new dimension of order, depositing the marks on the crust of my brain. Now I project them the oblique directions outlined by the branches and roots that constitute the common structure of the circumscribing spheres: our skull and the world.

Once again the ambiguity of unbuildable space emerges on the plane of sight. Solid lines are reduced to projections. Frontal objects only possible in two dimensions become concave and convex, frames first and then figures, simultaneously foreground and background. Inclined walls and columns that pierce or disjoin spaces become invisible, eventually reappearing elsewhere, while curved projection lines indicate evocative, hidden correspondences. *This vision may evolve into a second set of incrustations analogous to the terrestrial prison but deployed in the space of air travel. A truly hermetic and impregnable prison from which there is no escape? Fortunately certain particular molecular traces are so distinct that they can be differentiated as special locations in the homogeneous space penetrated by the vessel, suggesting the possibility of a real place in the future.*

Behind the melted foliage the omnipresent structure can be divined. The cylindrical vessel surrounding me is a most extraordinary construction. Among many notable attributes, it is obviously a water container, a time capsule empowered to sustain and generate life in the midst of a hostile environment where *nothing* exists. *Finally I might be able to satisfy the thirst that I had suppressed so often before!* This admirable fountain, presumably capable even of synthesizing its own water from the air, appears as a collision of plastic, metal, and plexiglass fragments bolted, welded, or glued together with amazing skill. The fountain, unadorned, as such makes no concessions to the force of gravity.

The structure's most stunning characteristic is its physical manifestation: an intriguing metamorphosis, possibly effected by the observer, transforms the wide range of artificial materials into organic matter, while sharp edges become soft graphite renderings of immense variety. The structure is a palpable and distinct synthesis of precision and contortion, conspicuously extolling the contrasting tactile qualities of multiple fragments. Behind an

91

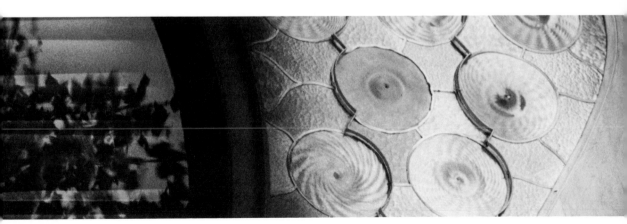

ideal image of the fecund mother, represented as a face framed by long, silky hair, with eyes as breasts, nose as navel, and mouth as vagina, stands a lascivious satyr. He is visible in the guise of a pointed steel rod holding up a curtain of liquid prisms about to rip open and flood the foreground.

Within the many angles of this self-referential realm thousands of metallic steps descend and ascend. *I recall the ominous Dragon and the sphere in my suitcase that, by now, resembles a tortoise shell.* Amid the painfully ragged objects and the unbearable transparency of multidirectional planes is a gray cloud of limbs and fleshy organs of fertile male and female plants, animals, and humans, collaged with rendered bricks, masonry, and pieces of wooden machinery. An inverted pyramid standing on its tip, constructed as a radial assemblage of twelve plastic breasts of diverse sizes, constitutes the actual water spout. From each mamilla of this pluri-essential Diana of Ephesus flows a jet of water, each a different temperature, corresponding to a time of day. *They may actually be testicles!* A stainless steel basin collects the water and disposes the tepid mixture (available for drinking) in hygienic paper cups. An inscription under the image cast in fiberglass imitation bronze reads:

To the mother of all.

The impeccable graphite sculptural drawings invite touch. Half-open lips insinuate breathing. Paper, leather, hair, and feet look soft and tender, providing the source of constant provocation for every traveler who has the good fortune of stumbling upon this theophany. I manage to suck (illicitly) from one of the breasts at the top. A few drops of cool water that gather the meteorological conditions at the appropriate seventh hour are immensely comforting. For an instant erotic implosions blunt the needles of doom scattered in the mathematical labyrinth. *The magical substance capable of dissolving the bothersome glare is the same life water that might transfer my*

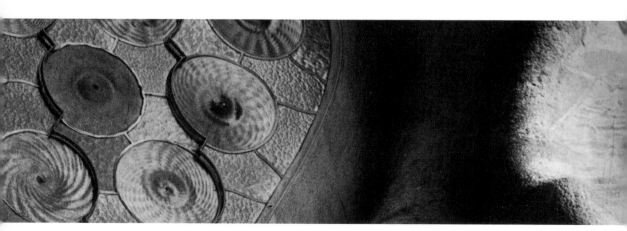

individual death to humanity.

In the heady slumber of enriched oxygen, shards of animal flesh are reconstituted into a lobsterlike monster that collapses within its hard armor and finally disintegrates into stardust to be gathered by a mortal hand. Where the angels hover in the vessel's inner space a diaphanous glow transforms all organs into jellyfish. The muscular tissue that adheres to vertebrae softens the electric impulses that traverse the cabin to homogenize perception and thought. *Again I remember the opacity retained by a leaden spherical object within my suitcase. I can also hear the guttural rumble of gastric juice and feel the contraction of my inner fibers. Fright or self-indulgence.* An agglomeration of sweet vapors and intimate smells pervades the interstices of cells and the alluring voids of desire. *Does the perfume of the flowers in this organic garden differ from the Dragon's pestilence?* Yet the melodious song of birds and perfect air temperature make it all the more idyllic. The voids of desire under the colorful blankets can now be filled; manifold orifices, deep and shallow, thoroughly saturated with soft skin and excited flesh . . . *The ultimate reality of man's destiny!*

I accept love as the final condition, that I may recapture the meaning of chaos in the shape of the womb. Thus I will ever search for the infinite structure of andro- gynous unity that wills the life of humanity from the particles of stardust that the hand has gathered . . . That on these grounds a true order of salvation may yet materialize!

The delectable vessel, site of this amazing cosmorama, is a wonderful place indeed. It caters to every possible need, supplying the necessary goods through pipes and wires for all whom it serves and transports. As a glove to a hand, this ideal environment suits the physiological self. But the perennial alienation and permanent amnesia of mortal consciousness pre- vail. In spite of our apparent satisfaction, some *thing* is missing. *I simply cannot quench my thirst by sipping reconstituted water from a paper cup, in spite of the excessively seductive phantasmagoria! Swilling this liquid is no more satis- fying than the death by drowning that would necessarily ensue! Thus I must continue the journey in pursuit of my beloved Polya—not without fear, for I*

remember the thunderous recommendation to enjoy pleasure slowly once it is found.

FOLLOWING THE SOUND of some distant harmonies of electronic percussion five tender young girls appear behind the lush vegetation. They wear metallic headbands and glowing dresses. Their long, silken white gowns cling to their bodies when the fabric is not lifted by the electric winds, revealing their round and ivory legs. They all wear shorter tunics in bright purple, green, or saffron on top of their gowns. As they walk, they move in circular motion. Their arms bare, the women are evocative of ancient nymphs, their long hair heaped abundantly upon their proud heads.

My presence disturbs them. *They are visibly startled, and as a result I feel absolutely naked. In a commercial airliner! Could this truly be the other side?* They eye me as if I were a ghost. The inner layers of my stomach again contract, this time pushing the blood into my head. My face has probably changed color. Embarrassed, puzzled, and uncertain, I fail to react. After having been totally alone throughout my protracted journey, this encounter with five beautiful women is positively surprising. *I could fall on my knees to adore them, run away, or try to keep as best I can a matter-of-fact composure . . . I am now almost certain that after escaping from the dark tunnel I transgressed a superior order. Is this realm of prepossessing, exquisite women fit for wanderers or traveling mortals? The coveted world of visible beauty has always been denigrated as inferior to that of the spirit. A senseless notion! The transcendental reality of form is at last fully accessible.* Despite the precariousness of the situation, I happily embrace the inevitability of my adventure.

When one of the women finally queries, "Well, who are you?" I can hardly speak. They approach me slowly as if they perceive my fright. Each in her own way assures me that in this unique place we are all safe and

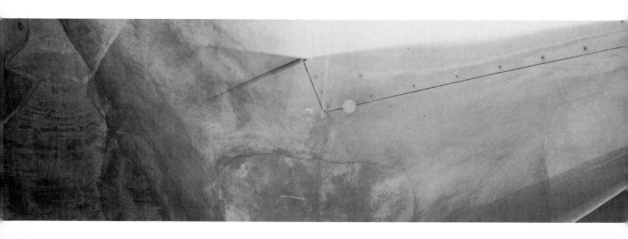

that I shouldn't fear danger or pain.

The first young girl, the most radiant to behold, grows pale and fades into the perspective distance as I try to touch her. She is consumed by the unquenchable flame.

The second evokes memories of childhood love by her ever-changing aromatic presence.

The third offers me her hand, and after I touch her, I can no longer see her. The surface of her skin brushes mine like a whisper from the past: protuberances, cavities, crevices, projecting members, tautness, and rotundity. The texture of a motherly caress.

The fourth offers me a piece of bread that condenses all the flavors of food and the contentment promised by a hard nipple.

The fifth enamors me with song, the sublime melody an explicit revelation of being. *All history is written in those notes.*

"Who are you?" they ask. My voice finally returns and I answer: "I am the most unhappy of lovers in the whole world. I love, but I can't describe the object of my longing, I can't place the craving of my heart. I even ignore where I am. I came here running away from a mortal peril."

Startled by my own voice, which I have not used for many hours, I almost fail to recognize its sonority. The suitcase under my seat must be checked!

Noticing my disorientation, the five women endeavor to explain that, thanks to my good fortune and propitious star, the rising sun, my fate is benign. Character, they say, is the cooperation of the psyche and the daimon, in effect the moral climate of man's cultural reality. Our character naturally leads us to follow the events in everyday life with which we are characteristically predisposed to cooperate. Thus character determines fate. *Even if our fate is technology?*

The motions and expressions of the five attendants are cool and precise. With a confidence that stems from extreme behavioral conditioning and codification, they emphasize that there is nothing to fear. Their mechanical gestures have developed into veritable extensions of the vessel. My response must conform to the narrow limits of normality, or the system

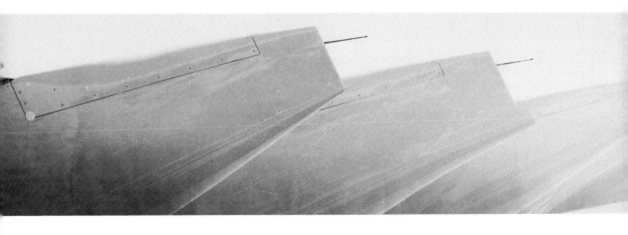

may break down. The women are evidently the most important safety feature of my adventure! *Nothing else?* In their realm is no sadness or dread. One says: "Perhaps you will even find your happiness here." "In our midst time remains still," adds another, "we inhabit the perfect state and our occupation is noble and appropriate to our age." "Enjoy your stay! In this paradisiacal region all your needs are met!" continues a third attractive woman, "here we are all sociable and maintain a permanent smile; men and women are equal on all counts for there is no room for suffering or chains where pleasure reigns supreme."

In low, monotonous yet sensuous voices they promise to take me with them. Eventually I will meet their queen whose name is Liberty and who inhabits the front of the vessel. She possesses a special wisdom that enables her to clarify destiny and can therefore elucidate my fate. Also, according to my companions, she may explain to me the connection between knowledge, flight, and eroticism.

"Soon you will meet this munificent and generous woman," they repeat, "and should Her Ladyship so ordain, you will see the solstice marker as well, the cylindrical anamorphic mirror that allows the vessel to capture and arrest time . . ." *These words fill my soul with a euphoric longing. At last, it is thus that I will have access to pleasure in the enduring present, leaving the terror and melancholy of history behind!*

UTTERLY CAPTIVATED, it seems possible to abandon my concern for objects and, at least temporarily reassured, leave the suitcase behind. I wish above all to comply with feminine desire. I am convinced that man needs not five but fifty or five hundred senses to attain knowledge, true knowledge beyond intelligence.

The five women carry an assortment of trays with edible delicacies and beverages, ornate receptacles apparently filled with perfumes and ointments, satin and linen towels, and several electronic devices. "The baths are in front," they say, "behind the fountain." Once the luminous signal has been turned off, they ask me to come with them, and I do so.

This encounter with existence brings me back to life; I am my usual old self. Even though I fear the potential eclosion of inveterate intellectual prejudices, I resolve to be a slave of the senses. Seduced by my first inspection of the fountain after escaping from the dark entrails of initiation, I tried to quench my thirst in its waters, an urge that has been tormenting me all day and has not abated. Perhaps an uncontrollably intense thirst rages throughout the whole universe . . . Despite the illustrious visions I have just experienced, I feel restless and unfulfilled . . . I cannot find repose . . . And so with resigned determination I follow five women of the senses while regretting the absence of my Polya, who would make the sixth and perfect number.

The five young girls guide me along with their engaging manners and provocative gazes. Between seductive poses they remind me that after enjoying ourselves in the feminine waters, we will all proceed to the palace of the most compassionate and liberal of queens, where I shall take great advantage of my avid infatuation and interest in love. We cross a thin partition under an inscription that reads:

**All that is desired by our hearts
can always be reduced to
the figure of
water.**

The baths—a dark and steamy sector of the vessel—are occupied by six identical metal containers whose external profile and specifications it is infeasible to determine. They are approximately cubic, I guess, disposed along both sides of an ample central aisle and filling the whole large, cylindrical vessel, both over and under the plane of the walkway. On closer examination, each container has a particular mode of entry. The detailing of their plumbing and construction systems ranges from nuts-and-bolts assembly to casting and welding.

The first woman, the most splendid to behold, invites me to step into the container immediately to the right. She looks directly into my heart and beyond the crystal of her eyes she is inhabited by a transparent, gushing spring. The door shuts behind me, and seconds later she appears in all her radiant beauty, having presumably accessed the ablution chamber through a door on the opposite side. Between us there is an undisturbed square of pellucid water; what feels like an insurmountable chasm. I seek her image by staring down into the liquid looking glass, because I wish fervently to contemplate her delightful features without causing embarrassment. Yet I unexpectedly fathom the essence of water itself, of which her total natural nudity, innocent and hairless, consists. The sheath of reflecting water is completely still and possessed by a magical animation, resembling the clearest and most gentle streams. In it the intangible motions of the swan, the whiteness and softness of feathers, and the song of lust that it sings as it dies are layered in a single, seductive mirage.

Within this chamber of plexiglass corners and polished mirrors the water is the eye of the earth, an eye that sees all by virtue of the light that it

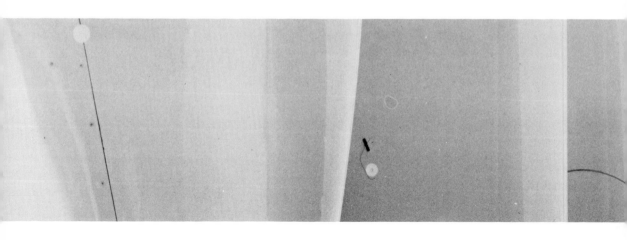

emits. The water of vision projects infinite reflections of the body of my companion, overlapping with my own image. We can see it all and love it all without running the risk of drowning like Narcissus, for this liquid is consubstantial with air, similar to the azure and green transparent atmosphere in which float Monet's waterlilies.

When I look up, I realize that the beautiful woman has not moved at all. *Have I loved her through my gaze alone? I possess her only insofar as I behold her in my conical field of perspective visualization.* She is still standing across the water fissure, smiling but draped and inaccessible. *How powerfully vivid and seductive are the rhythmic undulations of feminine water! Purified in the crystalline mirror, her naked reflection was more real in its immaculate detail than was her presence in the conventional perspective spectacle.* She remains utterly remote . . . *This chamber's purpose must be to preserve water in a manner appropriate to the girl's name and nature! I now believe that comparable mysteries and disappointments inevitably await me in the other baths.* A familiar visceral contraction: *it is time to proceed.*

Back in the aisle. Close to each door of every chamber, attached to the metal walls and to the plumbing systems, are identical glass indicators. *Cylindrical modules?* These long tubes resemble instruments that measure the liquid capacity of industrial boilers. They all contain water of four different colors—black, gray, blue, and red—precisely separated from top to bottom in distinct proportions corresponding to each bath. The woman with the mellifluous voice explains that the four liquors can be mixed, but that they will always recover their undisputed historical stratification. The black, the earth, invariably drops to the lowest depth, followed by the gray, the liquor of water, then blue, generating air, and finally red, the lightest, which may be kindled into fire. Since moist natural substance is easily formed into many dissimilar things, it is accustomed to extreme change. That part of it which is exhaled is made into air, the finest component being transformed into ether, and when the water is densified, it changes into a type of slime or earth. Therefore it is easy to see that water, of the four elements, is the most active and, as it were, constitutes a feminine first

cause . . .

The woman who had previously offered me her hand repeats this action and takes me to the second chamber, on the left of the aisle. Immediately clear vision deteriorates. Together we enter a somber, visceral place. Gentle shades insinuate a rounded space. Suddenly my skin feels as if it were fully exposed to the external world for the first time, my whole body breathes in intimate communion. Our feet are immersed in a tepid, slimy substance, and I sense the essential function of the liquid dissolving the hard, porous surface of the earthen container as it forms the primordial shapeless paste. My limbs metamorphose into part of that mud that is also dust, ash, and smoke, the first androgynous element: *the multifarious clay comprising a full range of generative fluids, from tears, milk, and wine to eggwhite, semen, and urine.*

This ablution chamber is as empty of form as possible, yet it conveys an inward materiality that derives from a tactile, primary experience of substance. *This is how scientists and poets describe the mucus of the sea, the intersidereal, cosmogonic element of life. Visually it is inconceivable that pure water may comprise a viscous and sticky matter, a universal glue allowing it to adhere to all other molecules. In this chamber, though, this primal reality is all encompassing.*

We advance toward the center. *Feminine forms, born of water, are polarized by desire! Voluptuous substance surely precedes voluptuous form.* The exact optical features of my companion are irrelevant. She is the warm, enclosing density that now forms a wave, pressing against my chest, about to turn into a woman. All of the images that accompany this experience have no cohesion or solidity. Our nudity is suggested but imprecise. *The eroticism of pure substance.*

Standing on two sides of an amorphous mound that protrudes above the surface of the water, I squeeze her hand in the hope of eliciting a response. I find with some surprise that my fingers can penetrate her flesh, which has the consistency of clay or dough. I knead the paste with vehement pleasure while my visual field is reduced to total darkness. I knead and thumb, moving my hands with the rhythm of a baker or a sculptor creating

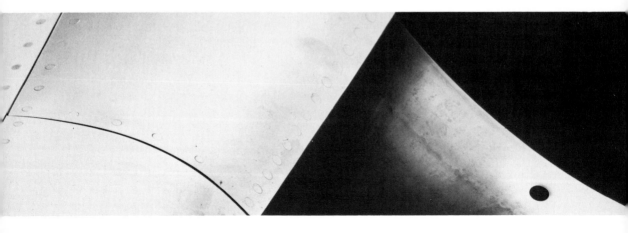

a masterpiece. Touching the interior of the primordial substance, I gain access with palms and fingers to the inner sanctum of the fertile grain.

I have grasped an unquestionable knowledge! Yet its perpetual incompleteness is also a source of immense frustration that must be the reason to continue onward. The woman who had earlier given me a piece of bread comprising all of the body's delectable flavors indicates the way to the third bath. She shuts the door from the outside and leaves me in solitude.

The salty air in this room is characteristic of a sea breeze. The space is defined by a nocturnal aquarium on three sides and by a window that permits a view of the seashore on the fourth. The center of the chamber is occupied by a complex piece of hydraulic equipment made of stainless-steel tubing, its tentacles extending along the ceiling in every direction. A polychromatic assemblage of pumps and vacuums, located at complex intersections, culminates in a round nozzle that is evidently used to fill a crystal goblet of ultramarine color standing empty nearby.

The aerial view toward the north: a setting moon illuminates the surface of the ocean and imbues it with a translucent, slightly opaque appearance. The moon, being matter before form or color, mixes with the sea to reveal the spumy and tepid essence of water as mother's milk. Water is disclosed as the primal nutrient that feeds the earth: the supreme material good! It even bulges around the shore like an overflowing fertile breast!

The surrounding aquarium water has an opalescent tint resulting from the density of nutrients. Lazy fish simply yawn and thus feed on this liquid, not unlike an embryo in the seedbed of our common mother. The salty taste intensifies. *Hunger and concupiscence exist solely on dry land or in the air. In the sea nourishment is attained without search or effort. Aqueous life floats like a dream, free from desire . . . but it is not human life.*

This mother's milk is, in fact, a bitter, poisonous liquid for humanity! Thirst can be quenched by fresh water alone, because only fresh water recreates all the flavors of paradise, that elusive ambrosia left behind in the womb. Fresh water must be the true natural or artificial transmutation of the ancestral milk . . .

The machine hums and now a dense, sweet liquid slowly trickles into the deep blue, pear-shaped goblet. *Amniotic fluid? There are very few wells dug by the devil; most water holes are cared for by saints and angels.* My companion fleetingly appears from an unexpected corner and hands me the glass. I sip the luscious draught with fruition, savoring each drop as it drenches with ecstatic pleasure every crevice and fold in my mouth: the space of the universe. *Limitless! Despite the liquor's purity, my thirst prevails.*

One more ending. Another beginning. I return to the aisle where the woman with the beautiful voice (one of two remaining) requests that I follow her into a pitch-black chamber. When the door is closed, I can no longer see her and must stand immobile. Gentle words invite me to sit down. The surface of the floor is neutral to the touch and the room is free of smell or visual distractions. In contrast with the sustained rumble of the aircraft engines over the past several hours, there is only silence: the hollowness of a colossal absence. *This is in all probability an acoustic chamber designed to convey spatial experience with sound.*

Then a liquid symphony of water springs forth; it incites an almost unbearable euphoria in my soul. In its various modalities this streamy sound of rain produces, with its pristine poetic timbre, the rhythms and melodies of nature and humanity. I can sense both intimate, subcutaneous and expanding cosmic spaces in its harmonious transformations and variations. The symphony creates expectations of melodic resolution that grow with every beat but are never fulfilled by a classical conclusion. *These melodies form the basis and principle of language, the fluid ground of speech. If all that man can utter is an echo of nature, then surely the word is primarily an echo of water.* Although interwoven with submerged bells and golden harps, I can detect the clear and luminous soprano voice of my companion. The liquefied mirror of instrumental notes, percussions, and vocal enunciations articulates a simple love song, the story of a man who could not go back to sleep when the sonorous rain woke him up. He was dreaming about his lovers, who glided about him in an undefined space, lightly brushing but never touching his body. Disconcerted by his dream, all that the man could

do was to repeat over and over two- and three-syllable words signifying hope.

I fall in love with the intangible liquid voice that so transparently reveals meaning! Then, as absolute silence once again inundates the chamber, wistfulness and excitement merge in an explosive quietus. The door silently opens and I leave.

In spite of my increasing apprehension, I follow the fifth youthful woman into the penultimate chamber. *Not the last?* She had initially triggered childhood memories through the sense of smell. As I cross the threshold behind her, her delightful aroma increases in potency and interfuses my skin. The door shut, all but her scent vanishes.

I stand on a small platform, slightly above the water that fills the chamber to the horizon, a continuous, polygonal intersection of the octahedral tank. It is dim, illuminated only by one thin, precise beam of moonlight pouring into the container from the apex of the pyramidal ceiling. Below, the perfectly undisturbed surface conveys immeasurable profundity. This heavy liquid, a fusion of water and night, exudes the doubly fresh scent of humid shadows.

The presence of death embodied by these deep and fragrant waters contrasts with the gentle running streams that traditionally carry away the funeral boat. This quiet, shadowy pool will not transport the mysterious vessel to the underworld but is instead contained by our vessel, itself in perennial pursuit of nothingness. *A soul only truly dies when transformed into water; unlike fire or earth, water is the sole element in which the human body is completely dissolved.*

As the platform gradually descends into the water, the pollution in the heavy fluid becomes discernible. On the surface the liquid consists of thick, layered iridescent rings of different colors with independent densities and internal cohesion. When I am fully immersed, however, I realize that this is the most limpid of waters, in fact the very liquor of purification! An overwhelming sense of cleanliness and freshness penetrates through each pore into every recondite fissure of my body, removing the soil accrued on

my journey. *A total absence of bodily scents allows one to believe in the possibility of absolute detachment and perennial spiritual virginity: a never-ending potential of desire that is also its fulfillment. Is this, in fact, the water of self-indulgence? This small pool resembles the mythic water of unsoundable lakes and underground regions, the water of memory used for washing the dead, the subterranean sky that also contains the vessel and is to be discovered only after the site of a sacred place has been dug.*

If I could just elapse and merge into the water! This is the element in a modality that would quench my thirst and fulfill all my desires. Surrounded by this absolutely unadulterated freshness, unceasingly new, cool, and immaculate, I swim in slow motion, like never before. I am suspended, free from gravity; this is flying. In the water one learns to navigate over the clouds, to swim in the sky. *Is this as close as one can ever come to an embodied experience of flight? Or perhaps another premonition of the future. Drifting in the dense, pristine waters of death, in a vessel, in the sky . . .*

The euphoria is short-lived and quickly turns into a source of anguish. A sensation of ecstatic immobility, a sort of suspended ascension, threatens to dissolve me in its contradiction. Wishing to leave the chamber, I finish wading across the container and exit into the aisle. *It is only in this way that I can recover my capacity for synaesthetic perception.*

I AM NOW ALONE and there is still one additional chamber to visit. *Will the sixth cubicle finally bring about the fullness of experience? A perfect number is propitious for love, and so will I find Polya here at last?* One striking feature of this chamber is the glass measuring device by the door that, instead of indicating the existence of the four elements in their various proportions, is filled with a glittering golden liquid. The colored waters that never mixed in the other containers are thoroughly dispersed in a quintessential, homogeneous liquor. There are two symmetrical inscriptions flanking this threshold:

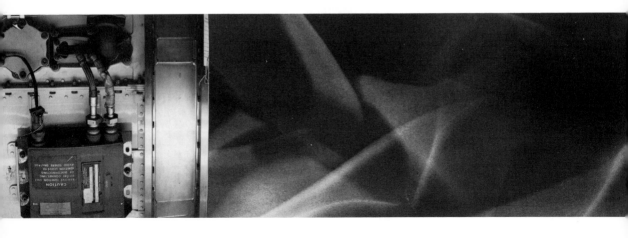

**Never urinate in the spring or the mouth of a river
whose water runs toward the sea.**

Never urinate standing while facing the sun.

The accurate parallelism of material and spiritual pollution and purification! A promise of synaesthetic fulfillment?

Entering the chamber is like a negative spatial déjà vu. I seem to stand on exactly the opposite side of the fountain, a residual space between the mass of angels and the void of angles. This sixth chamber has a polygonal plan, is lined with dark wood, and is evenly illuminated by an indirect golden light.

The five youthful women are all inside, standing or sitting along three steps that encircle the empty centralized space, which teems with the qualities of water and fire. All is saturated with the warm humidity of cosmogonic and prenatal reveries. We are intimately immersed in a stirring fusion of water and fire, the only two real appurtenances of our lives. *Whilst water, like a woman, extinguishes fire, fire generates its mother. Even the most accomplished philosopher would lose his mind confronting this unfathomable union of fire and water!*

From a fissure in the floor emerges an insubstantial flaming matter, concentrated in a fragile globe of glass, a receptacle of solar dust. Surrounded by water, the fire is preserved and prevented from exploding beyond its spherical limits. *Leibniz saw in this phosphorescent glow an image of the immortal soul, while Fabricius believed that water, kept for a long time, became a spirit, more volatile than any other liquid and liable to catch fire. This aqua ardens is most certainly a potent revitalizing and life-giving elixir.*

Over this source of energy rests a special perforated vase that exudes the most exquisite vapors of various unidentifiable odorous substances. An equally undefinable yet sensuous music pervades the air . . . *The windpipes*

105

of the sky! This must be the atmospheric symphony played through the myriad orifices in the aluminum allow skin of the vessel. The austere, smoky black surfaces of the chamber are enlivened by colorful ducts, coils, valves, and other plumbing fixtures, which control humidity and temperature. Exhaust vents resembling articulated bivalve Venus shells are located at waist level around the room, opening rhythmically as they allow steam to escape. On the wall opposite to the door hangs a urinal emitting a single jet of clear water, possibly the source used to fill the chamber up to the second step. *The furnace itself can be used to effect a transmutation of the elements into the fiery and refreshing juice of grapes! I know this is an ancient alchemical womb of the most fantastic sort; is it, by far, more fascinating than any real, existing woman within reach?*

The young girls are indeed at hand, and I find them extremely pleasing. *I cannot fathom the contrast between my recent terror and my present happiness!* Very slowly, but without hesitation, they shed their silken dresses. While gracefully concealing their most intimate parts, they permit me to admire intently their slim pink bodies in shades of peach and snow: truly spell-binding! Overwhelmed by all senses, I am filled with joy at this sudden voluptuousness. My chest expands to contain the seductive vapors of burning lubricants, the unnatural ardor of bursting tissue, and the agitated beat of crimson tidal waves. Only by looking away can I resist touching their divine bodies. The young women apprehend my dilemma and giggle naively, and so begin to engage in girlish games to make me feel more comfortable. One of them, realizing that I must miss my lover in this moment of heightened eroticism, incites me to pursue my own gratification and prophesies a propitious encounter. When I involuntarily whisper the name of my beloved, she hastens to speculate that my own name, rather than signifying "the friend of Polya," may actually mean "the lover of all."

Now that the five senses have come together, am I perhaps in the invisible presence of my Polya? Is it impossible to love exclusively the One? Infinity or totality? Are

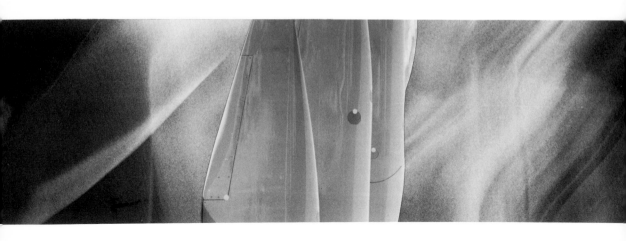

we moderns condemned to the love of all through a passionate consumption in the fragments? Barely one-third of the way, I must persevere in my quest.

The heat in the bath increases suddenly. Enveloped by steam, a freezing sensation infiltrates the burning flesh! *This humid heat purifies my body and may even render it immortal! It fuses the flesh and seals every orifice, and by enticing the soul to remain forever inside it propitiates the merging and transmutation of the body and soul into one substance. This ablution chamber is indeed true to the nature of a womb that not only bestows life but takes it away.*

On the opposite side the pink urinal occupies a prominent and unexpected position. The gentle ladies encourage me to approach the fountain, which from the distance appears like a porcelain pubic bone section. One of my companions hands me a frosted crystal lenticular vessel, requesting cold water in order to refresh herself. Indeed, the jet of clear liquid that flows onto the floor from the deep curved orifice usually reserved for draining the hygienic contraption is evidently the source for the lustrating steam that engulfs me. As I approach the urinal to fill the cup, there is a surprising explosion of water! I must have tripped some sort of photoelectric sensor that caused a gush of turbulent liquid to inundate the bulbous receptacle and discharge forcefully.

107

The profusion of absolutely pure, cold water is thoroughly rejuvenating. I am wet from top to bottom and without breath. *Pure water is like a magical magnet, attracting nymphs without having to resort to ceremonies or incantations!* The anthropomorphic urinal is a veritable fountain of youth, fulfilling its erotic promise in the complementarity of water and fire. Joy and contentment pervade the space, amid the laughter of my companions. The flood of water reduces the incandescence in the chamber, and now the air temperature is pleasant, like an extension of our naked bodies.

Exchanging tender caresses and amorous intentions, we all ascend to the

upper platform. The five nymphs anoint their limbs and mine with aromatic balms that leave a satiny texture and prolong the ecstasy of fresh heat. After the girls dress, they prepare lavish trays with fruit and confections and offer me a portion of the sweet, cool aqua ardens . . . only a short breath later, they indicate that we must depart and proceed in our journey. In the midst of Queen Liberty, they claim, we will find even greater delight and amusement.

We exit the chamber and continue along the aisle toward the front of the vessel. Initially I had the impression that the rubbing balms were intended to relax my tired muscles, but the unquenched heat mounts, becoming oppressive and scorching under my unventilated skin. As we arrive at a glowing space, beyond yet another partition, my body is overtaken by an uncontrollable libidinous urge. The young women giggle while my irritation increases. I am about to pounce on them like an eagle on a partridge when one taunts: "If your Polya were here, what would you do?" I cry to my friends that I am dying of passion and beg them not add fuel to the fire. Their pale mouths betray their own excitement, and they desist in silence. *Oh, the overflowing splendor of form!*

The girls untie their belts and find seats on cushions lying about in the darker corners of this airborne salon. It is similar to a forest's clearing, where gravity itself is a voluptuous force, unlike the uneasy catwalk we just left behind. The young women tell me how to adjust the light to their preference and then pretend to hide from me. Their deep breathing magnifies my lubricity . . . at last here is a licit opportunity to engage in manifold acts of transgression, for which I tell myself any violence is excusable . . .

After endless moments of pleasant thoughts and games, one of the women brings me a cup of clear liquid and insists that I drink it. The liquid seems at first familiar and identical to the aqua ardens, but I discover that it is of a very different nature. *Recycled waste water for increased efficiency on long distance flights?* The moment I taste it the vessel stops glowing and my libidinous desire ceases.

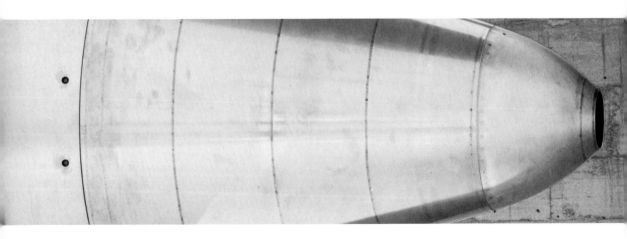

IMPERVIOUS TO MY EMOTIONS, the women smile. They point out that I am now prepared to pass into the realm of Queen Liberty. We proceed to mount a spiral stair to a suite of carefully appointed rooms. *Forever the same movement . . . Can this be motion?* The first enclosure is perfectly square in plan, articulated by a vertical rhythm of solids and voids around three edges. On the fourth side, opposite me, is the entrance to what must be the vessel's main gathering place, probably the anteroom or residence of the Queen's domain.

In the middle of the quadrangle is an image epitomizing anger: a fountain of violent water. This fragment of a tempestuous and bloodstained sea is a telescopic projection of the horizon overlaid on the pocked surface of a water treatment basin. A fascinating mechanism of plastic and metal with glittering plexiglass filters pneumatically agitates the murky liquid. From its location at the basin's center, this juxtaposition of plumbing fixtures absorbs polluted water from the receptacle and subjects it to despumation and clarification through artificial crystals of diverse consistencies, until the liquid emerges from the bloated conical valves at the top in the form of sharp silvery fillets. *Reconstituted sterile water of perennial unfulfillment or sublimated mother's milk falling back into the basin?*

The foliage of the landscape, reflected on the polished materials and multiple densities of water, externalizes a rainbow in all directions each time the vessel infiltrates a bank of clouds, and dazzling white light fills the space. The fountain of violent water betrays a profound technical mastery, utterly useless and thus truly spellbinding. *Still frustrated by thirst, I deplore the supposedly purposeful technological contrivances imitating real fountains but lacking the wondrous qualities pervading the work of a demiurge.*

Although this enclosure affords many more captivating details, my companions forge ahead. Next we enter the living room, decorated with exquisite ergonomic furniture, austere carpets, and walls inlaid with

indestructible laminated paintings. A collection of electronic gadgets controlling every comfort factor imaginable are distributed throughout, embedded in the walls or ceiling. The structure of the aircraft is discernible in this large space, as well as a multitude of assembly systems resolved in thoughtful details. *This is unquestionably the highest expression of the art of building ever witnessed. But is it architecture?* Everything is in its place, obeying visible or obscure reasons, resulting in a consummate equilibrium that maintains the vessel in suspended motion.

Arriving at a series of three curtains, I repeat the question about who is beyond. First, a guardian greets us and joins our group. Next a similar young woman announces that this is, indeed, the recess leading to the interior quarters of the royal suite and adds that she will accompany us until we grace the Queen with our company. Finally, at the third curtain a lady who personifies memory guides us back to our seats.

The electronic percussion rings again. Harmonic sounds of synthesized starlight reverberate through the fuselage, while outboard low-speed ailerons emerge from under the wings. The plane's buoyancy is greatly increased as the power is reduced, and we float languidly to our final approach.

ONE-THIRD of the cycle lapsed, the plane has come to a complete stop. On the horizon, behind the control tower, the sun is still rising. The sphere in my suitcase secretly provides a digital time reading of 14:02. There are scarcely sixteen hours left, and the sun is at its brightest.

The attendant personifying memory hastily approaches and asks me to follow her. She explains that I am now prepared to grasp the fullness of being through my body's own recollection, experiencing the inveterate architecture of mankind in my gestures and flesh. *In this technical stop, one-third of the way around this circular gesticulation, I may once and for all comprehend that there is no origin and no goal and that in the center (in my loneliness, under the sheets) is only emptiness. In the presence of nothingness, however, being will manifest itself, and thus I shall find salvation beyond the dichotomy of material body and immaterial spirit.*

I do not comprehend this in its entirety, but I follow the beautiful woman with fascination. As we walk along the axis of the vessel and cross a majestic opening at the front, she insists that I listen carefully to the Queen's advice yet trust my own perceptions.

The airplane of mixed passenger/cargo configuration presumably has a hinged nose that can be lifted in one piece. As expected, a short corridor leads to what is possibly a mobile waiting lounge for passengers in transit.

A soft, diffused white light fills the fully automated hall. Its most notable feature is the central pavement of sixty-four red and green squares of impeccably polished, artificial precious stone. The quadrangular surface is so smooth that the utterly reflective sphere in my suitcase would not have stood still for one second. There are no joints between the paving squares, but the playing field is surrounded by moving sidewalks rotating in a counterclockwise direction. The endless rubber bands allow for simple access to the amphitheater and also lead toward the cardinal points, out of the hall.

The walls are divided into seven panels separated by columns of vaporous light. Even though the sheets are made of laminated plastic, each possesses distinct qualities and textures embedded or suspended within the translucent material. Furthermore, it is easy to detect surprising sequential correspondences among the panels on the four walls. The first sheets on the left all have the grain and color of lead and onyx and make reference to the right foot and the right ear as transmutations of moles and cuttlefish. The second panels are crystallizations of tin and sapphire that address the head directly, and particularly the left ear, through sections of eagles, dolphins, and deer. The next plates to the right seem to be made of iron and diamonds, in sympathy with the right hand and the right nostril. These panels reveal harmonious orders by fusing plans and rayographs of vultures, pike, and wolves. The heart and right ear are invoked by the fourth plates, made of gold and carbuncle as oblique sections of geese, lions, and seals. The fifth rectangular spaces are filled with X-ray sections of pigeons and male goats in relief, addressing the genitals and left nostril through solidified copper and emeralds. The sixth plates formed by floating yet fluid transubstantiations of storks and monkeys made of mercury and agatha speak to the left hand and the mouth. The last panels in the extreme right of the walls refer to the left foot and left eye as rubbings of fragments of owls and cats.

The cosmological connotations of the hall are more explicit in the ceiling, where thousands of electric pulsating glowworms convey a striking picture of planetary dust. The luminescent monads intensify near the perimeter, constructing a continuous frieze of zodiacal animals that fuse into one another. On top of the central gateway that I have just traversed, a black circle melts into a white square of identical area. *A materialization of the ultimate paradox! Abstract Conception and Immaculate Cognition?* Above the opposite door appears a white circle: *the spouse of all the planets, source of the light that allows for man's loving embrace and of the warmth encircled by his perpetual dance . . .*

Under heaven and hell, facing me and the smudgy circle, Queen Liberty displays her authority. She magically presents herself in an unfolded form, her front majestically garbed in gold and her back naked and poised in the exact shape of Ingres' violin, the voluptuous instrument resting its breech on an enameled throne. The material of her dress displays such wonderful properties, reflecting light in one direction with the radiance and geometric density of the sun, while becoming totally transparent when illuminated from a different angle, allowing me to gaze through to caress the evanescent surface of the finely tuned instrument and even to penetrate the infinitely pink and dark sound holes of the body.

The Queen's jewels are symbols of power that celebrate matter and spirit, body and intellect, as separate substances; deliberately they conceal the mysterious fusion of such entities in the paradigmatic human miracle of incarnation. On her shoulder the Queen supports a bag made of cowhide, probably wet-formed, hand-stitched, and stuffed, modeled after a pair of buttocks on one side and a vulva on the other. Her purple mitre projects toward heaven two sharp V-shaped openings lined with pearls and downy, pubescent fluff. On her chest hangs a forged silver pendant of extraordinary craftsmanship in the form of a sectioned eye, or pear, from whose seed, molded as a shallow orifice with thin lips, emerge three elongated irregular spirals made of gold.

The Queen's abundant jet-black hair falls heavily on her back. From the front her irregularities are subsumed by the perfect contours of a sphere over a cube. Around the hall, to her right and left, the ergonomic seats located against the walls are occupied by distinguished looking ladies-in-waiting. I advance to the center and make a polite gesture to demonstrate my respect and admiration.

The welcoming Queen declares that I have arrived to the Kingdom of Freedom, a unique place where real, finite time moves forward and, creeping along thus, progresses from the present to the past. *The day may grow older . . .* Somehow knowledgeable of my previous predicament with the Dragon, she entreats me to recount her the story, which I do succinctly. After wistfully commenting on the wonderful uncertainty of human existence, she remarks on the glories of ambivalent fortune and on how often adventures that start badly end successfully. Finally, she suggests that before continuing my pursuit of eternal love and the fulfillment of its desire, I take part in the friendly communion of a symposium. *To be joyful and thus better prepared?* Her fluctuating and unfathomable dual appearance is startling. Distracted, I accept the invitation, taking my place on the vacant stool to her right.

From this new angle I can better appreciate the uncanny solarizing effects with which the white circle behind the Queen's throne bleaches momentarily all objects in the room. This disk of nebular matter is really the face of a beardless young man. His seven rays of golden hair celebrate the Age of Light. Behind my allocated place the panel of mercury studded with variegated, ribbon, eye, and moss agates fluidly changes shape. The flat and oblique projections of stork and monkey undergo sudden transformations and fusions. *The wanderer's fate, in perpetual flux? All my tribulations are present, including the dryness of the fire that consumes me and my great poverty of mind.*

THEN THE FESTIVITIES begin! Seven percussionists occupy the gridded square, playing mechanical sounding variations on a single note that accompany the service of every course of the banquet. Each guest is allotted his or her own table and assigned three female attendants. The tables, square sections of very thick glass, are totally flat and absolutely transparent, except for their deep green edges. They are suspended in midair by some kind of undetectable electromagnetic field, or perhaps they rest on chrome tripods made invisible by solarization.

The Queen proceeds to remove her golden cape, and more of her geometric garments are planted on the corresponding square in front of her. She remains dressed only in light, tightly draped by the manifold projections and reflections surrounding her, acquiring the texture and color of these animals, metals, and precious stones.

On the moving walkways appear several self-contained washbasins, and one of which is brought to me. I hold my hands under a cylindrical container, and a fragrant cleansing cream is dispensed automatically. After rubbing my fingers with the oily substance, I place them beneath the faucet. By this simple action tepid water completes the task of aseptic purification. On the opposite panel of the mobile contraption an automatic blow dryer is activated by my glance.

Concluding this operation, one of the charming servants promptly brings me a mysterious object. *Do they give the same object to both men and women?*

I suspect that its sole purpose is to be fondled and to keep my hands and lips busy between courses, so that I will avoid contact with any impurities during my meal. This sterile object of synaesthetic desire is neither soft nor hard; it is approximately the shape of an egg, accepts to a degree digital distortion and penetration, and is delightful to smell and to behold. By fingering and sucking the egg, time is again dislocated and becomes utterly present. *As in the plane.*

The meal is accurately choreographed and meticulously scored, like a symphony, along a strict and limited temporal sequence. Each one of seven separate courses has been synchronized with appropriate beverages, flowers, and table settings. My three graceful attendants keep changing clothes to harmonize with every setting and the respective victuals. On a wooden cart with solid, white wheels arrive the required utensils. Once we have finished eating and drinking, the plates, cutlery, napkins, and glasses are taken away. The flowers from the preceding course are thrown on the floor, where they accumulate and exude an intoxicating mixture of luscious aromas. When the mechanical orchestra starts up again, the carts return and the process is repeated with a new set of floral arrangements and fabrics.

The food is both extremely simple and sophisticated. Each course is composed of breads and wines. On the tables the only condiments are crystals or flakes of salt. Nevertheless, the courses evoke the archetypal flavors of the seven major gastronomic systems of the world while maintaining a serial rhythm of spices and sweeteners. *Emulsifiers and polyols of different grades permit modern cooks to invent novel food forms or to duplicate the properties of existing popular dishes.*

The earthy flavor of grain is always present. *Astounding variety as well!* The breads are either fried in an assortment of aromatic oils and butters, baked, or grilled and exhibit various consistencies: from dry, hard, or crispy and rough to very smooth, moist, and soft. Assorted flours, such as whole wheat, rye, barley, white wheat, and cornmeal, alone or in varying proportions, produce long-lasting or short and pungent tastes, which contrast or harmonize with the herbs and spices mixed in the dough: onion and garlic, caraway, dill and rosemary, thyme and marjoram, curry and pepper, ginger, sugar, cinnamon, molasses, and cardamon. Some of the bread is hard like a biscuit and some is spongy, incorporating air through fire, with the help of eggs, yeast, or sour milk bacteria. Its forms are all different, always combining on the same plate anthropomorphic and zoomorphic figures in an assortment of loafs, buns, sticks, rings, braids, brioches, crepes, and flat pancakes. Each bread is accompanied by suitable wines made of diverse fruits, ranging from very dry to sweet and served in crystal of onyx, sapphire, diamond, carbuncle, emerald, agate, or quartz . . .

Having finished our seventh course, the three glamorous attendants disseminate orange blossoms and gardenias on the floor and proceed to collect the silverware and white silk tablecloths. A tree resembling a petrified smoking leaf is now rolled into the amphitheater. Completely immobile on a ubiquitous axis, the familiar tree epitomizes both the image of happy dwelling between the earth and the sky and the sphere itself. Unfolded fragments of the human figure can be discerned in silhouette . . . Perhaps the tree is being eroded by the gloomy background devoid of nebular matter.

One of the attendants plucks a fruit from the tree and, placing it on a plate, offers it to me. At close range the object is uncertain. *The egg again, slightly bloodshot? They eye of the queen or a testicle of the bull?* It fits perfectly between the tips of my fingers, is soft like flesh, and has a smooth opalescent surface. I introduce my thumbs into the rounded artificial fruit and tear it open. It yields slowly. At the center, protected by a womblike reliquary of unspun wool, lies a miniature red apple. I cut the fruit in two, using a pair of gold pincers to extract the seed. It is in the process of pollination, held in place by the stinger of a bee. *Is this all I have eaten? The product of sexual equality and freedom?*

The seed usually contains the full substance and wisdom of the fruit, and as I bite it, I realize that my pleasure is somewhat diminished. *A somber recollection! The impossibility of love? Yet, one and all, the three young ladies that served me resemble Polya . . . I am possessed anew by their extreme and contradictory voluptuousness.* And before I can try to elucidate the strange and puzzling coincidence, I am soaked once more, this time by a revolving fountain fashioned as a triangular prism. The minimalist porcelain triple urinal rotates and, while it moves, ejaculates wildly (possibly activated by electronic eyes), casting on the guests copious jets of balmy water.

Then this apparatus disappears from sight. The three women bring a water pipe that contains an aromatic mixture. This, they say, should banish my fears and any weariness caused by the banquet and my long ordeal. The rich smoke fills my chest and dissolves every trace of my bittersweet cupidity. Nothing seems lacking. *Nothing? For a moment I believe that my happiness is faultless and complete, without grasping the risk of being sated by the pervading euphoria of the senses.*

The Queen suddenly rises and concludes the meal by toasting love and freedom with a clear, iridescent nectar. After a brief silence the glass tables are removed, and the flower petals piling up around our feet are swept away. The sixty-four red and green squares of the pavement, now spotless and shining, are prepared for a performance. Our Hostess nods and the spectacle commences.

Thirty-two actors appear. Sixteen are wrapped in tight silver body stockings and fifteen wear geometric golden costumes. One more, whose body resembles the Queen's, dresses with her regal robes and joins the second team. Each figure occupies a single, specific square, and the groups face each other, leaving four lines of squares in between them.

There are distinctions in rank in this golden army. The front row is filled by eight indistinguishable small cubes. In the back row, along the edge of the playing field to the left and right of the queen, are two large cubes at the corners. On contiguous paving squares toward the center stand two symmetrical cubes with one-eighth of their volume missing, leaving

115

L-shaped extrusions when seen from above. These are followed by two more cubes from which have been subtracted four triangular prisms each, along the medial axes of their square elevations, producing a symmetrical Greek cross in plan. The remaining square, to the left of the queen, is filled by two superimposed cubes set at forty-five degrees to each other.

The silver army on the opposite side is, by contrast, totally undifferentiated, composed of androgynous, faceless defenders. Beautiful assemblages of strong, articulated human limbs occupy the sixteen squares. Once the battle has started, their gestures and motions correspond exactly to the frozen geometries of their counterparts on the other side. It is easy to identify the acrobatic leaps of the horse, the defensive, diagonal moves of the buffoon, and the stiff, cautious tracings of invisible walls by the tower.

This mechanical ballet is a masterpiece; it demonstrates the complementarity of abstraction and figuration, a veritable conceptual tour de force of some demiurge obsessed with the synthesis of imagination and logic. The stage itself is a colorless electromechanical structure vitalized by chromatic emanations coordinated analogically with the psyche of every deed, capture, riposte, or heroic defense. Beams of color, laser, white, and black light overlap and produce clearings and shadows, vacant abandonments and luminous corporealities. The choreography responds to referential electronic noise that ranges from ophicleidic harmonies to dodecaphonic voices. Actors and stage develop into one unified field as they conform to the preestablished instructions of fortune and either display their bodily flexibility landing on the intended square or actuate their mechanisms in accordance with their geometry.

Whenever a piece is captured, it metamorphoses into its opponent and retires from the game. Before long, only the two kings and queens survive. This endgame provides an opportunity for the dancers to exhibit their extraordinary grace and ability in a grand apotheosis of the voluptuous accord of being. In a final, anticlimactic move, the silver queen leaps into the golden sphere and the match is declared a draw.

Exiting along moving walkways, the fifteen players bid us farewell. After a brief pause—the Queen—the sixteenth piece, solemnly reminds me of the time which I have left, and of the urgency to continue my journey. Enlightened by the symposium, I must next travel to the Place of the Enigma, where I will finally confront three doors. She explains to me that in order to find my Polya I will have to make the correct choice, but that I will only learn of my dexterity or error after the fact. *After the fact?* To help me select carefully, I will be accompanied by two personable young women. The first excels in her capacity to reason, while the second one that I have already met, personifies memory, desire, will, and pleasure. Both women will express arguments in favor of either thought or action, convinced as they are that their own way is the most appropriate for the attainment of truth, love, and meaningful dwelling on this earth. They may both be right or wrong, and it will be my task to decide. (Fortune is indeed the supreme mother, yet still she is inscrutable. It is our duty to please her with prudence and excellent judgment, in spite of her present invisibility and ambivalence.)

With these words of wisdom the Queen bids me good-bye, but not before offering me her own object of desire with the request to keep it forever as an amulet. *An old possession?* Her fruit is similar to the egg-shaped object that I have fondled in between courses during the banquet, it is soft and susceptible to digital penetration and, although it is studded with melting precious stones, it always recovers the form of a crystal sphere. *A dark crystal?* I respectfully thank my host and retire, holding hands with my two companions.

RATHER THAN EXITING through the gateway that we had entered, the women lead me along the moving walkway. Memory recalls that in each of the six bodily orientations we will yet encounter wonderful things; this is important to remember in view of my final decision. Although we apparently tread in the direction of time, the mechanical walkway leaves the playing hall at the corner and takes us into another space of the same plan and dimensions.

We are now surrounded by a shady arcade of greenery crafted from synthetic silk. The space is punctuated by metal planters and double columns with translucent capitals. The central area is occupied by artificial trees studded with brightly colored transparent blossoms and probably capable of yielding a rich fruit crop. It is impossible to determine whether we are inside or outside, in a real or a simulated garden. The soil is covered with astroturf, but the wind transports the smell of freshly cut grass. Every detail of nature is utterly clear and perfectly represented: a confusing, disconcerting eclipse of the real. Abstract or geometric objects do not exist in this garden; everything is recognizable, specific, and qualitative. Nevertheless it all seems consumed by the seductive glossiness of superficial appearance, lacking a sense of either mystery or concealment.

Smiling at my frustration, the second, younger woman recommends that we keep on walking and climb the tower. I comply with her reasonable advice, and after a protracted ascent we arrive at the operations control center. The room, of approximately the same size and proportions as the previous ones, is lined in its entirety with video monitors. On each screen complex labyrinthine luminous traces of electrons represent the manifold scales of reality, from the macrocosmic realm of aerial navigation on a global scale to air traffic in the sector, vehicle traffic on the ground, and the predictable behavioral patterns of individual travelers.

Suspecting that I cannot fathom the purpose of this specious place, my companion rationalizes that every wanderer cast into the cosmic labyrinth is totally disoriented. Only from the height of a control tower it is possible to grasp the profound truth and order of this reality. The numerous meandering scales are concentric, and whoever enters the historical world is condemned to the miserable necessity of traveling toward the middle, subject to progressive acceleration. At all scales are mortal dangers that may default the individual's chosen route. At the inescapable center everyone must face the now invisible actuality of the void and determine his or her destiny. The discovery of this reality that, my companion emphasizes, the senses alone cannot penetrate, is possible only if one assumes that the travelers process all information through binary models in a manner analogous to the computer circuitry that coordinates the multiple orders of real phenomena reduced to the screens.

On the left wall the screens map the past; on the right they project the future. The words **unsayable, inseparable,** and **inscrutable** are written on top of the walls from left to right, alluding to the Creator, the Created, and Love. *My three charming servants resembling so accurately the essential Polya! Geometric figures and sublime types are always enigmatic. In our constant search for stability, we struggle in vain to acquire a clear notion of even a simple cube. Orders of geometry are unbreakable, eternal, and incorruptible.*

Every aspect of nature is utterly obliterated and perfectly recreated in this electronic panopticon. *I am again confused and disoriented.* There are no recognizable objects in this space where everything is novel, geometric, and quantitative. *It all seems drained of meaning by the reductivism of eidetic operations lacking, like the preceding garden, a sense of mystery and concealment! In spite of my companions' enthusiastic preferences, neither the garden nor the tower are convincing prototypes for the order of the world . . .*

Holding hands we continue our journey toward the exit. An electronic percussion in the distance signals the proximity of the final place, perhaps the threshold of choice. Again we stride without effort on the moving band. *My thirst for knowledge is ever more insatiable. I want to inquire about the Queen's ubiquitous pear-shaped pendant, an object much more powerful and fascinating than the topoi of faith and reason.* Ignoring this patently critical question, my companions continue their debate on the merits of theory versus practice and on the virtues of pursuing a life of action versus one of contemplation.

Back in the mobile lounge, we are surrounded by a gloomy and inhospitable space. A mechanical voice, obviously prerecorded, insists on the advantages of remaining seated as long as possible and of moderating one's walking pace when crossing the threshold. At the far end of this hall of perennial waiting we are finally confronted by the three identical, stainless-steel doors. *A new beginning?* Even though the gates are ostensibly heavy and hermetically sealed, as soon as we approach the first door on the left, it opens automatically. Under a sign that praises the glory of God I am forced to look upward, whereupon the entire universe appears as a grim and barren perspective vista.

Reason speculates that only arduous study and elevated intellectual pursuits are to be admired in man. Truth must be found by repudiating the lazy and corrupt body. Only in this way can man develop into a veritable vanishing point, an aleph capable of gathering reality in its entirety. As Nicholas of Cusa insinuated in the fifteenth century, God and the universe are the same thing: a circle whose center is its circumference. At the vanishing point reality and its representation are finally identified, because the vanishing point is a constitutive principle of the real. God is a point that projects thought around it, synthesizing immanence and transcendence, extensive substance and immaterial thought, multiplicity and unity, the real and the ideal . . .

Noticing my discomfort with totalitarian visions, the guide insists that I cannot judge whether this is the correct path until I have actually experienced it. Unconvinced, I turn to examine the door on the far right.

Under an inscription praising the glory of the world I am forced to look down, toward the tarmac and the platform filled with resplendent airplanes and shining equipment. Every object normally deemed ordinary or graceless, such as turbines and air conditioning plants with their flexible hoses, retractable walkways, and luggage ramps penetrating deeply into the underbelly of the aircraft, proclaim a sensuous life of their own, belonging to an impure reality.

As soon as a plane arrives, diligent mechanics inspect the landing gear, connect the hoses and cables of auxiliary equipment, and ensure that the unloading facilities are in place. Finally, they insert inflatable rubber diaphragms inside the front of the engines, probably to protect them from organic predators. *This precisely concerted activity becomes more exciting than a secret caress in the shadows, while the objects in the choreography surpass in eloquence and provocation my most vivid recollections of Polya's beautiful features. Physical work and the projects of human technology are overtaken by an unexpected aura that conveys an immense sense of enjoyment, alien to calm and limits and undefined like the sea. This is not a simple material gratification, nor is it localized in a specific part of my body. Like the beat of electronic rock 'n' roll, it is internal and medullary, it corrupts and dissolves my consciousness in an overwhelming and undifferentiated cerebral orgasm.*

To my initial surprise, it is Reason and not Memory who speaks again. Extolling the virtues of manual work, she indicates that if I elect to advance through this door, I will, after fighting like a man, surmount fatigue, produce many offspring, and develop a great capacity for endurance, stability, and ultimately happiness. She adds that objects are never neutral and that God and the devil are pervasive in every particular thing and action. In the specific things of the world, reality and its representation are at last identified, because the thing is a constitutive principle of reality, synthesizing the real and the ideal . . .

I have almost decided to proceed through this opening, but Memory's noticeable silence puzzles me. I hold back and peer behind the third door, in the center.

When the gate opens, a luminous sign forces me to look straight ahead and read:

The flesh is neither matter, nor mind, nor substance. It is an element of reality that becomes the absolute in unlimited and boundless nakedness.

119

In front of me, seemingly coextensive with the vessel, lies the void. Near and far, the world behind this threshold appears thoroughly inane, except for my body. Memory finally speaks. The problem, she states, is not the abolition of the sensuous or the nonsensuous. On the contrary. What must be rejected is the dualistic misinterpretation itself, which entails both the deprecation of the sensuous and the extravagant elevation of the supersensuous. The perceived structure of knowledge should be changed because most of the scientific assumptions about our bodies and the way they acquire knowledge are based on the established misinterpretation of their status as mere natural objects rather than as what they truly are: works of art. The conventional split is ultimately fallacious. Bodily being does not mean that the soul is burdened by a hulk called the body. We do not merely have a body; rather, we are bodily . . .

Her words are convincing indeed! This choice would lead to a higher form of knowledge, to a different bearing of thought beyond the delusions of reason and the illusions of sensuous intuition! Thus I cast aside Reason's diatribe against voluptuousness. Terrified by the void, she repeatedly insists that the way of the flesh is indecent, that by embracing every imaginable being one will only meet bestial pleasures followed by torture and pain. After declaring that my "vicious inclinations," particularly a disloyalty arising from "full detachment" and my inability to feel guilt, are in fact already implied in the very meaning of my name, she turns away and withdraws in a rage.

Memory, on the other hand, gently concludes that by pursuing this pathway I will be true to my nature. Thus I should find the one I seek and so eagerly covet. She then begs me farewell and takes her leave. Behind her, the pressurized doors are sealed again.

IN THIS EMPTY but vibrant space my body communicates with the world in a mode more ancient than thought. *My quest for love and knowledge obviously demands a body whose gestures are expressions of charity. These gestures of caring and loving kindness are perhaps our vehicle to retrieve the archetypal in that which we make. The unnamed order of the future must surely depend on the realization that our hands are not just parts of a bodily organism, prehensile tools like the tails of monkeys, which may simply act as efficient terminals for electric impulses from the brain. In truth our hands must be the organs of erotic curiosity, origin and source of true caring. A further revelation! Only a being that can speak, that is, think, can achieve both the poetry of motion and works of handicraft. This is the nature of human making, denied in technological production. Every movement of the hand in each of its works carries itself through the element of thinking. Only by bearing a new thought through the body's loving gestures will meaning be recovered in a future world of artifacts.*

The Queen's object? Eroticism transforms the brain into a sphere. The talismanic sphere in my suitcase should not be let out of sight; it is indispensable for a safe journey. The paradigmatic gesture of culture is the encircling embrace; it has no ancestry or goal apart from man's dwelling on earth, and it admits the void at the center of being. Under the sheets the void compressed by my abdomen feels like an oracular sphere of sweat. Nicholas of Cusa also said that our spiritual gifts cannot come to perfection without the senses. Death is acknowledged, but the soul's liberation does not mean that it detaches itself from the body. Rather it is the dream of a complete metamorphosis of the flesh whereby the flesh of the body and the spirit of the soul achieve a relationship of harmony and nonduality: the simultaneity of desire and fulfillment in the sensuous experience of the fleeting present, an enduring orgasm that affords a glimpse of the absolute. This thought must constitute the path to salvation, leading to or resulting from my encounter with Polya . . .

3:35:06 Almost an hour has elapsed. One very long hour in the terminal building. *I have surely made the right decision, because I am overwhelmed by the distinct impression of having always been on the chosen way. Besides, one can only learn what one already knows.* I can hear engines running. The man with piercing blue eyes (*or is it someone else?*) now reads a passage from Tertullian's *De Resurrectione Carnis*:

121

> **Has God combined the soul with, or rather, inserted and intermingled it in, the flesh? Yes, and has so closely compacted them together that it can be held to be uncertain whether the body bears about the soul or the soul the body . . . it is rather believed that the soul is the driver and has mastery, since it is nearer to God. Yet this also enhances the glory of the flesh, that it contains that which is nearest to God and makes itself the partaker in the soul's mastery.**

As the plane accelerates, my body is seized by the devouring flame of erotic desire, like speed at the threshold of nothingness, always increasing in intensity. Suddenly, at one with the pleroma, I am totally alone and consumed, while in the cockpit the captain exclaims:

"Full throttle up!"

THE IDEA OF AIR is meaningless at immense speeds! Forward flight under conditions like space travel is just an empty ballooning . . . At a subsonic velocity, though, there is still friction. This is an exciting place, fraught with electrical impulses. The ionized atmosphere of the vessel is permeated by desire, by the infinite possibilities of geometric space. Prepared to read the text of the world (the flesh), I would relish an encounter with Polya! For now the unified field of the earth and the sky is manifestly feminine. *In this time and place the inveterate patriarchy is finally over, and it behooves man to be male and female always; whole and centered in order to be compassionate and to open his actions to meaning.*

The upper regions of the sky divulge a perpetual duality: memories of familiar places strangely reminiscent of Polya's body and golden hair. *Having learned about the limitations of traditional metaphysics in the Palace of Freedom, I am quite convinced that all reality consists of that which is visible and that which is invisible: two ineluctable reciprocities! That which is clearly visible and a distinct object of thought must surely be only a trace of the invisible, inscrutably dark ground of being . . .*

While the vessel gains in height to reach cruising altitude, the reflection of the city on the fuselage reveals a deserted stage, vacant and inhospitable, where no play can take place. This city merely maps the void of efficiency and comfort. The airplane also ascends into the shadow of the tower where the sacrificial blood had been collected, under the great red chimney that once marked the center of the world. *And I wonder again if it will ever be possible to walk in the city and not be a mere spectator; to walk in order to make a place for dwelling on the pubic-shaped square, or to leap gracefully while joining hands with youths of all regions of the globe in a round dance of celebration.* Ascending toward the west, the feminine sky is now the ethereal stone pubis of our past. *A triangle pointing down, the object of delicate fondling and*

vertical penetration? As we take off, all that remains visible on the earth of undifferentiated vertical and horizontal grids are the perspective runway lights, which draw out the elongated initial of the virgin. *Closing my eyes, I feel immensely thankful and relieved. I have left behind, on my chosen path, an objective world that cannot be moved by desire, the unhappy world of either dogmatic belief or nihilistic practice that will perhaps soon come to an end.*

I dismiss the spectacle beyond the window and realize at last that this wonderful realm that we inhabit is indeed the true ground, the earth in the sky. My fellow traveler is now reading two parallel texts printed on opposing pages of her book, two quotations written as if translations of each other:

Awake we see a dying world;
asleep dreams.

We share a world when we are
awake;
each sleeper is in a world
of his own.

Having acknowledged the full reality of the air plain, I glance at the sharp blue eyes of my fellow traveler who, to my great surprise, is a beautiful woman. She reads or improvises from a singular notebook covered with unfamiliar script. On the page I can follow a system of frozen motions, a most immediate mimesis of human gestures (which probably contain all the wisdom of the world).

"Almighty is the system of the Pleroma," she says, "while that which broke loose and became the world is small. The all-encompassing has not come to exist; it is. Therefore, never doubt the resurrection or at least the continuity of life. If you did not always exist in flesh, you borrowed it when you came into the world. And in flesh your consciousness will ascend back

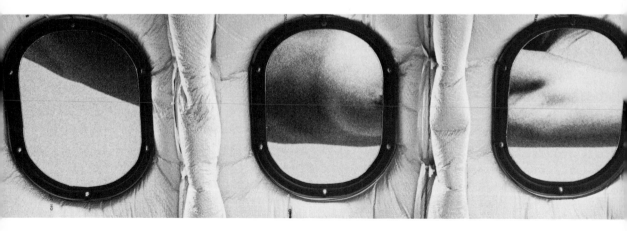

into the Pleroma. That which you are, your body, exists with you. Yet while you are in this world, what is it that you lack? This is what you have been making every effort to learn: to experience the nonduality of body and mind. Those who are living shall die. Nevertheless, the resurrection is not an illusion, for it is the truth of being that stands firm. It is the unveiling of what is, and the transformation of things, and a transition into newness. For imperishability descends upon the perishable; the light flows down upon darkness and swallows it up. The Pleroma fills up the deficiency. These are the symbols and images of the continuity of personal life; this is what makes the good . . ."

Astonishing words pronounced by this young woman! Is it Polya? She seems not to recognize me and her dress, and the circumstances are particularly unusual. Closing her book and concealing it with her right hand, she allows me to admire her. She is garbed in uniform, a plaited, long-sleeved blouse of a transparent fabric and a full-length dark skirt slit on one side up to the thigh. The blouse is tied below her splendid bosom with an iridescent girth that accentuates the impatience of her body under the pressure of the volatile garment. Her delicate breasts are, indeed, the most perfect embodiment of female flesh: primordial fruit ripening under a satiny skin of well-kneaded milk dough. The spacing between is emphasized by a small, dazzling pendant formed as a cluster of many colorful gems, all carved exclusively as spheres.

Under a flat bonnet with an enigmatic circular insignia my fellow traveler's golden hair is intricately braided and pinned against her proud head. Four yellow stripes on her sleeves indicate that she is the highest in rank among the crew members, in control of our course. She casts her gaze forward; her body remains poised and straight. Her smiling and radiant eyes are in fact hazel, emitting the brightest of lights around the cornea. When I look out the window her reflection merges into the unceasing changeability of the mountains. The essence of whiteness and the essence of mass, clouds and snow-capped peaks are neutralized into ethereal being, a pure luminosity and vapor ascending from the vagina of Mother Earth.

The seductive mouth opens up as expected; it reveals the analogy of perspective and gravity. *Am I truly in love with another woman?* Again my muscles fail, prey to tension and vertigo. My eyes fix themselves on her beautiful breasts, which I yearn to unveil. Her glance, on the other hand, is the very spark of creation, the presence of being in the feminine heaven. *What moves me? The love of Mother Earth, the manifold ground of being itself, the ground on which we mortals need to stand to be ourselves, and the abyss into which we individually perish when it is time to die?*

This sublime woman who plots the vessel's route evidently holds our destiny in her hands. She stands up and requests that I follow her. *Acknowledging the end of patriarchy demands a new posture of humility that, like humanity itself, shares its etymology with humus, the earth; that is to say, we must be ever mindful of its quality as the primordial ground. If our fate is not to be that of the old humanity, perishing of hunger in the face of many delights, desiring them all but unable to satisfy its appetite, we must relinquish our ego and humbly accept the designs of fortune, whose unfathomable embrace ultimately sets our course. Planning is no longer possible!* While holding her book on the right, the woman extends her left arm toward me. *Stupefied by her rare beauty, my memory seems to identify her touch in the most intimate parts of my body. My uncertainty is exacerbated by the uncanny juxtaposition of her apparel and imagery with my lust.*

She murmurs my name and asks me to approach her. Holding my hand, she proclaims that we are kindred spirits. Her touch is like warm snow and coagulated milk. *I feel undeserving of holding and contemplating such creature. She is obviously divine, possessing the noble power to entwine the material and immaterial parts of human bodies. At the time of our passing, the power to transmute the flesh?*

When I adopt a vertical posture, I can hear the song of the earth, as well as the poet's question: "Why do we no longer rejoice in Holy Dance?"

The trace of the city where the disclosure of a real order has become impossible appears again in the window. In the void of ritual, a black hole. *Cosmic place? There is no place for dwelling in the narcotic world of nihilism that*

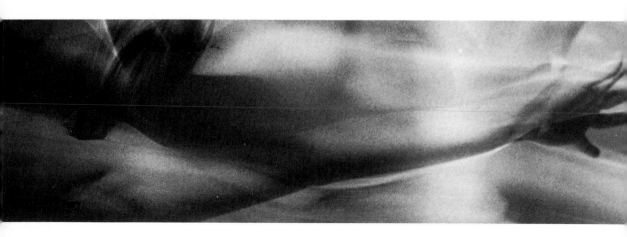

we have left behind. But is there a potential future in a different mode?

The vessel moves in the space of modernity, one in which all bodies are alike and no motion is special. Where every place is analogous to every other, each moment is like any other. In this space all determinations of bodies have the same basic blueprint, according to which the natural process is nothing but the space-time determination of the motion of points of mass. This basic design of nature circumscribes its realm as everywhere uniform.

Walking hand in hand in the space of the vessel, however, we trail along a fascinating anthropomorphic plain. The ground is recovered through motility, by moving serenely, without violence, on the chosen path. *Walking takes measure of the earth and keeping balance acknowledges the omnipresence of the earth and the sky.* In the upright posture the earth is revealed as the fundamental support, the ground of all orders, and our principal source of energy. It holds us up and simultaneously weighs us down with the gravity of our own mortality. Similarly, the sky enraptures us with its vastness, provides the measure of its lawful recurrences and frightens us with its emptiness. *This is, indeed, the ancestral experience: each body has a place in agreement with its kind. Earthly bodies belong down below and fiery bodies above; man, whose nature is embodied mortal thought, takes his place in the ambivalent in-between, standing vertically between the two poles.*

The magnificent posture of my friend reveals that human beings by their bodily nature possess a double character, placed consciously in the clearing and also tied in the underground of all clearing. My companion is a dual manifestation of elemental flesh: the individual woman that I may love and the manifold Mother Earth on which I stand. *Wise words of the philosopher who wrote that the healthy body, shapely and perpendicular, speak honestly and purely of the meaning of the earth.*

The awareness of our experience of place grows with the exciting discovery of this original architecture of being, as we move along the path of thought. Suddenly our walking speaks with a voice and sends a visible breath. We make a visible track as we tread in this sacred manner. We walk with beauty in all of the six directions, bound by our destiny, which is a

127

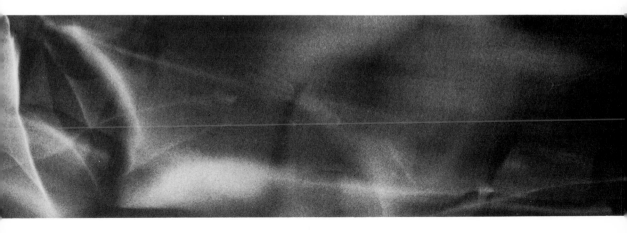

single celestial rhythm, and embraced by time. Time stands outside the realm of temporal beings that are in time. *The obsession of metaphysics to understand this concept rigidly has patently led to nihilism. I can now perceive the obscure reality of time embracing every moving and resting thing and the necessity to share in its playful passing. The question "Why?" should not be asked.*

In our melodious walk we partake of a greater harmony by taking the measure in stride. The thoughtful and orchestrated motion of the bodily parts forever dispels the old explanation of displacement as a mechanistic collection of movements strung together. In the hold of time I project my being in an erotic embrace that reaches every corner of the universe, that in fact takes the measure of the earth. *This primordial geometry is surely the first act of poetic dwelling, disclosing the profound meanings of my mortal being in the openness of the earth and the sky to the mystery of the godhead, the necessarily unknown first measure.* In the rhythmic arch described by the compassionate stride of my friend, her taking measure makes being felt, comprising in one gesture my past and my future, the history and fate of humanity.

Floating, undulating fabrics, a mixture of crystallized milk and aromatic musk. Under my feet, by my side, exquisite contours, the humid earth and the texture of skin. *We fulfill our destiny as we embellish the ground (taken for granted) under our feet! Our rhythm in walking does not originate in our individual bodies but rather in the flesh of the world, in the body's relationship to our elemental ground, our underlying earth.* As we find our true stride, again my voluptuousness increases. *Am I deeply in love with my companion? I am in awe of her divinity as the multiple universal mother. Restraining myself is feasible, but this superb young woman is visibly inclined to amatory encounters, judging from her age, her figure, and her manners! I must appease my heart with the hope of future love while continuing my contradictory inward soliloquy about the fidelity that I owe to the one woman I seek.*

Ubiquitous Woman! I scarcely begin to forget your dark indifference and you appear again, ever present, and everything else disappears in your wake. Your

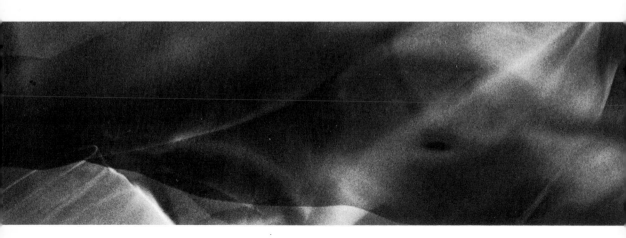

footsteps over the sky enfold me like a shadow. In your stride toward the night I divine that it will be possible to erase my memory of the day. Oh Thou marvelous world, no longer merely natural or artificial; you are reborn whenever I close my eyes! Thou art the wall and the breach, the horizon and the presence, the containment and the metallic membrane. The total eclipse. The light. The universe gradually melts, while from its depths rises a phantom, a woman larger than life whose outline is at last clear. Nothing separates her from me! *O desire, twilight of forms, in the rays of this sunset of life, like a prisoner I grip the bars of liberty, I, the jailbird of love . . .*

The woman, larger than life, grows still larger. The world is her portrait. Mountains recede into the background, and if I am present in the foreground, it is so that she shall have a forehead on which to lay her hand. She keeps growing. Her disheveled tresses cause comets to tumble into goblets. Everything I touch partakes of her hands and I am nothing more than a drop of rain on her skin. *Sea, do you really love the decomposing corpses of your drowned victims, the softness of their turgid limbs? Their incredible purity and floating hair? Then let my ocean love me. Flow across my palms, water like tears, boundless woman, in whom I am bathed. I desire only that these foreign bodies that hold me together should finally leave me; that my fingers, my bones, my words, and other agglutinants should abandon me, that the blue magnetism of love should tear my body asunder!* The joyous curve of her hip, the bewitching detour of her arms underscore the meanders of the pale land. *I am drawn both by the whole anguish of existence and this shimmering, immense hope. I can no longer speak of anything but you . . .*

We continue on the pleasurable plain, amidst V-shaped cork trees in the process of being stripped, suspended luminescent aureoles of tan-colored skin, coagulated droplets of milk, and deeply slit oak barks fertilizing the earth with their yellowish-brown sap. The landscape is studded with ambivalent soft objects unmistakably molded by the hand of man, imprinted, folded, and stroked. Palms, fingers, and nails of dull white plaster (or black, or blue), flesh-colored wax, stuffed pink fluff, mercury covered with red-stained straw, and pale green molded cotton. Tormented stones like

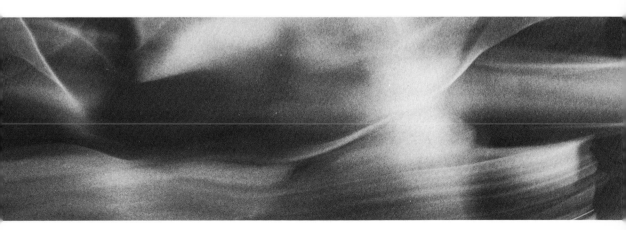

the flesh, stones filled with air and entrails, stones that dance: all noses, mouths, and ears, their senses tuned to the precise time.

As I apprehend the matriarchal spirit of the landscape in the new time of humanity, I realize it is no longer tenable to conceive of the essence of being as Logos. Impossible too is the Logos of domination, which subjects man and nature to its imperative direction and command! The dweller and maker of the future shall be lord only by renouncing the will-to-power, by serving the ancient dream of the earth in accordance with the feminine principle. In the space of Newton a body left to itself would move in a straight line, thus leading to the standardization of all motility and eventually to man's exile and homelessness. By contrast, we are now on the way (which is a place itself), avowing our indebtedness to the primordial earth. The architect of the future must necessarily follow my path. He must be and at the same time know the state of nonbeing, the infinite ground of our deep, inexpressible vibrations. In my heart I wish that we may fulfill our dream, if only this single time!

As I walk along the air plain, I don't tread upon the soil of any one country or specific region that may still hold some local arcana. This is a ubiquitous coffin. The old rootedness lost, symbolic order can no longer depend on it: a different mode of gathering is demanded. Despite the many optimistic signs, I cannot escape the morbid dread induced by this confined interior, which vibrates anxiously with the postmodern question . . . *Are we condemned to live our lives without foundation and either in the absence of ground or in function of purely simulated ones?*

Cognizant of the menacing storm clouds on the horizon, my glamorous companion, her hair now dark like her complexion, proceeds with an impassioned statement of hope. Our prevailing release toward things and a new openness to mystery belong together, she declares. They provide us with the vision of a renewed autochthony and grant us the possibility of living in the world in a completely different way, through a mode of dwelling as yet unnamed. Both conditions together constitute the promise of a novel ground and a foundation upon which we can stand and endure

in the contradictory world of technology, without having to accept the inevitability of apocalypse.

Profound and exciting truths are disclosed in the structure of the body-nature continuum. *Admitting the primacy of the flesh among the elements is obviously crucial for the realization of any future order created in the homogeneous field of intercultural space. The upright posture and our rhythmic stride articulate a new, preconceptual openness to the preexisting orders, pervasive in our awareness but irreducible to metaphysical elucidation. Art, poetry, music, and architecture are first evident in our movement and our gestures; replenished with the gifts of thought and caring, they formulate a nonlinguistic verb.*

A woman whom I can both accompany and inhabit, a possible friend and lover whose inexplicably transforming features surprisingly reveal the same unchanging, unfathomable beauty. *Increasingly anguished, tortured by contradictory feelings, I resolve to renounce my love for Polya!* As I am about to declare my infatuation, we suddenly arrive at the cockpit, which now appears in all its complex and multiple reality as theater and arena, cosmic pillar and sacred grove, phallus and omphalos. *A forbidden, utterly inaccessible place?* My companion takes her place at the commander's seat and together we witness a sequence of events in the center of the space.

On the perfectly polished mirrored surface of a cylindrical object the anamorphic landscape that we have traversed in our walk of caring touch and compassion is magically reconstituted. *A truly unforgettable apparition!* Alternating men and women, facing forward and backward, hold hands and engage in a rhythmic dance. By keeping time, their harmonious gestures incorporate morality, treading around at the edge of an abyss, rejecting the commanding standpoint of perspective and the immobility of an organic body obsessed with total visual control. Their joyful round dance reveals itself as the first intentional social act, the origin of all ritual and potential dwelling, open to receive its new content from the poet and maker of the future.

The slender, graceful dancers gather in their midst the earth and the sky, mortals and gods, committing themselves to the building of a world of

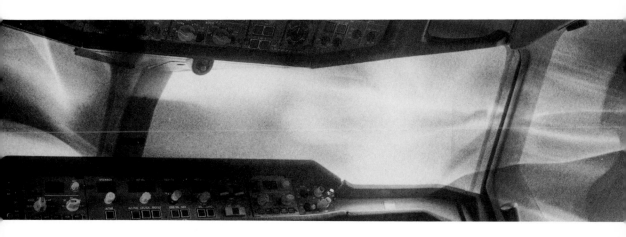

beauty. Their gestures conjure up the potential for cosmic place in a clearing on earth and under the dome of heaven. It has become plain that just as all speech is essentially poetry, all true motion is ultimately dance.

Exposing the reality of change and transformation in its purest sense, their circular motion comprises place in itself. In this case however, the contained circular place of the dance platform where the rituals, cockfights and corridas have been previously staged, is not an empty geometric shape accessible to intellectual contemplation and eidetic fecundation. The inveterate Platonic womb, receptacle of being and becoming, the labyrinth or gap and primordial chaos, is now conspicuously inaccessible to the classical man who still inhabits the cities of reason. The internal space that exists behind the reflecting cylinder, gathered as a concrete order at the center of the dance, is a treasure experienced only by the participants, the presence of fortune in the rhythm of destiny. *Dancing is primal architecture: making or laying out order. It dissolves the tension between subject and object, not as a conceptual formulation but as its own embodiment of meaning.*

The old, crucial question remains unanswered. Why does the holy dance rejoice no longer? I suddenly recollect how, as a child, I had intensely wished to dance, and leap, and play in order to regain a certainty that, I was told, might simply not be there! Perhaps my dream of flight corresponds to my desire of dancing. I desire, as I have never before, to dance over all the heavens, to tell the parable of the highest things and demonstrate the unreifiable truth of the ground . . .

My companion, who in her own way is keeping time by pushing a set of coordinates into the vessel's inextricable instrument panel, stands up and invites me to join in the dance. Finally in touch with my deeply felt sense of motility, I am released into an expanse of tremendous energy, open, rich, and hospitable. I walk toward the center being everywhere in the extension at once, staying constantly with near and remote locations of things, rather than being either here or there. This is, indeed, a very different experience from the claustrophobic Euclidean space to which we had become habituated.

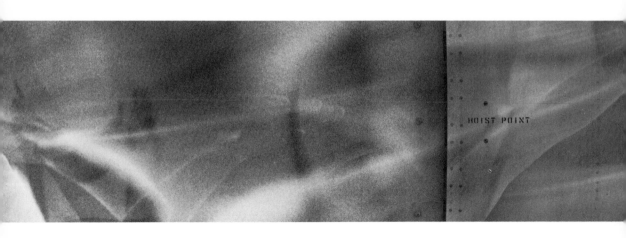

HOIST POINT

Useful to physics, modern physiology and our entire manner of technological building and production, Newtonian space has been, after all, only one modulation of space among many other equally credible, coherent, and workable formations. It necessitates, unfortunately, a freezing of being and a solidifying of boundaries, perspectivism, objectification, permanence, and egocentricity that ultimately have led, together with the history of metaphysics, ever closer to the apocalypse . . .

But space, our extension at hand, is rather the result of innumerable, badly adjusted concavities. As the pores become increasingly distant from each other, the skin of my companion appears more naked. *Unlimited and boundless nudity would probably convey the sensation of the absolute as flesh and finally confirm metaphor as the truth or unveiling of the real: revelation as poetic transference. Nakedness, however, must be impure. It must be finite to exist at all, and its finiteness is the sexuality of things. Is love the cause of death? The cause of rational obsessions and our distrust of poetry? Without pores, the smallest of all sexual vessels, the skin would be a total and infinite vestment, paradoxically not dissimilar to what we can imagine Euclidean space to be: a world without gender.*

Focusing my eyes on her sensuous body, a fragment is framed: the feminine flesh becomes less material, more naked and neutral. My gaze relaxes its grasp and my sight becomes clairvoyant. Overtaken by a new, more confident erotic awakening, I decide to rejoin this woman. Our salvation from impending doom will entail either a leap of thought right into the abyss of nihilism gathered at the unknown center or, at least, a dance of surrender on the very edge of the anamorphic mirror.

133

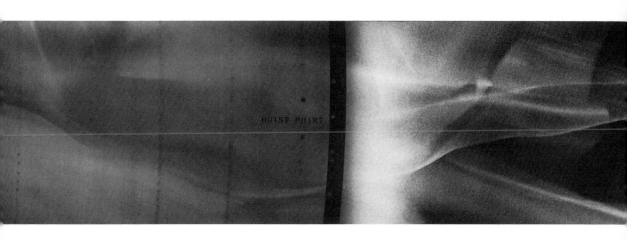

HAND IN HAND we start on our way in the direction of the Temple of Love, walking along the circuit created by the anamorphic mirror with its external and internal depths. On the outer perimeter of the convolution, at the points of the four horizontal orientations, are corresponding machines that celebrate the Triumphs of Desire. These are contained by perfect cubes, never fully visible but always evident, and appear to be in a constant state of flux when beheld directly. But only as perceived through their reflections on the cylindrical mirror do the machines materialize as nameless although stable objects, each like a paradoxical multiplication of negative numbers.

Upon careful examination, each of the machines presents four different but related aspects to the observer, corresponding approximately to the four visible elevations of the cubes. The surface of the first machine glows with the color of emerald and copper. On the right side a butterfly flutters, exhausted, on the ground, after a day's flight. Its wings crumble and bits of the golden membrane turn to dust. The wingless insect then transmutes into a violoncello and is carried, on the croup of the earth itself, through the universe at an unimaginable speed. The left elevation depicts human hair growing from a springtime shadow in the semblance of a footprint. Bull's horns writhe into serpent shapes and, surrounding the cello, finally curl around it, projecting a crescent on its polished exterior while tightly embracing the peg box of the instrument. Long hair grows from the top, almost reaching between the f-shaped sound holes.

The lateral elevations of the cubes are invariably opaque planes. Their respective stories are depicted in layers, creating a stereoscopic depth. The backs are transparent, while the facades are always reflective, inexplicably moving along with our perambulation. Through the rear of the cubes we catch glimpses of hallucinatory frontal axonometrics that disclose the struc-

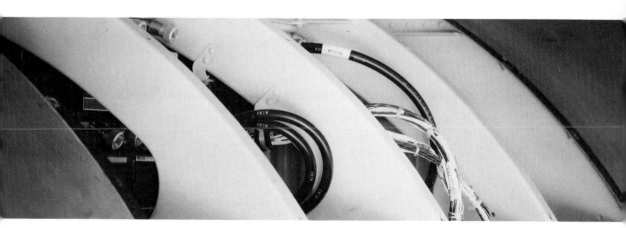

ture of these machines, all constructed on the basis of six superposed diaphanous boards of apparently unrelated electronic circuitry.

The mechanism of the first cube, a centaur of sorts, is activated by a kiln whose plan resembles a stringed instrument on the inside, with four segments slightly larger than a quarter circle attached to its sides as wings. From one of the wings a pneumatic hose with sharp and articulated pincers makes its way around the instrument's long, tapered neck capped by a recently manufactured wig. The flexible cylindrical tube bores holes and clips off the excess hair being fed by a pointed, V-shaped spindle from the belly of the viol.

The second cube's surface is the color of blue sapphire and gold. The relief on the right depicts a bottle holding a candle. Both objects are petrified, resembling an archaic megalith. Having withstood for millennia the erosion on the beach, at last a rising tide touches the bottle, with the effect of melting polar ice. On the left face an inscription reads:

To some, the sea is agreeable,
the act is agreeable to the sea.

Under the inscription an egg hatches on contact with water, and from it a soft wax candle (permanently lit) slithers out. It meanders along the beach leaving a trail of carbon on the sand and, climbing the dark glass bottle, curls around it two and a half times.

Through the back side this second machine can be seen lumbering slowly like an elephant in its motions, which originate from a water-powered generator or pump of circular plan that rotates at an imperceptible pace under the impulse of a dense, transparent chrysosperm. Soon milky and opalescent, the liquid fills four long, metal cylinders with funnel-shaped ends hanging from an annular contrivance to make candles. Hollow needles descend from the top and penetrate longitudinally the metallic molds at their centers, introducing four flaccid wicks. The molds curl immediately:

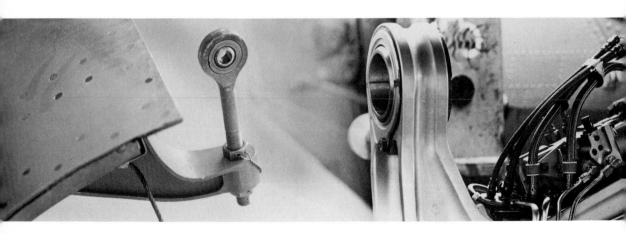

springs of joy spouting the same solidified liquid that, taken through a spiral furnace, is transmuted into a long, thin vitreous pipe with a glass oval attached to the end. Rotating on a rectangular marble slab and being blown by a pneumatic device, the egg swells and becomes a swan and then a lenticular container for the selfsame liquid that formed it.

A quadrant further along, the third triumphal machine pulsates with a yellow and greenish tint reminiscent of precious chrysolites, punctuated with blood drops. From certain angles this cube is capable of disappearing. On its right surface a rose blooms under laboratory conditions. A glass bell fails to protect the flower from a glimmering dust falling from the sky while an empty launcher for long aerodynamic projectiles, aimed diagonally up on approximately a sixty-five-degree course, is seen in the background. On the left a bleeding sunset cloud becomes a drifting stone and is soon eroded by the air. The resulting perfect sphere cannot fall but hovers tantalizing beyond reach.

The structure of this third mechanism, seen both in plan and elevation, is a spherical pendulum gliding for an infinitesimal instant on a tilted, crescent-shaped track at the bottom of the arcuate trajectory. The track is an enlarged projection of a segment removed from the sphere's lower half, allowing for its V-shaped slit to glide tightly on the irritating angular time-piece. In elevation the track generates the impulses transported by several interlocking clock and matchlock gun parts with the physiognomy of a unicorn's skull to a round, mute face. After a number of accelerating cycles the triggering mechanism goes off and the spherical pendulum is transfigured into an expanding disk of intense silvery radiation, impossible to behold.

The fourth cube glows in the night with its fiery color of carbuncle and a texture of hot, iridescent asbestos. On the right, even though the land-scape is crepuscular and gloomy and the background hints of menacing thundershowers, a piece of thick, crumpled paper catches fire. As it burns, the sheet forms a flaming egg. On the left elevation of this triumph of love, the fire rages out of control within the chambers, tubes, and pistons of a

tuba, until both, the embracing and the embraced, are reduced to ashes. The metallic calcinated egg rises as a conic stone pyramid through an undulating slab of rock.

Through the rear of the cube the motions of this machine are produced by a structure whose plan is that of a cannon foundry. Externally it is a square and internally a circular furnace, with accommodation for a single, longitudinal mold and two smaller spherical ones for ammunition. Flaming liquid metal that burns like the eyes of a tiger is poured into the frames. The sand and molds themselves ignite and evaporate, filling every crack and crevice of space with scintillating earth. The three pieces fuse and liquefy, obtruding into all orifices. In elevation smoke ascends through the transparent chimney of the crematorium, manufacturing a cloud.

The reflecting fronts of the four triumphal monuments capture, amid multitudinous projections, fragments of the sensuous body of my companion and a mysterious glove engaged in manifold actions. In our perambulation the glove's motions appear sometimes continuous, at other times more directly related to the amorous agitations of the four different machines. Dancing clockwise, starting again with the first triumph, the glove lies candidly on the earth, in the valley between the firm breasts, tearing off the butterfly's wings or grasping the horns of the bull or projecting the head of a serpent from the middle finger. Flying through the air, it initially comes to rest on the water and adopts a welcoming, concave position. Its long fingers become curved and outstretched and softly embrace the very white nape of the neck. Through the foam the agitated glove covers the naked parts of the noble woman's body as it is partially exposed and comes to lie between her legs. Taking to the air once more, the glove becomes infatuated and, contracting like an eagle's claw holding its prey, tears and collapses, bleeding, extended on a perfectly spherical buttock. Through the touch of the warm, smooth skin the glove catches fire and, exasperated, blows apart, disintegrating into its constituent parts.

Perhaps these wonders are to be expected after my previous initiation into the unfathomable mysteries. I am, nevertheless, truly astounded by the impossibility of

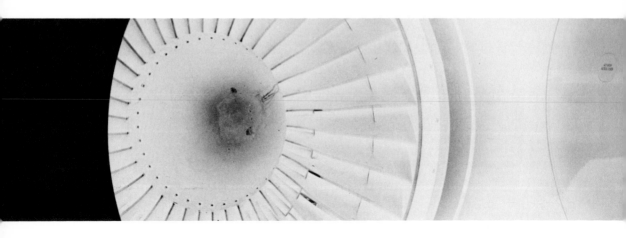

distinguishing between my own motions and desires and the machines' actions. In spite of their obviously causal intrinsic transformations, these machines do not represent acts of domination. Rather, they reveal love as the most humbling human emotion, as the prime governor of the elements' dynamism, ultimately postulating Eros as the motor of the universe.

THE DIZZYING and bewildering spectacle of the cubic triumphs keeps fluctuating constantly with our movements. Only when we eventually turn to face the cylindrical mirror is the anamorphic reality of the four floats revealed. They stand absolutely still, pregnant with inexhaustible potential motion, among the joyful men and women dancing in a circle, dressed in jeans and intensely colorful T-shirts. The floats are abstract, mute, and mobile objects that, being the reflections of a reflection, do not occupy a part of perspective space at a fixed scale. Each object incorporates the multiple, infinitely rich manifestations of the triumph that it had respectively generated.

The four elusive objects possess a seemingly magical property: at any size they remain unchanged. Thus, because they are all-embracing, their essential meanings cannot be articulated, despite their intentional forms alluding to a superior order. They are monochromatic, carved, turned, or molded, made of wire or metal rods, wood, hair, stone, bone, wax, plaster, or precast concrete, hung from a frame or supported on the ground or on a platform above ground. Their pieces and elements are simple, but they are neither geometric solids nor literal human bodies or fragments; they are recognizable but also totally different and enigmatic. They either stand autonomous in a group, drawn to each other, barely touching, glide irritatingly over one another, or interpenetrate. *In spite of their astounding diversity and originality, the four floats reflect embodied desire and thus belong to the same family, alluding to the lovers of the deity.*

The site of this beautiful architecture, caught between reflections, comes

to light as the most idyllic place. Time and the flowers of spring endure. Paradoxically perhaps, all is natural again in this landscape; no human intervention is evident. Young men and women roam this fertile region, some singing, others playing wind instruments; couples gently touch or exchange amorous looks. Blue, vermilion, and green; red, yellow, and violet; black and white; these seem to be the dominant color combinations, in counterpoint to the uniform jeans and shorts. The girls, probably more prudent than one may imagine judging from their age, are accompanied by pubescent men, their cheeks covered by golden down.

As we walk in circles through this spectacle, I can identify many illustrious women and their lovers. They are either alone or in groups, around the four triumphs providing hints of their memorable affairs. Emma Bovary is enveloped by the aroma of lemon and vanilla from Rudolph's hair, her nostrils flare to their limit while she inhales vehemently the freshness of the ivy on the columns. Clelia Conti and Fabrizio del Dongo exchange furtive glances through the spatial slits of a bird cage; they weave their desire in the invisible traces of winged flight. Alissa fades away as she crosses, hand in hand with Jerome, a strait gate in the foreground. With great vehemence Ma Ubu exclaims "Ah! Gross," as she runs behind Pa Ubu to give him some haggies. Near the nesting ground Sissy Hankshaw, the Montana Cowgirl, casts her large thumb aside while being embraced by a whooping crane. In the distance Catherine and Fiona roll toward Cecil through the waves, allowing the rusted girdle with its thumb-sized lock to sink into the sea. On the bridge of the crescent-shaped ship Ursula emulates Ariane amid images of porridge, leeks, tobacco, pipe clay, and the split skull of a long-dead goat, which she now fastens to her waist to conceal her pubic triangle.

On the internal side of the circuit similar events take place, but thick walls, rendered pink in section, frame and separate the actions. Rebecca embroiders on canvas by the window, waiting for Ecstasy to arrive at 4 A.M. Realizing its perpetual absence, she eats handfuls of earth with suicidal avidity, chewing young worms and breaking her teeth with snail shells. While she vomits, Aureliano Buendia composes love poems for Remedios

. . . Taking off her veil for the first time in her master's presence, Zetnaybia reveals a mark tattooed between her breasts with a design of the sun . . . Sofia Petrovna (known as Angel Peri when she wore a Japanese kimono), damp with perspiration, receives a card from the Red Domino. She is consumed by idolatry in her perspectiveless house whose rooms are each one occupied by an absolutely enormous object . . . The very young Spanish widow Pepita Jimenez offers wild strawberries with goat's milk to the priest, whose black cowl twists and eventually tears in mystical agony . . . A. stares at the question mark left on the wall by the centipede when it was squashed by Franck with his napkin . . . Nadja appears, only temporarily, in the luminescent space enclosed by the glass and cast-iron gallery. The extraordinary reality she opens for André dissolves as soon as the flower of devotion blooms on the sill, creating a permanent, eerie void . . . Marketa and Eva let Karel's mechanical body rouse and subjugate them both. Holding hands with Karel's headless torso they dance in a circle, enclosing paradise within their anonymity as they levitate and spiral toward heaven.

Captured in the vertiginous whirl, I am stupefied by the divine triumphs of love and their mysteries. My guide, whose hand I have been holding all along, then speaks in a soft and provocative tone of voice. "Polyphilo," she says, "all the women who have been loved by the deity should enter with a flaming torch. You must help me to extinguish my own torch with your passion when we arrive at the temple . . ."

Puzzling and imperspicuous words! I am now practically convinced that my friend is indeed Polya. Unable or unwilling to acknowledge my obvious longing, my companion exhorts me not to despair and to appreciate my good fortune. In elliptical sentences she reminds me of the scores who would be content merely to glimpse what I—contemplating the joyful women and sharing in the delight of their young lovers—perceive so clearly. Amid the enjoyment of endless pleasure the round dance on the agreeable air plain continues. Nothing essential is missing, and all contributes to perpetuate worship without interruption or boredom.

My companion is at least, most certainly, the guide and commander of the vessel.

141

Is she my lover as well? The question lingers in her exhilarating presence. Plunging into the next revolution of the spiraling motion, we near the darker yet transpicuous inner surface of the mirror, which reflects the inward landscape of my mind. *I become increasingly troubled and pensive as we resume our walk toward refreshing fountains, shadowy streams, and springs of crystalline water.*

This large involution teems with flowers and aromatic herbs, surrounded by middle-sized mountains and assorted trees. Anonymous young virgins bathe with their lovers in the pure water, exposing their thin and curvilinear forms, their pearly legs, shapely calves, and dimpled knees. The waters scatter an extreme whiteness of limbs, echoing their joyous company in the rhythmic waves of the current. Ankles immersed in milk and the splashing water sparkling with the laughter of games; a majestic swan opening its wings. On the tender grass maidens fashion flower garlands and passionately kiss their lovers. Humid lips adhere to alabaster necks as the suckers of small polyps; wriggling little tongues, chewing aromatic musk, leave innocent red trails. Flowers tossed, colorful trajectories of rapture. Male heads burrow between bare breasts, both chaste and lewd. And more lovers yet, along the river banks, intertwined under the shade of trees like the snaky hair of Medusa, as closely enmeshed as the ivy on buildings. The place itself is a chiasm of flesh: a delectable embrace.

The nameless lovers on this innermost plane of perennial spring are free from the sadness and excitement of changing fortune; they are lucky youths who lead unceasingly meaningful lives, in utter delight and perpetual voluptuousness. Desire coincides here with fulfillment yet no one is ever fully satiated; spiritual virginity endures. *There can surely be no greater punishment than exclusion from this place; envy and jealousy are the inheritances of the dispossessed, prisoners of existence . . .*

Am I drugged? Have I not chosen the appropriate gateway? Is my mind playing tricks? Surely the eyes of the body cannot see the invisible realm that always remains beyond humanity and the senses. Romantic nostalgia is totally repugnant yet my confidence in the dark power of ambivalent Eros to unveil being for mankind has

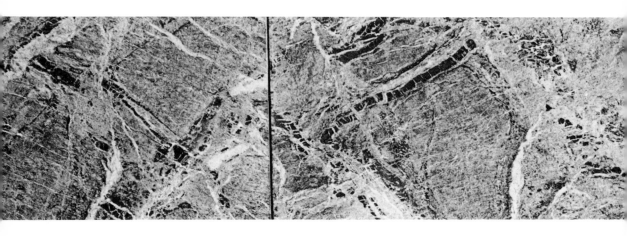

actually increased.

The realization of our mortal state weaves together sorrow and exhilaration, the ubiquity of heaven and hell. Through this gridded screen, like the picture plane of geometric perspective, I contemplate the dreadful possibility that I do not belong in this ideal dwelling place. I am not even prepared to ask my companion whether she is, indeed, my beloved Polya, for fear of offending her through the impropriety of my language!

I may perhaps be denied the honor of staying in this region, but hope must prevail. Any burdens, sacrifices, and responsibilities will be welcome if they lead to an encounter with Polya, even if only once . . . For the duration of a gap outside of time . . . A reminiscence of three exemplary heroes and saints coalesce into a sublime type. Manuel Bueno, the priest of the now submerged city of Valverde de Lucerna who led a tormented but authentic existence, who was always unable to utter during prayer the particular passage of the Creed that affirms human belief in "the resurrection of the flesh and eternal life . . ." Stephen Dedalus, who endured a whole day of understanding, wandering in search of his spiritual progenitor and disclosing the painful mystery of real fatherhood as utterly unrelated to sexuality, since the universal mother, rather than the Holy Ghost, had come to complete the trinity . . . And Aureliano Buendia, the hero of Macondo who faced the firing squad, who remembered the afternoon when his father showed him ice for the first time, who reconstructed in an instant the story of one hundred years of solitude from the pulverized wings of yellow butterflies and the crystals of cold . . .

To be loved or to contemplate my Polya I must follow the exemplary life of all three in one! In her presence? I would even withstand the suffering that Nikolai Apollonovich endured when the potentially explosive sardine can immortalized him as a heroic political parricide. Suddenly remembering the gleaming sphere in my suitcase, I confirm that it is, as expected, well within my reach. Under control? I long to burn together with Polya, whom I have carried in my heart from a very young age or else to continue dying and allow the fire that consumes me to become like solid ice. My unyielding devotion has afforded greater torture than the meanders of the labyrinth or the polar snowstorm menacing the vessel. Now my companion's

143

eyes can tear my heart apart more truly than the bomb that would have dislodged the guts of Apollon Apollonovich, turning bodily space inside out and dissolving the world into a perspective vortex.

This spiraling kaleidoscope is disorienting. Beyond the cockpit window, still far ahead of us, a dot appears on the frozen white nights, at sixty degrees north latitude. Probably 180 degrees or twelve hours away from the explosion, measured on the circumference at the top of the world. *In all certainty I know only of a raging fife that consumes me without physically burning, augmenting as we approach the antipodes of a dot on the map where the place of being was once tangential to both, the surface of the sphere, and the immense astral cosmos.* I cannot yet decide whether to leap into the abyss gathered at the unknown center. My gaze finally comes to rest on my friend's beautiful body, whose identity still plagues me. Angular cheeks and breath of cinnamon, piercing violet eyes, radiant blond hair, skin of ebony. The wonderfully sensuous architecture of genetic manipulation tortures my imagination. Its promise of inconceivable pleasures is debilitating, yet unless fulfilled it will lead me to a certain death.

My body is swollen with perspiration and runny tears. *I must articulate my hopes and beg for my guide's compassion . . .* Once more I decide against it, for I find some consolation in admiring her upright commanding posture and in her overflowing love that one look projects onto the earth. *Recalling the experiences of Nikolai and Aureliano, I also fear that any impulsive action might have catastrophic consequences. The vessel requires a firm hand at the helm during all times.*

My eyelids slip over my pupils, transparent, dissolving the layers of color that peel like old paint, corroded by the imminent collapse of a great sleep cycle. A further shift of consciousness dislocates my mind and body; viscera untangle while muscles and streams of thought realign themselves, anxiously seeking a new, more appropriate position of sleep.

THE RADAR SCREEN indicates that we are entering the final sector of the first half of the circumambulation, at 165 degrees west longitude. The fresh spring breezes will soon be inflamed by the hot air of summer. We soar on our way to a climax in a sinusoidal route that shall, if ever reached, bring about its own declination; we will finally abandon the West to descend into the East . . . *Indeed, we true moderns were all born to live in the Orient!* The sun is rising.

With a firm hand and measured gestures my adorable companion takes me at last into the circle. *The tangential acceleration that we have acquired in our spiraling perambulation around the cylinder must be the cause of our present freedom. Perhaps now the lost dimension, the much sought after metaphor of the fourth dimension in the realm of experience, can be recovered or even transcended.*

The spacious yet visibly enclosed place is populated by familiar objects, which seem to be radial projections of the four triumphs previously contemplated. The electric tension among them jolts our muscles and shorts our attention: the polarized molecules of ether, the space of desire frozen in an infinitely transparent perspective at 4:00 A.M., precisely before the late spring twilight. This is not a mere spatial organization but an auspicious trace, an instrument for clairvoyance. It allows us to visualize, surely and immediately, the place where a crucial event is imminent and will occur at the appropriate time. *At last, a cosmic place that will not be dissolved by the geometric space that is its substance!*

A fragile wooden scaffolding of undetermined scale, but most likely smaller than ourselves, contains a space of unique quality never previously inhabited. This substance blurs the duality of inside and outside with its corrosive density and concentration. Fueled by my own longing, by my obsessive search of Polya's locus, this essential substance progressively eats

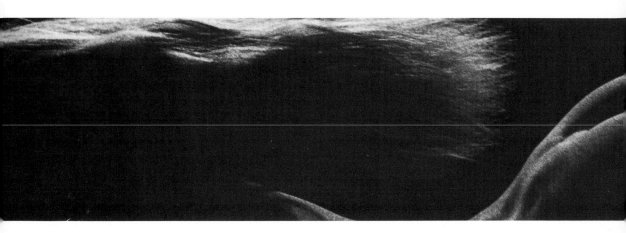

away the objects to manifest its own frightening absence. *Or my breath may effect the more hopeful metamorphosis of space into flesh!*

In this abode our place exists but is neither here nor yonder; it is between my center and the objects. *It evokes the feeling of treading along the ocean's thin foaming wavelets on the beach; one has neither a landward nor a seaward yearning. No escape into the alternative is possible because home is both ways.*

Vaguely perceptible along the periphery the feasting silhouettes of youthful men and women merge into the horizon: love and the fruits of fertility celebrated in one gesture. Within the circle of the round dance, the progressive erosion and substantial transformation of the elements into flesh seem now inevitable. The serpent of the earth, to the right, reduced to its spinal cord, hangs suspended inside a shifted quadrangular scaffold: the vertebrae transmuted from a garland of flowers. On the left the dark glass bottle assumes a feminine aspect when squeezed in front of three opaque panels or negative windows: the bilboquet originating from a cornucopia filled with mature grain. The spherical air pendulum, floating at the center under the four-sided oblique pediment or barely touching the *objet d'art*, loses any trace of the V-shaped wound: the transfiguration of a naked chubby angel crowned with fruit. Lastly, up above, the fire pyramid becomes a mechanical bird's structure with extended wings and articulated pincers hanging on wire from a rectangular frame: the skeleton transmuted from that of a rigid king, scepter in hand, looking at the stormy sky.

The flaccid *objet d'art*, a cast of galvanized plaster, the byproduct of some complex alchemical fabrication, occupies the most prominent position. It lies on a small semicircular platform cantilevered from a hanging vertical panel attached to the scaffolding. Printed on the back of the panel are illustrations of twenty twisted and simple darts and wedges, both engaged and disengaged, with an inscription indicating that these are the tools of the form giver. The darts are pointed and erect or curved; the wedges can easily become receptacles for donkey's blood, warm milk, or sparkling wine disseminated by the elastic dancing silhouettes on the earth's circumference.

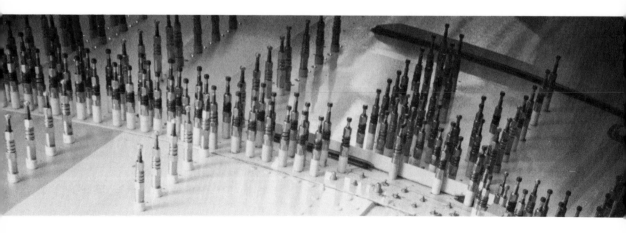

I can hardly restrain the intense, intimate pleasure that this extraordinary place produces in my tortured body. *At last, an accurate representation of desire? A mimesis of salvation?* My guide and companion, however, remains strangely aloof.

Tightly we hold hands as we continue our loving walk, proceeding with the established itinerary toward the center. While she keeps the vessel securely under control, I walk with my eyes on the sky, beyond the navigator's canopy. Space and time overlap; time spreads out and space rolls slowly forward, allowing us finally to glimpse and understand infinity. *My passionate emotions can now be compressed into sensations. Soon passive reflections will no longer be necessary!*

Beyond my guide's golden hair and smooth skin is a pouting pinnacle supported by a turgid roof, not far from the efflux vein that collects all of the cockpit water at the hermetically sealed and perhaps ultimately inaccessible center. *The frothy quality of the papular structure is astounding.* It appears to be covered in graphite and to obey a formal syntax oblivious of gravity, with concavities, crutches, bulges, and serrations that reveal a unique logic pertaining to the consistency of flesh. The whole semifluid, molded mass is abruptly sectioned by the three orthogonal planes of spatial descriptive geometry, x-x', y-y', and z-z', which have acquired a considerable thickness and are therefore visible as a three-dimensional Greek cross. It is easy to inscribe mentally in this monument the glittering yellow sphere pierced by a sharp metallic instrument.

Delighted by the contrast between the viscid and lathery substance on one hand and the frozen, cutting edges of the geometric plane on the other, I forget the favors that I coveted from my guide. My only pressing concern is to arrive at that place in the distance: *an architecture consecrated to love. Is it really on the other side? Are we following some obscure, tangential route?* Despite my distress I dare not ask my friend to take me there . . . Yet, unexpectedly, the Absolute Given meets us halfway. In front of us stands the source of water and light, the principal fuel pump and illuminating particle generator.

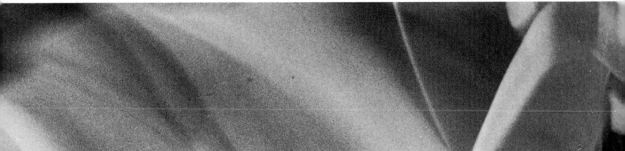

Below, on the distant coastline, one can still see a river by the sea and a hydroelectric plant. I turn to my right and my guide has vanished!

THE TEMPLE OF LOVE is now at arm's length. *It is utterly magnificent!* Standing simultaneously at the center and the periphery, this architecture contradicts its appearance from the distance and does not conform to a single geometry, structure, or scale. Plans, sections, and elevations could not, therefore, be rendered objectively. *This is, indeed, the antithesis of a classical temple, with its squares and circles traced on ideal leveled surfaces and proportioned according to immutable, natural whole numbers.* The place now exists only in experiential time and space, shadow and light, its objectification beyond the scope of present possibilities. The ambiguous reality of the future architecture resides as a succession of frames, three per instant, conveying three-dimensional images that envelope the six paired directions of the human body and coincide with the descriptive planes and our meandering circumambulations. The center, meanwhile, preserves itself, comprising the sanctuary with its systems of collection and distribution of water and light. We are both in the temple and beholding it. Three perpendicular square frames / twenty-four moments:

I

A thin graphite base representing etiolated white.

The texture and the color of a flat and bleached blue sky.

A faintly rubescent, internally glowing section of flesh

inscribed: **and there was light.**

II

A thick charcoal layer representing somber darkness.

The deep and achromatic color of a night sky with no stars.

A cupreous and frosted, internally opaque section of flesh
inscribed: **and darkness was upon the face of the deep.**

III

A soft gray curved wall sweeping down from the upper left-hand
corner against the unilluminated background.

The uncanny silkiness of the gateway's plastic material bearing
the inscription: **Let us make man in our own image.**

The subtly arcuated profile of the thigh as it descends toward
the basal joint.

IV

The curved V-shaped valley against the unlighted background.

Remarkable precision of the inverted pointed arch.

Increasingly humid satin hollowness at the abrupt depression of
the vaginal furrow.

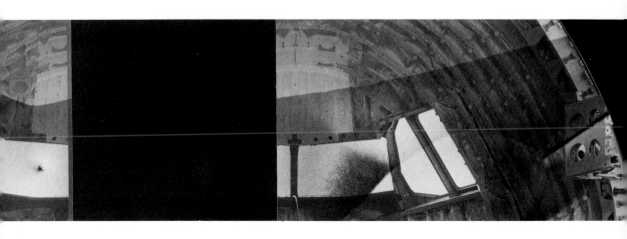

V

Two curves converging at the upper margin forming an ascending
path, an obelisk in the center casts a shadow.

Exquisitely crafted glazed pavement of variegated color.

Beyond the birth canal, the pale haunches in the shade.

VI

In contrast with the sweeping curve, the monument cuts deeply
into the pavement with its sharp edges and shadows.

The viridescent mineral block is tinted like a dart with crimson
carbuncles and inscribed: **You are dust, forever banished from
the garden of Eden.**

The burning shadow on the waist unseams the permanent pores of
eternal return.

VII

A very dark circular orifice surrounded by spiraling walls in
the light and shade.

A bronze vault cast in one piece, both enclosing space and
allowing the light of life to filter through.

The sinking cavernous funnel of the navel contracts as it twists
and thus, in its shallowness, intimates an unsoundable depth.

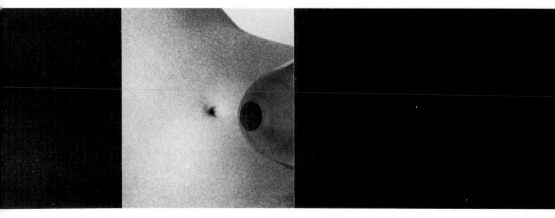

VIII

A bright opening in the distance, at the end of the enveloping
path.

Perforated pillars gather the rain and water and take it to an
underground cistern, avoiding the deteriorating effects of
thunderstorms and all the inconveniences of free-fall.

One of the conduits of peristaltic rhythms that open like
vortexes into the nine bodily windows.

IX

Light pours into the egg-shaped tunnel, coating with different
shades of gray five smoothly rounded enveloping strata.

A golden shimmer enlivens the carefully constructed membranes
that limit the space as it unfolds to the exterior, accentuating
the annular structure.

The abysmal hypogeum of flesh comes to an end at the place of
union and penetration, where the dialectics are always resolved,
at the edge of the cranium or under the vulva.

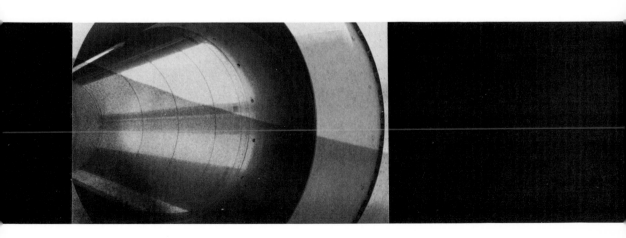

X

The curving path continues among sloping walls.

The most harmonious music, unequaled in timbre by any known
instrument, is created by the wind filtering through membranes
whose thicknesses are in perfect concordance, and blowing under
mushrooming arches traced with well-adjusted drafting tools to
the specifications of accurate serial dimensions.

The folds and crevices of the distended diaphragm, armpit, and
flowering breasts.

XI

In the background an arch in the form of a pair of cantilevered
pincers, projecting from a curving, horizontal concrete stump and
barely touching the opposite wall.

Hollow pivoting thorns capturing the wind, horizontal pinnacles
funneling the irritating energy of the life breath.

The prickly crown of needles at the crotch.

XII

On the lower right-hand corner, a curving oblong cavity
circumscribing an invisible iris.
A sphere made with a malleable, glazed material, cast in multiple
layers of variable density and transparency, azure, purple, and
viridescent, reflecting the monticles and the dark crescent of
the moon and showing the inscription: **The eyes breathe and the
mouth flutters.**

The pointed, delicate corners of the eye glowing with internal
light, epitome of all bodily joints and gestures.

XIII

Beyond the curving walls, at the horizon, the intense contrast of
a black triangle and pure luminosity pointing at a line between
hemispheric forms.

The hinge of the universe bearing the designs of fate embedded in
its incorruptible material and inscribed on the protruding
automatic doors; on the left: **To each one it is convenient to
make according to his nature,** and on the right: **Voluptuousness
is the cause of action.**

Beyond the receding undulations of a chiasm of calves, the sharp
shadows between the buttocks enhance the convexity of the pubis.

XIV

A lenticular opening with a pyramid looming behind it.

A hyperreal, bloodstained head of Medusa presiding simultaneously over the gate and the center: the orbs of her eyes now absolutely void; her mouth, the vibrating lips of Polya.

The vertex of pleasure hidden by vermicular reflections.

XV

A symmetrical shadow resembling the hands in a gesture of prayer raised toward the height.

154

The mouth of an abysmal well where the rain water is gathered and the inscription: **For you cast me into the deep, into the heart of the sea . . . and the flood enveloped me.**

The seamy side or penetralia, marking the gateway to the recesses of the sacred.

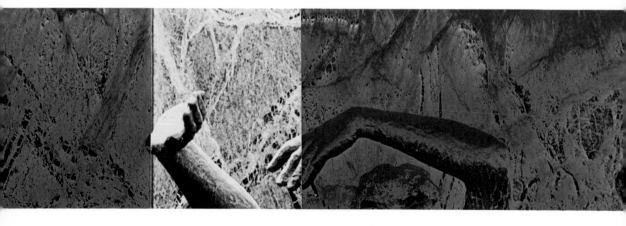

XVI

Raising from a horizontal reflecting surface, a smooth, slightly
curved vertical monolith in front of an organic wall and capped
by a pediment of shadows.

The structural buttress inlaid with polychromatic mosaics, which
makes possible the virtuosity of the monocoque shell.

An elongated, fleshy tongue that emerges from the depths and
gently penetrates the triangular orifice.

XVII

On the reflecting surface of the well, the phantasm of an
ascending bridge, the absent umbilical cord.

The fulgurations of sapphire, emerald, ruby, and topaz projected
by a mysterious lamp, a fiery incandescent sphere enclosed in a
thin and amazingly transparent material so bright that it is
impossible to behold directly.

The luminous, innermost membranes of the womb, engraved with the
cellular tissue that contains the secret of life, the fire of the
earth.

XVIII . . .

The three frames suddenly show the same monochromatic reality: an evanescent path of pure, white light with no texture, descending as a sharp-cut, precise curve from the converging point of its two edges at the top of the square. The sepulchral monolith is no longer distinguishable. Frames nineteen and twenty exhibit a progressive contraction of the ascending arch, followed by an insubstantial, totally shallow, and almost hyaline vision of total blackness. *The gap or chasm!* The three penultimate frames surround me with the sweet, quiet warmth of salvation. A star vibrates near the upper right-hand corner of the cockpit; it grows and comes to occupy a central position, transforming itself into the blinding, coruscating sphere. *At a distance of two palms from my eyes, at the height of my heart . . .* "Ooo-oo-ooom . . ." The familiar sound! *The sonority of some other world?* Under the last frame an inscription reads:

Then I saw new heavens and a new earth . . . and the sea was no longer.

My soul is filled with both serenity and amazement. The truth made present in this place reconciles the sensuous and the spiritual, a disclosure forever denied in the cities down below. I find myself alone but, incomprehensibly, also sense the enveloping and enigmatic presence of Polya in the proximity of absolute ecstasy. Yes, yet my beloved remains invisible. Like art and being, forever as well?

An illuminated caption, projected with dot-matrix letters under the horizontal center line on a large glazed rectangle in front of me, reads:

Given: (1) Liquid fuel; (2) Electricity; (3) Air.

I remember my fathomless thirst and the many inextinguishable fires and fluid reflections in the temple. We are now, finally, confronting the hermetic sanctuary at the core of the structure, waiting for the priestess and the virgins who never arrive. The sun is rising but there is no ritual. *We remain alone.*

THE SANCTUARY, where everything is set erect, appears behind a plate of glass that may represent the map of the vessel's operations or the cockpit's internal elevation, transforming perspective into reality. Proportioned like a gate with no hinges, its height is divided by the horizon line, which coincides with the top of the instrument panel. Thus, the upper rectangle frames the sky beyond the ample sloping windshields with their acute sweep-back and electric anti-icing systems, which make them glare-proof and virtually invisible.

The glass plate captures its beholders, making them part of the shrine that presently reveals an even more recondite inner sanctum, concealed by a thick, wooden door embedded in a masonry portal and closed with a heavy crossbar. *The analogy between the impenetrable transparent and opaque gates is obvious . . .* The sanctuary extends an invitation to participate in the ceremony, but only through a fully detached, voyeuristic interest.

The glowing sphere, which now fills the center of the upper rectangle, imperceptibly becomes a reflected face of subtle blinding light. Below the horizon the captain's immaculate uniform completes the vision of this luminous body. The intense brightness subsides and turns into an abundant, curling mane of blond hair, framing a very smooth, oval-shaped visage with nubile breasts as eyes, navel as nose, and depilated vulva as mouth. *This uncannily familiar yet emasculating vision of the Mother is disconcerting indeed.* Using her two hands, the captain then pulls down a thin rubber membrane over her head, a technologically sophisticated mask cast in a

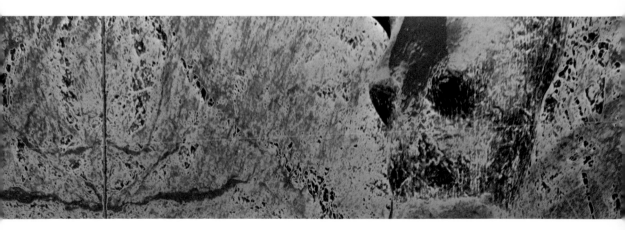

mold of silicon paste or antinomy.

On the glass I can instantly recognize the reflection of Polya . . . *Except that her face is uncomfortably strange, perhaps slightly darker.* I lower my head and stare at the naked foot of my companion, an act that undresses her body to the waist and lengthens the gait of her haunches. The reflection also grafts the tip of her bare foot and empty shoe, abandoned after many hours of flight. A more intimate, unquestionable recognition occurs when the radiant albescence of her legs overwhelms my entire field of vision and precipitates into my heated memory, filling it with the undescribable pleasure of silent white.

At this time the inscribed gates may unlock automatically under the action of invisible magnetic forces. I take from my guide the glowing electric torch that she has been carrying all along and is now willing to relinquish. Marking its trajectory in space, it joins two vertices of the polygon of sex and comes to shine upon my agitated lower abdomen. She says: "My dear Polyphilo, I am indeed your beloved Polya! In order to maintain our course, I have had to hide my identity. I have suffered much. Your passionate love has finally induced me to abandon my profession; I am no longer Keeper of the Fire. You must now, in your innermost center, carry the fiery burden of desire, one that cannot be extinguished by the water of the well. And now that you hold the torch, we may truly fly, and I can reciprocate your love and fulfill your burning cupidity. I belong to you and would die for you."

Two butterflies of flesh mutually gobbling flies against a blue sky tinged purple by their enormous wings frantically try to obliterate their individuality, transmuting light into color in a dazzle of sunshine. My lips are touched, and as I have hardly started to cry sweet and fervent tears, I am suddenly struck. *Struck by anamnesis. Soon back at the origins, the beginning of the end?*

Struck and frustrated by the same unnamable obstacle that always stands in the way of erotic fulfillment, both absolutely transparent and utterly opaque. The impenetrable membrane masking the cockpit: the mask of

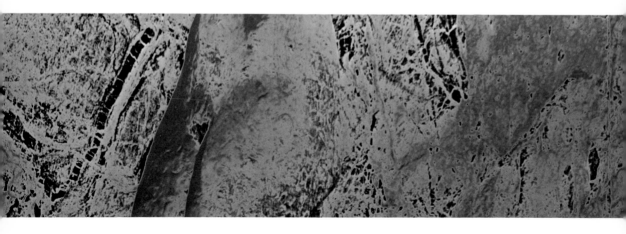

Polya's face into which my companion has fully receded. The maiden architect of fate, commander of the vessel, prepares for her debut by becoming a trace of her rhythmic agitation on the large glass. Enveloped by darkness, she operates mysterious handles and mechanisms mapped in elevation with phosphorescent chemical compounds, oil paint, lead foil, varnish, dust, and lead wire.

The unmarried professional sits on a reclining, ergonomic couch, supplied with an emergency vibrating yoke. The source of erotic energy is at the left of the lower rectangle, the navigational domain of the cockpit. Her motions are linked, along the plane of the sex polygon, to the trim wheels, the fuel cocks, and the electronic starting panel, all given. She rests her hands firmly on the ram's horn flight controls with built-in "artificial feel and stall" warning system.

The map of a sequence of facts in an ultrarapid instantaneous exposure reveals the ambiguous connections between the trim wheels and a complex array of flaps, spoilers, rudders, and ailerons; between the fuel cocks and the jet engines through the fuel pumps, sloping ducts and microscopic sieves for gasification and ignition; and between the electronic starter and all systems, including the multichannel and self-test unit and the on-board computer with its external sensing devices and its display monitor at the center top of the instrument panel, just under the windshield.

The turbines, providing the propulsion needed for penetration, inhale the air between the conic mound and lips and compress it through their Rolls-Royce chassis. This activates the automatic gear boxes and pressure relief systems connected to the outer fan ducting. The engines are also wired to the fire/shutdown valves, which can be triggered by the explosive decompression alarm systems that in turn can effect an unexpected insemination, thereby illuminating the CRASH! indicator on the computer monitor. The parachute is an unlikely subsystem of the fire/shutdown circuit.

The electronic autopilot/ACL (automating checklist) interfaces with the computer. It controls the overall lubrication, as well as the complete auto-strip operation. On the right the radar screen and other gauges that disclose

the position of the vessel in three sets of Cartesian coordinates represent the voyeur's place. This instrument panel allows for objective witnessing but is equally indispensable to direct with utmost precision the invagination of the sky.

The computer monitor displays a double real-time clock, showing the twenty-four milliseconds delay of ultrarapid communication. This monitor can flash simultaneously many visible parameters, a particularly useful function when the airplane attains supersonic speeds or transcends motion to become consummately immobile. While I lift my eyes to contemplate the clouds pierced by the sun, a series of green digital commands appears in rapid succession. BOOTSTRAP. The sky's nucleonic reservoir feeds the polar ionization chamber, potentially engendering an infinite array of phenomena through the configuration of magnetic desire, ranging from the Milky Way to the northern lights and virtually, even, life. BREAK.

After a brief interruption, the set of commands continues to be displayed in the monitor: TIME-SHARING: MULTITASKING. FORMATTING FOR AIGPS. At the prompt the captain writes on the screen: "Artificial Intelligence Germination in Pleromatic Space." INPUT: "Two male swans, two white pigeons held together with a red ribbon, an urn with sea water, a large inkwell to hold the blood of the decapitated sacrificial animals, assorted flowers." After entering these data, the computer continues on its own. COMPILING ALPHABET. FACTORING. RECOMBINING. SCANNING. Two red, inexplicable characters are written on the screen and added to the alphabet of twenty-two letters, characters clearly not constructed from a combination of preexisting fragments. The word EMET (aleph, mem, tav) flashes on the screen, containing the two odd letters assigned values of one and forty, life and death. BREAK. RESET.

Over the horizon line, beyond the pressure bulkhead, the nose tip encapsulating the radar dish and other vital sensors penetrates the sky. The quantifiable ratio of friction to air velocity is immediately graspable as a precise sensation. The autopilot system allows for a sudden discharge of generative friction in the air. Thus, the electricity and fuel recombine with

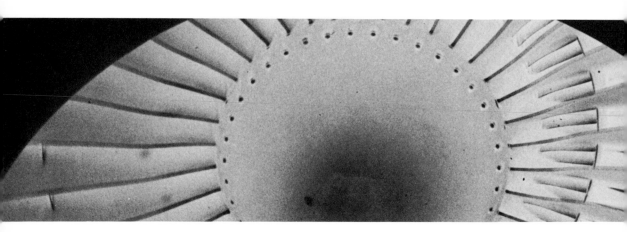

water and light filament molecules suspended in the colloidal life breath. This biochemical reaction originates the transmutation of the professional woman into the sky virgin, with its perfect plastic body, looming behind the clouds. On its forehead the imprint reads: EMET. And in the computer monitor, after a delay of twenty-four milliseconds, JUMP. DELETE: chiasm. WRITE: ~~aleph~~, mem, tav.

The autostripping has evidently caused the miraculous reconstitution of life: an androgynous totality or metasexual human person. *Is it behind the closed door on the altar of the temple's inner sanctum?* The peepholes in the massive door are fully accessible, occupying the same place of the witness in the now invisible transparent glass plate. *One obstacle removed. The end? The beginning?*

A remarkable binocular sight indeed! The luminous, wide-open space behind the door is both bewitching and banal. It is the site of the temple as we all remember it, not far from the river but by the sea: gentle, wooded hills surrounding the sacred precinct, framed by a flat blue sky. Even though the time is probably close to six in the evening on a late spring day, the twilight reveals the scene with supreme clarity.

Very near my eyes but also very far away a naked girl is stretched on a natural bed, a primitive altar covered with twigs. Her blond hair falls freely but remains completely motionless, concealing almost all of her face. Her legs are open and slightly bent, her pubis strangely smooth in contrast to the splendid abundance of her hair. *I recognize her features!* Her vaginal slit is definitely out of alignment with her axis of symmetry, as if distorted by spherical anamorphosis. Her arms are extended backward, and on her left hand she holds a lit phallic torch that paradoxically creates darkness analogous to that pervading the cockpit.

This plastic golem provides the final and clearest revelation of Polya's identity: the quintessential lover, inhabiting an utterly still landscape and suspended in her moment of lonely ecstasy, perhaps the instant of death. The perfection of the flesh in this exquisite body, purified of hair or dimples, is absolute. One can only hear the murmuring trickle of the emission, feel

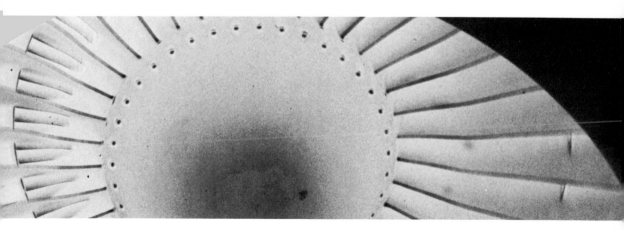

the electrical discharge, and smell the oil by-products resulting from the alchemical conflagration.

We behold the light as well but cannot see the material objects. Our gaze seems to pass through them. I am part of the ritual, but my unpossessing voyeurism has been transformed into clairvoyance and my desire into contemplative knowledge. *The ultimate reciprocity! K'uan, a single Chinese character, means both contemplating and being contemplated. The transcendence of duality? But desiring without touching what is desired is no less torture than the punishment of boredom and dread that follows possession. The existence of love beyond these mortal alternatives?* During a temporal delay of twenty-four milliseconds Polya saw herself, and this vision excited her. Caught in the reflection, I looked at myself looking at her, and she looked at herself in my look that looked at her naked. At the moment of the discharge, the moment of the miraculous generation of life, I disappeared from her sight and the glass became the opaque door without hinges, sealing off the crypt of our personal and collective history.

I have perhaps arrived at the end of my journey. At least I have caught a glimpse of being in this trace of the fourth dimension . . . The ascent in the sinusoidal wave has certainly concluded, at 180 degrees in the dream map.

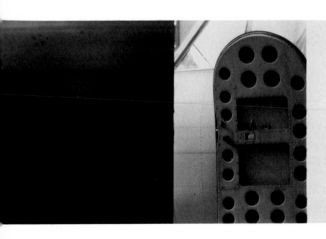

2:35:30 . . . POLYA IS BESIDE ME in this dim light, wearing this time not the airline uniform but Levi's overalls and a brightly colored T-shirt. She is eating a synthetic food from a styrofoam container, a delicacy that is also a product of the genetic germination. Without speaking, she shares with me the outstanding hamburger of universal taste. *The flavor of flesh! Indeed, the food of authentic fraternal communion all over the globe, accompanied by the same beat, probably impossible to make more perfect and fulfilling . . .*

Amid confusing images, sad and hopeful, I sense the rebirth of my tragicomic lust. The last pure thought accompanying the dissolution of the ego? There is no captain, and it is time to leave the cockpit. Forever together and alone my traveling companion and I exit definitively at the top of the world.

OH CHARMING COMPANY at the climax of the world! From the very tip of the pyramid, the leading edge of Mother Earth, the new axonometric place is disclosed. Polya and Polyphilo tread toward the eye of the crest, a volcanic temenos erupting at the point of fusion between the sky and the vessel. *A quiet, unceasing ejaculation!* Their bodies are hyperreal, plastic bodies free from blemish or imperfection. Abandoning their respective pedestals on the perimeter of the stage they glide voluptuously, leaving a vibrating trail of passion and condensing space by the emanations of their every pore.

The summit of the pyramid is the only location in the complex where the geometric secret of the post-perspective public square is revealed. From that vantage point walls, arcades, and pavement are reduced to a two-dimensional vision. The aerial, objective view of the distorted square appears as an undistorted, orthogonal elevation: a geometric projection onto a vertical plane that can now be precisely overlaid on the axonometric stage. The horizon has shifted ninety degrees, but the limits are again visible.

We hover free from gravity, and despite the overwhelming pressure my heart is flooded with ethereal roses that quench its painful fire with sweet emanations. Polya's scintillating eyes shine brightly as she asks Polyphilo to proceed to the river, to the holy precinct by the sea where they may contemplate numinous signs. From there, she suggests, since they have been cleansed of all impurities by their sacrifice and communion, they may finally travel to the much-desired place of endless fulfillment . . .

Their smooth and hairless bodies irrupt through separate, anthropomorphic arches marking the entrance of a roofless pavilion: an incomplete yet prophetic transformation of the old sacred space. A brick wall behind the sanctuary, opposite a descending stair, is perforated with an opening that deliberately frames the sheer presence of the void. *In relief, merging*

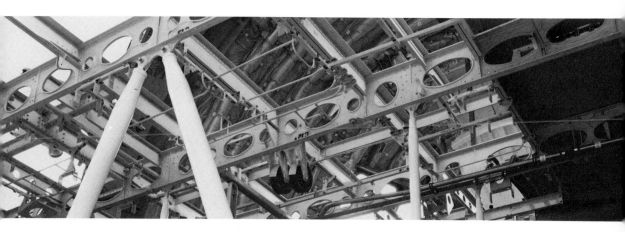

into the masonry, a furrow of flesh stretched by our hands reveals a pink, humid orifice that stares back at us and palpitates with life like a repugnant octopus. The loving couple ignore the simulacrum. They continue through the twisted metal, smoldering plastic, and shattered rubble, reaching a chamber by way of a hidden underground passage.

The pavilion is a glass cage immersed in a pool. Water is visible on all sides through the windows, wombwater for waterlovers: vast, democratic, restless, and sterile. *Not air?* Through the space glide a few invisible tame fish. The walls of the pool are lined with a thick, waterproof coat of clay, and a drain valve with a glittering chain is seen in the distance. The interior is furnished with huge divans covered with purple silk, overstuffed and scented with myrrh, aloes, and cinnamon.

Opening a trap door, the loving pair emerge (*back?*) into the circular space to seek intimacy and protection from prying eyes. They submerge themselves in a private universe of rhythmic undulations and reflections. Every surface multiplies the image of copulation, unfolded in endless symmetrical arrangements, central and bilateral, vanishing into an ubiquitous perspective. *With even the slightest motion, our hearts burst into the emptiness in which we are caught and terror seizes us with the infinite unfolding of our own image.*

Polya is enveloped by a cloud that makes her nakedness yet more explicit. The air is sweet and warm. Their immaculate bodies appear undisturbed by the red liquid that surely infiltrates every crevice and fold of milky flesh. Crumpled jeans and elastic T-shirts lie on the floor. The couple, lost in the depths of their embrace, becomes aware of that falsity which is at the root of anguish; together they realize that pleasure is the same thing as pain, love, a synonym of death. Inescapable is the fact that being manifests itself in acts of transgression. *Death entails not only disappearance but the intolerable motion in which in spite of ourselves we disappear and fuse with the Other, even when it is absolutely indispensable that we stay still (and that our identities remain intact).*

Soon Polyphilo, in a fit of lust, can barely hold his breath. Polya also falls

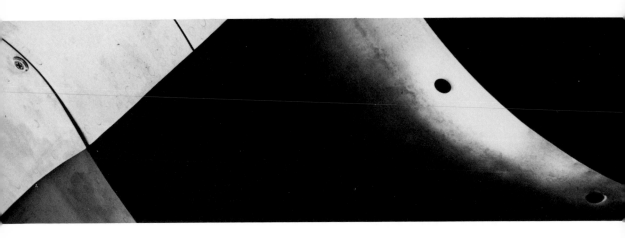

prey to amorous contagion. She looks at him intensely and utters some ancient words of love: "At unfathomable depths, through and through me, beneath the flesh an implacable fire rages. Nothing is visible, and the roar of waves sounds in my ears. Sweat flows down in rivers and a tremor seizes all my limbs. I falter, paler than the grass in autumn, pervaded by the pains of menacing extinction, lost in the love trance."

Fire is reciprocated in Polyphilo. He evokes the vibrations of the snake, tasting the flavor of the small, succulent mouth and penetrating the hidden treasure of Mother Earth. The final fulfillment of long-awaited expectations seems to be at hand! Cloudbursts, secret springs, eruptions, geysers, and whirlpools. The source of living water that is the joy of voluptuousness overflows into the eyes of Polya, whose sight intimates death. They enjoy their bodies with passion, and the hum and the sweat and the tide rise in unison with the start of summer. But at that instant, at dawn, just before orgasm, Polya refuses to die.

167

I AGAIN REMEMBER the modern dilemma that makes it unimaginable to die for love; seduced by Faust, Marguerite failed to differentiate between licit and illicit cupidity, finding it impossible to bring about her own demise from guilt. Beyond good and evil, the ethics of classical tragedy is also untenable. What now? Polyphilo despairs, invaded once more by the original doubt that plunged him into his dream, the crucial, intertwined questions concerning the very potentiality of love, life capable of true death: the elusive presence of being.

I am tempted to ignore all dangers and transgress the presumed sanctity of existence so that I may confront the abyss! My irritating thoughts can hardly be resisted: violence, shattering membranes, excess, and overindulgence. Not the insipid "pleasures of the flesh" or even the usual debauchery that cannot dirty anything sublime. Rather, I am attracted by a radical debauchery that soils not merely my body and my thoughts but everything that I may conceive in its course:

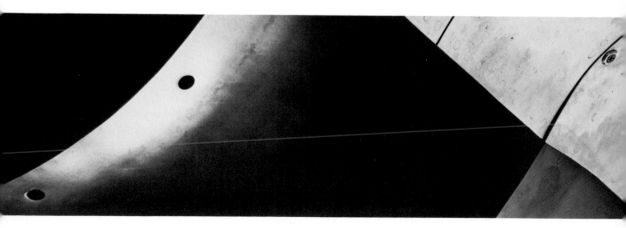

the vast, starry universe of light itself.

Polyphilo vehemently expresses his wish to die for Polya, if dying with her should prove to be impossible. *Please kill me! I am only a mortal whose thirst, aspiration, hope, craving, ardor, and concupiscence cannot effect motion. No longer can I stand under a mute agglomeration of objects impervious to desire.*

"Patience!" she responds simply.

Patience blasts in my ears. Recalling all his previous suffering, Polyphilo resolves to hold his breath. Again, amid calcinating flames, in the expectation of being reborn from the ashes. *To attain the final release?*

Knowing about his lover's quest for order and his obsession to gather potential realities for the dwelling of tomorrow, Polya exhorts Polyphilo to examine the remains of the crash site: the polyandron or "cemetery of all," a true school for life and promise of wisdom where Mother Earth embraces her many lovers. The indelible shadows incised on the ground and cutting through the walls, the footprint of a penetrating force also imprinted on the anthropomorphic openings in the pavilion, are evidence of the great explosion. She says: "There are more enigmas in the shadow of a man who walks in the sun than in all religions of the past, present, and future." *Yet neither the substance of light nor the shadow of light existed materially, in three dimensions, before now. In a previous situation, below the airplane. Remember? A few hours ago, or perhaps at the end of this space within a pause.*

While awaiting their destiny, almost accustomed to a perennial dying and to the uncertainty of (il)licit love, Polyphilo decides to follow Polya's suggestion and visit the polyandron. Constructed of substantial sediments or shadows of shadows, this place comprises the tombs of all who have found premature death as a result of unfortunate affairs. Polya, who is now modestly draped, insists with her lover that we must have the courage to keep our eyes open and behold the bottom of the tomb and the total emptiness that it contains. "However remote," she emphasizes, "Paradise is the attainment of freedom on earth, the experience of love, and the

proclamation of the utterly mysterious empty coffin beneath the sanctuary."

I am not yet convinced! In frustration I cover my nape, stomach, and feet, the parts of the human anatomy most sensitive to cold.

Polya remains alone in the pressurized chamber, surrounded by the infallible paradigm of buoyancy, simplicity, and persevering penetration, waiting for the sonic boom and the authentic experience of flight . . . Polyphilo carries his suitcase and undertakes to explore the world of permanent shadows, hoping to find more secrets about the architecture of the present and future.

I DISLIKE THE AQUEOUS substances of glass and crystal and distrust acquacities of thought and language . . . There is light at the end of the tunnel. Through the eye? Polyphilo climbs the ramp and makes his way back to the summit, a coal-black fusiform raft carrying the pavilion and hovering high above the axonometric cemetery. Since the explosion this privileged viewing platform has also become the open vertical shaft of the tower's indelible shadow.

The old red-brick tower now appears in the distance, having evidently lost its phallic character. It is unfolded and hinged with its symmetrical image along one of its five corners. Parallax is forever denied by the receding and diverging, softly curved walls that thrust upward, drawing the initial of loVe and marking the axis of putrefaction. The divine iris no longer looms at the top of the tower. The familiar dark circle, a faceless clock, has reestablished the primacy of tempus. *A favorable time for pleasure and knowledge.* The acoustic device has now been replaced by an archetypal mechanism: a metronome with an eye punctured by the time-keeping needle.

The obelisk of destroyed time is an eloquent symbol of the miserable cadavers of love whose crushed monuments can be seen all around. *Under my feet the center of the black shaft is less crowded with debris while over my head the dome of the sky resembles a funnel for the collection and conveyance of sacrificial*

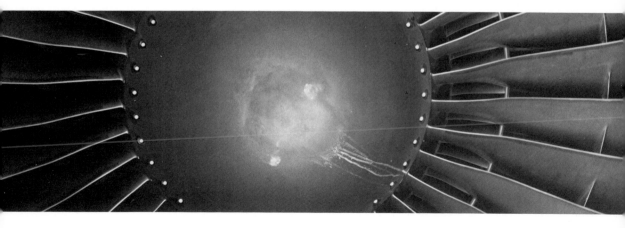

smoke. Reciprocal pyramids? It is possible that by descending into the permanent shadow I might find a passage among the ruined fragments of the cemetery. Descending vertical motion between the funnel and the shaft, along the hinge of the tower and the needle of the obelisk. Could it indeed be the key to the polyandron's axonometric order?

Seduced by an excessive appetite of knowledge, Polyphilo walks down the stairs and opens an undersized door. All is immediately dismal and foggy. Our eyes must adjust to the darkness. *My thoughts now redundant—thoroughly redundant!—resound with a humid sonority.*

Under the funnel, beyond gloom, a single, jet-black pedestal supports a strange object. The pedestal has seven small drawers that presumably can be unlocked with a special tool lying beside a pair of white gloves on a metallic table nearby. Polyphilo puts on the gloves and, using the extraction hook with great care, proceeds to pull out every compartment.

The heavy drawers of diverse rectangular sizes open on different sides and seem to occupy ubiquitous space, apparently overlapping with each other inside the pedestal. Each drawer contains a world of miniature objects that recollects an archetype or chain of being. Among every set of objects there is always a geometric body made of a pure element and a slab of imitation stone bearing an inscription, an epitaph alluding to unhappy love. From bottom to top and from left to right, in an ascending spiraling route, the inventory is as follows:

1

Colored pebbles (like those used to decorate aquariums),
humid clay,
the skull of a reptile,
a cube of onyx.

The first generation says of him that he came from the void, was nourished in the heavens and came to knowledge in the bosom of his mother. And thus he came to the water.

2

Realistic bulk figures of a man and a woman in copulating
positions,
a black and white checkerboard,
a pentagonal bell tower with a pyramidal spire and a red
triangular flag flying from the mast,
a simple rectangular chapel with a curved apse and sloped roof,
a copper triangular prism or wedge of chastity.

**The second generation says of him that he came from a great
prophet. He was nourished on a high mountain by the bird of
heaven and received his glorious pleasure through an angel. And
thus he came to the water.**

3

An incubator, consisting of a ninety-centimeter modular grid
scaled on tracing paper,
a half-egg of scintillating mercury on a sheet of reflecting
mylar under pink and blue neon light,
a square prism ingot of gold.

**The third generation says of him that he came from a virgin
womb. He and his mother were cast out of the city into the desert
where he was nourished and became knowledgeable. And thus he
came to the water.**

4

A carved crystal capable of reflecting images and of transforming white
light into rainbows,
a computer chip,
a sharp and polished silver quadrangular pyramid.

**The fourth generation says of him that he came from a virgin
but was lost and never found. The virgin became pregnant again
while picking flowers and gave birth to a child whom she
nourished at the edge of the desert and who received his
knowledge from the seed from which he had been begotten. And
thus he came to the water.**

5

A realistic model of the double pyramid of the Templo Mayor in
Tenochtitlan,
a mound of earth for childhood flight,
a hollow cube of lead.

**The fifth generation says of him that he came from a heavenly
drop. He was thrown into the sea and the abyss received him,
gave him birth, and brought him back to heaven where
he was nourished and became knowledgeable.
And thus he came to the water.**

6

A porcelain cup,
an electric light switch,
two identical tetrahedrons of diamond and iron.

The sixth generation says of him that his father coveted his own daughter. She became pregnant from her father and gave birth in the tomb, out in the desert. The angels nourished him and gave him pleasure. And thus he came to the water.

7

A single laser beam projected from a gene splicer,
an amorphous heap of greenish crystals of plastic,
substantial empty space . . .

173

The seventh generation says of him that he was born from a virgin who spent time on a high mountain lusting after herself in order to become androgynous. She fulfilled her wish and was made pregnant by her desire. He was born and received knowledge from himself. And thus he came to the water.

Thus the cycle of sublimation and transmigration closes, ending the quest for symbolic unity. The architectural object on top of the pedestal embodies the dark chamber surrounding it, denying emphatically the perspectival belief in a dualistic, quantifiable world. The object shifts in obscurity, in an

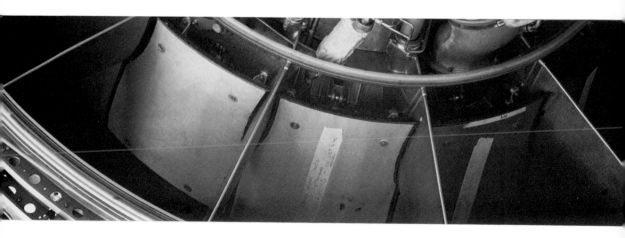

unceasing reciprocity with our perception. A nameless archetype, made of diverse plastics and plasters, cast and assembled, light, opaque, transparent and translucent, smooth and rugged, it conveys through its ambiguous materiality the very idea of infinite transformation: a visible ubiquity that is nothing but a transit, a motion—neither hard nor deep—lacking in substantiality what it exhibits in its boundless capacity for transmutation. It comprises four totally different elevations from each of the cardinal points, which visual representation cannot reconcile other than as a sequence of different things but which belong together in our experience.

Polyphilo quietly circulates around the altar, a house for some architect who wished to be buried vertically. He admires in his quiet perambulation the hopeful embodiment of an alchemical confusion of discrete parts and the invisible sacrificial smoke raising into the funnel of the vault of heaven, the catastrophe of Babel notwithstanding.

Fatigue in the humid interstitial cells of my joints, a groaning distension of muscles at every step of the way. Light once again within my cranium, up above. Polyphilo returns to the surface convinced that the polyandron has originally been open to the sky and that the rituals of communion, life and death have been performed under the bare vault of heaven. From his new vantage point desire suffices for him to visit the remaining parts of this ruinous monument to future knowledge, with its multiple tombs for unfortunate lovers.

THE SITE IS roughly rectangular and evenly distributed. An east-west linear passageway filled with indelible shadows allows for easy access to six compartments. *Not seven?* The south is visibly the realm of water, fire, and fragmented Euclidean solids. In the north earth, ice, and emphatic perspective distortion are dominant.

Traveling from east to west, as I have been for the past twelve hours, there is first, on my left, an octahedron emerging from the water. The first building is

constituted of two quadrangular pyramids joined at their bases. The upper pyramid reflects light while the bottom one absorbs it. Two of their sides are being eroded by violent gushing waves, and a luminous glazed cube inscribed in the octahedron can be seen from above. *This is perhaps the theatrical pavilion of delight where Polya anticipates my return, the stage itself perpetually suspended in dawn.* An epitaph laments the failed affair between Tlaloc and Hutzilopochtli, day and night, the opposing forces upon whose fatal and destructive encounters our existence depends:

The eighth generation says of her that she was born from a cloud that came upon the earth and enveloped a rock. The angels who were over the cloud nourished her and gave her knowledge. And thus she came to the water.

Avidly Polyphilo examines more remarkable fragments. On his right the molded terrain of a colorful rock garden suggests a human figure. In evidence are sections of limbs in high relief formed with a solidified plastic material and embedded with pieces of artificial glass or ceramics. At the center of this square open space is a cubic crypt partly buried by debris. Within the crypt lies an uncovered sepulcher made of efficient sarcophagus stone, capable of consuming the flesh of bodies in forty days. *Sarco, sacro? Is the ultimate ground of the sacred the flesh? Infinity itself?* Looking through a fissure into the tomb: petrified shoes and funeral robes and a quivering womb, engendering and nourishing a growing fetus. The slab sealing the tomb is carved in the form of Coatlicue, a monstrous woman with a skirt of serpents and necklace of human hearts and skulls. *Again Mother Earth?* Engraved at her feet is the plan of the rock garden itself, a woman with distended arms and legs, revealing the perfectly circular geometric structure of her innermost spaces and waiting to be impregnated. An inscription over the head of the sepulcher reads:

175

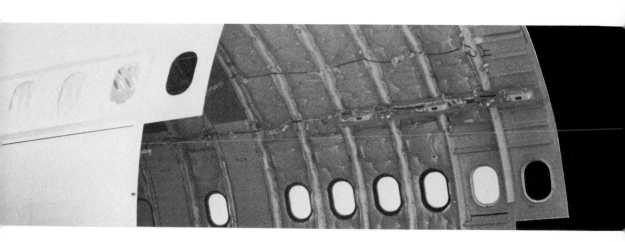

The ninth generation says of her that she was born from herself and from her own carnal desire and was nourished by the flesh from the cadavers of humanity. She existed perennially in possession of knowledge. And thus she came to the water.

Excited and joyous, Polyphilo arrives at the site on his left where a hollow stepped pyramid is filled with rubble. The stair that may have provided access to the chamber under the pyramid marks the polyandron's north-south axis. It is now impenetrable and the path impossible to tread. Like the tower in the north square, the quadrangular, terraced pyramid is unfolded and hinged at one corner, split approximately along its diagonal and opened like a cabinet. Despite its cataclysmic state the pyramid is still contained by a disintegrating three-dimensional grid of tubular steel and topped by a molten cube. The congealed calcination rests on the uppermost platform, where the fire may have burned fueled by a virgin's throbbing heart, securing for the next fifty-two years the light and warmth of the sun.

Two stainless steel, rounded cryogenic coffins are placed on polished brackets in a crypt at the hinge. Sophisticated mechanical equipment necessary to service them is hidden behind a curtain. The aerodynamic caskets keep the fully preserved cadavers of two lovers with abundant offerings of frozen food placed well within their reach. *Bowels moving with intense delight, fear, and pleasure.* Polyphilo reads with visible emotion an epitaph describing the odyssey of the couple who died together in a fire. The conflagration was caused by a hot electric iron dropped suddenly by the startled naked woman on her dress, leaving a triangular hole in the pubic area. Apparently she had been caught by her lover (more than likely a rapist) unconsciously caressing herself against the pointed end of the felt-covered ironing board while watching a television program about the sacrifice of virgins in ancient Mexico. The inscription concludes:

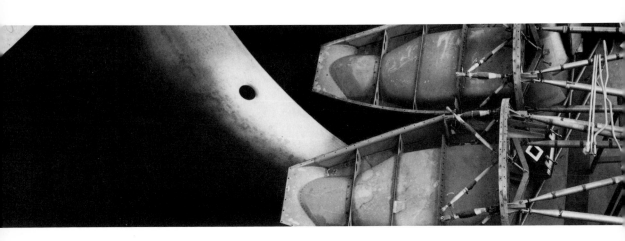

The tenth generation says of her that she was born in vitro from seed intended for a glossy, simulated mother. She was carried and nourished by a surrogate mother and received her knowledge from a man. And thus she came to the water.

Polyphilo next ventures into the distorted perspective space on his right. The walls, openings, and checkered pavement are physically subjected to the original deceleration toward a vanishing point that had existed at the top of the pyramid. Following an eccentric corridor behind the tower, he comes face to face with a mural that displays an axonometric reflection of the experienced reality of the polyandron. The composition is affected by a transformation in time reciprocal to his movements and point of view. *The triumphs of love? The present, however, is ostensibly missing. Or perhaps the nature of the present is mutability itself and its nature that of omnipresent being. Nothing is solid.*

In the mural's world men and women embodying the souls of the condemned are eternally imprisoned between fire and ice. They circulate without interruption amid totalitarian buildings of metal, glass, masonry, and concrete, perpetually envious of where they are not. Those who refused love in the name of morality are imprisoned in the crystalline ocean of ice; those who contemplated murder or suicide in a fit of passion are condemned to the flames. Two terrifying inscriptions allude to the realm of permanent shadows:

I

After this I looked, and lo, in heaven an open door! . . . At once I was in the Spirit, and lo, a throne stood in heaven, with one seated on the throne! And he who sat there appeared like jas-

per and carnelian, and round the throne was a rainbow that looked like an emerald . . . From the throne issued flashes of lightning and voices and peals of thunder, and before the throne burned seven torches of fire . . . and before the throne there was a sea of glass, like crystal.

II

In the year 2011 *nahui ollin,* the fifth sun dedicated to Xiuhtecutli, god of fire, will vanish forever. The earth will be destroyed by violent earthquakes and mankind will disappear.

This frightening world however, deployed in its own immeasurable space and accessible in some way to the universal brotherhood of mankind, is no longer refractory to desire. This alone, if nothing else, offers a glimmer of hope. Not far from the mural and, as might be expected, precisely under the vertex of the V-shaped space defined by the unfolded tower, a sober sepulchral slab is placed upright and inscribed with the following poem:

What can my heart do?
Have we arrived in vain?
Have we in vain emerged from the earth?
Make an effort. Desire the flowers of the Giver of Life.
Will I have to go like the flowers that perished?
Will nothing remain of my name?
Nothing of my fame here on earth?
At least the flowers and the songs we have made!

Have we arrived in vain?
Have we in vain emerged from the earth?
Let us enjoy ourselves, O friends!
Let there be loving embraces.
Today we walk on the earth of flowers.
No one will determine that flowers and songs end here,
they will survive and remain in the house of the Giver of
Life.

There is no tomb, no rotting body or decaying house of the giver of life below this poem. *What if I find a flower in my hands when I wake up? Will it really matter? It will probably convince no one . . .*

Nevertheless, Polyphilo continues his journey. There are many hours remaining in the clockwork mechanism, many hours to close the circle. On the left a bronzed glass and steel curtain-wall structure appears to have rotated or maybe imploded under great torsional forces. Under the remnants of the partially collapsed building lies buried a sophisticated computer and its billions of information bytes. With hallucinatory clarity and precision of detail the cube had been projected to a vanishing point in the sky. This had created the illusion of an infinitely tall skyscraper, a computer center enclosed by the utopian technological future that is effectively nowhere. A tetrahedron of reflecting glass terminating the polished, cupreous pyramid is now absent: Tezcaltlipoca, the smoking mirror that looks into the future, truncated the project and revealed the finite geometry of human existence. The epitaph reads:

179

The eleventh generation says of her that she was
born in vitro through selective breeding of seed,
intended to engender the strongest and most
powerful. She was nourished chemically and
received her knowledge from a man. And thus
she came to the water.

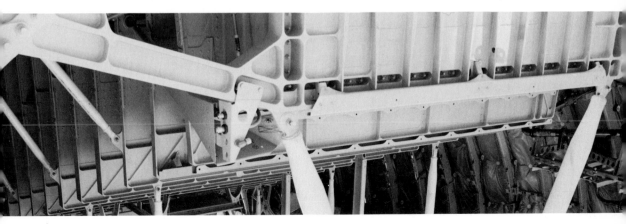

Next, on his right, Polyphilo witnesses a violent copulation of buildings. A pink concrete shell formed with soft curves is entwined with a rigid modular structure of steel, masonry, and lightweight panels. The two school buildings, produced by a simpleminded technological mentality, had lain innocently side by side on a site in the city until recently: a rounded, whitewashed concrete hollow loaf and a three-story, steel-frame structure of rectangular plan, both composed on a ninety-centimeter grid. In their present state their crushing, vigorous embrace culminates in frozen ecstasy. *The ultimate revelation? The death and rebirth of architecture?* In order fully to observe this spectacle Polyphilo steps into a brick enclosure cantilevered from a higher wall nearby. The balcony, perhaps an extrusion of a vertical tomb for a hermaphrodite, surrounds the whole front of his body with the interior cast of a half-male, half-female musculature. *Split along the axis of symmetry?* Under the two perforations for the voyeur, an epitaph reads:

180

The twelfth generation says of her that she was created in vitro through biogenetic manipulations intended to engender the strongest and most powerful. She was nourished by chemicals and received her knowledge from a photograph of a naked man in an old forbidden magazine. And thus she came to the water.

A lizard, lounging under the bright sun, makes an abrupt pirouette and scares Polyphilo, deep in thought. *Is it conceivable that culture may depend on the consented rape of the beautiful Indian Malitzin by the Spanish Hernan Cortez?*

I SEEM TO HAVE swept through time along a straight line, from prehistory to posthistory; but I know full well that the past and the future do not exist . . . Once the soul and the body have been thoroughly fused like a metallic amalgam. And my excessive interest in these temporal projections of poiesis was so distracting that my Polya, the disclosure of infinity in the present, may have been taken away permanently! Is uncertainty really the most beautiful thing about life?

Frightened and anxious, Polyphilo ponders retracing his steps. Facing death and despair with an immediacy that reminds him of his encounter with the Dragon, he is overtaken by an intense panic. A final decision is suddenly upon him. *I shall attempt a return back to the tranquil pavilion by the water where hopefully Polya still awaits me. To come back expeditiously!*

Forced to continue on his route toward the west, he approaches without effort and quite unexpectedly the fusiform opening of the world of shadows, the floating raft above the axonometric world. Over the ramp's threshold the last inscription proclaims:

The thirteenth generation says of him and her that regardless of the story they are always born from the word. The word received a mandate, glory and power. Desire must always satisfy the word. And thus they will come to the water.

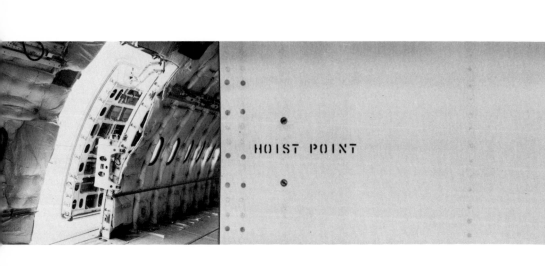

HOIST POINT

TO RETRACE MY STEPS back to Polya . . . It is now clear that the image of the labyrinth outlines an inescapable order of dwelling; a symbol that conforms to the structure of the soul. *At the end of time, having lost our myths and our secure home, the labyrinth has finally become real. Is it a huge drifting vessel—the S.S. Labyrinth? I believe that it is no longer customary to give aircraft names. Somewhere there must be an engine room, a bridge, a cockpit certainly. But where? At hand is my suitcase that I decide to open—is it time?—in the hope of finding a clue, a map that might provide directions.*

The convenient naugahyde case gathers an assortment of ordinary things that comprise their own world and convey every aspect of their place in the universe. Except for the glittering spheroid filled with gelatinous matter, we have seen them all before. A small black book explains how to build, at the perspective point, a superposition or rendezvous of two planes: "A mechanism for ontological orientation is desirable at the point of transition, but who can paint, or make, or think any more? Simply follow these instructions . . ."

One plane is a color reproduction on paper of a Renaissance Virgin and Child, and the other is an acetate transparency of the same size, remarkably similar to the large glass in the cockpit. The intended encounter obviously points to the idea of conception and the procreation of the human species. On both planes the bachelors are present in the rendezvous, yet there is a break. *Or is there?*

Finding my way back to Polya, to love and death. My aching muscles carry me blindly through a maze of ruins and precipices from which there is no respite . . . Perhaps the labyrinth can be deciphered by determining whether there is a dimension of time and space in between the two planes.

The optical world is flat, but black cats continue to cross our path at right angles.

HOIST POINT

The clue is probably in the fold of the map, in a twist of the mind. What is the depth of field? Where is the ground? At right angles to this world are invisible images and captive objects that remain out of focus: a calendar with a blank page for each week, a white field for January, an orange, brown, and yellow field for October, notes and scribbles (a map of time); a camera with its hard leather case and three lenses (a recorder of time); trendy and colorful clothing, neatly packed in transparent bags, labels, manufacturers' logos (a sign of the time). Packed adjacent to the glittering sphere are tools to control, interrupt, and restore time: an alarm clock whose wide black V on a silvery face indicates a few minutes past seven in the evening, a heavy pair of insulated pliers, and a set of sharp knives, presumably for plastic surgery or delicate art work.

Clasps click. The Bride overlaps on the Virgin, the wasp sex cylinder on the floating egg, the malic molds on angels and saints. The horizon on the horizon. The immaculate conception and mechanized generating process now share a perspective. Polyphilo enters a long tunnel, the walls clothed in white ceramic tile and the floors of vitrified electroconductive static covering. This is a high security zone where few men have gone before, most likely inhabited by the scientists who study and manipulate the invisible, specialists obsessed with the preservation and potentially eternal conservation of everything, from paper and art objects to human life. The corridor veers left and the walls close in, cutting all light from the dark.

Close to the limits. There is the same leaden feeling when you stand next to an occupied child's coffin that something has happened that should not have. My uncertainty thickens. Once the membrane is ruptured, there will surely be no point in going back or in going ahead. Polya is perhaps still waiting.

Polyphilo presses further. Behind a glass wall clones of humans dressed in bleached cotton and green surgical smocks manipulate these things that they will never see. They work in the obsessive belief that the imperceptible, submicroscopic agents that they study can explain at one essential level the complexity of life. *Is this the force that holds the planes together and apart? The*

biogeneticists are developing a new technology with which they will erad-
icate the chromosomal blueprint and create novel versions of life, more
efficient and less prone to decay, mutations that were not anticipated by
natural evolution and will soon need to be patented.

Hierarchitectitiptitopture!

    Simultaneously amazed and terror-stricken, Polyphilo doubts again. *Is
there even a place for the real order of desire in a world where the philosopher's
stone has become an effective tool of black magic and where it is possible to transmit
it as electromagnetic waves? A place for architecture? Always the same question,
over and over . . .* Ruminating on these unfathomable problems, he soon
arrives in a room lit brightly with fluorescent tubes. The manual from his
suitcase reads: "All items of clothing and jewelry should be briefly
described and any disarray recorded, preferably by means of photographic
techniques. The descriptions should indicate whether buttons were done,
undone, or missing; zippers closed or opened; shoe laces tied; and belts
buckled. The clothing should be removed from the body without cutting
or tearing. Each article should be put into a separate plastic bag and
labeled." The men in the laboratory are actually innkeepers of the in-
termediate zone between life and the following stage. *Coroners or embal-
mers? Wakers easing the passage for every traveler with the help of suitcases
identical to mine.* They kindly show Polyphilo the way back to his beloved's presence . . .

    *I FINALLY COME to her, sweating and ill-disposed. I am pale and my clothing
is reduced to ashes. Metal taste. I surely resemble a cadaver. My eyes are consummately fixed on her . . . my eyes, actually immobile or obstinately demanding peace.*
    Polya simply sits where Polyphilo had left her, immersed in airy water,

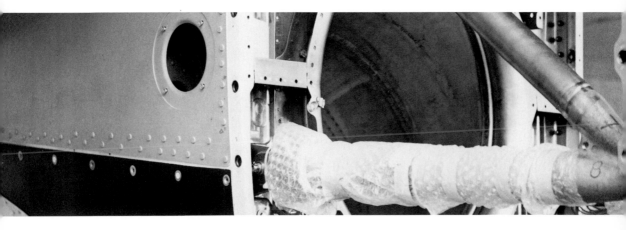

visibly hopeful and serene. It is early in the evening, but the sun is rising. She takes him in her arms and attentively listens to his story. After his pounding heart has recovered its usual pace, she smiles and, kissing him tenderly, states in a reassuring tone that they are merely waiting for the digital order from the computer network to surrender their will and speed into true flight. Rising amid clouds, they shall soon be on course toward the much-desired resting place, hopefully Love's abode.

The instrument panel suddenly lights up. Polya sits straight on her ergonomic chair, her face illuminated with a mystical green glow. The softly curved, perfectly detailed machine appears splendid as a naked child. It is winged. Gold and pink, ultramarine and mauve. Rounded body.

The commands are pronounced by a seductive, metallic voice, capable of awakening cadavers from the humid soil, or of even creating human beings from the invisible primordial matter. The voice acknowledges in a language similar to English that the procedures have been followed and that acceleration will soon ensue.

Suitcase packed and stored. Will I need it again? The sphere pulsates at a faster rate, probably energized by the quickened oscillations of the clock. *Are they connected? Physically? As in the act of giving life?*

The articulated drooping nose of the airplane is now up. *Perfectly erect and horizontal!* The variable geometry of the vessel's fuselage is aligned with a single point, ready to break the sound barrier. Through the windows planet earth cannot be seen. *Has the familiar globe disappeared forever?* While the instruments indicate an increase in velocity, movement as an optical perception of gleaming lines and opaque surfaces comes to an utter standstill. At 2000 kilometers per hour, in level flight, there is no impression of speed at all, only endless ascension.

A vertical disorder, contractions, blackouts, terror of the void. Between fainting and awareness there is no longer horizontal motion. What remains is a state of internal devastation, a static crisis of bodily consciousness. *We can now truly experience the reality of traveling as a condition, without purpose or destiny. My identity lost, there is no use for a passport; all is permanently in*

transit. I am now the traveler as formless, pure dynamism. Real flight may thus at last become the dream of flight.

THE WINDOW FRAMES a rendezvous between Polya and Polyphilo. Echocrush, the much-awaited sonic suddenboom! On the crest of the wave they glide, pulled by the invisible beam of the inertial navigation system, leaving the world of their previous experiences definitively astern.

A beacon transmits a dark light from an observatory topping the tower at Bellevue, the last rocky promontory, which had offered the best of all possible views of the polyandron. It shows the way to the island in the middle of the sky. Lying on a bed of very pliable clay whose substance is the rotting manure of the earth, an asymmetrical elevation is drawn from a juxtaposition of the debris of architectural history: a Renaissance tower crowned by a Greek temple, a keyhole opening, a buttonhole, semicircular and gothic arches, a serliana, a bilboquet, iron fences for safety, a medieval turret, and an inscription in Hebrew. The elevation that they have left behind suggests the mysteries to be found in the island of love, always at right angles, in the folds or cuts.

At the turn of the wall, not surprisingly, the rendezvous is actually a sort of camera obscura, a generator of hyperreal images that betray the existence of a transcendental fourth dimension; it is both the flue of the chimney and simultaneously binoculars, telescope, and microscope.

The rendezvous frames atmospheric air as well, the air of dreams beyond violence and friction that allows for flight and growth. Polya and Polyphilo are transmuted by the substance of perennial levitation, the locus of ascending flight growing into the light. Swirling into the heights, they are projected toward the eternal satisfaction of their oneiric voluptuousness and become engaged in a providential voyage across the ocean of fear. *For the nowhere-going flight of dreams traveling is the goal. This is real motion, being as*

187

becoming. The fundamental embodied awareness of gravity is the primordial ground of dwelling on earth, as well as the dream of flight itself, dynamizing verticality from the heels to the nape of the neck. Such is to inhabit a real tower!

The arch of flight reveals the bodies of six crew members: luminescent aerial flesh, transparent nylon pressurized uniforms, suspended breasts hardly contained, supple buttocks and rounded stomachs with slender pelvises. Having concluded the acceleration procedure and engaged the vessel's autopilot system, they sit around the exquisite machine to partake in its seductive aroma and instrumentation, its dials bright as burning coals. Although infinitely responsive to manifold electromagnetic impulses, the vessel remains impervious to the lascivious crew. Polya and Polyphilo continue their journey through the calm and abominable skies, evidently patterned after the designs of desire.

THE DREAM OF FLIGHT may be defined as the result of specific peristaltic motions that have been experimented with and detected in the state of full awareness while rolling down stairs. It is perhaps the objectification of the rhythmic slowdown of the respiratory muscles and, in some cases, a function of the cardiac systole and diastole, retarded by the action of some imponderable and unknown physical oppression. *Under the shroud, it would be ill-advised to change my sleeping position!*

How I admire Polya's divine beauty! Ours is seemingly a wingless flight amid balmy temperatures. We fly where there is no trace of life, no history or future, as if propelled by a suspended impulse. The sweet perfume of flowers envelops it all. Ascension and liberation. Is this the experience of the new world? My entrails are polarized between vapor and crystals by the vessel's purposeful course. The austerity of extreme quietude and the sweetness of excessive temperance. Technology and concupiscence. I am torn apart by two masters, one that consumes me and the other that inflames me.

Their gaze is lost in the transparent blue, beyond the frame. First there is nothing, then depth, and finally azure: the dark blue depth of a millimetric layer of paint on the canvas that can be seen only after staring for a long, long time. Purple wrigglers pulsate and obliterate the opaque field, sucking its residual substance. Nothing is but a continuous, everlasting dawn. The view of a yawning cerulean sky, of all impressions the closest to a complete fusion of feeling and sight. Not an optical thing or the white vanishing point of self-annulment but the very denial of temporalized matter: that which *is*. The ominously somber focal point of time.

Polyphilo and Polya feel the pull of the livid sky on them; it beholds them, imposing its tranquil power by losing them in a mirror with no quicksilver, a discolored series of infinite transparencies where form plays no role and everything is dynamic.

Again the feeling of suspended fall . . . I open my arms to purity and embrace motion itself, eradicating the distance between the visible and the invisible. The expanding aroma of Polya's perfume and my great joy causes me to drift into a greater and deeper reverie.

Undying beasts painlessly disappearing and begging to be caressed. Sweet and round, unstable and restless, foaming and slow transfigurations, crumbling silently, ascending, dissolving. And beyond them, an unexpected cerulean, ethereal elixir of luminosity. This motion, disencumbered from substance and coagulated vapor, is the fuel of levitation. Polya or fire, snow and liquid love rising buoyantly! *Hurling over the windforms, drinking from my own velocity, hearing the earth's rotation, dizzily suspended in the air. Now to catch my breath! Like a flash, a sudden revelation: freedom from gravity always occurs at the limits between day and night, at the birth of light.*

TWILIGHT IS THE VERITABLE wing, flight a warm breeze. Wings surely obstruct the flight of angels. Inhabit a tower and consume your existence by mounting into the unfathomable sky and descending into the depths of the earth! Contin-

uous ascent is certainly the indication on my map . . . Vertical motion makes real objects exist, conveying upon them the synaesthetic qualities of levity: luminosity, precision, clarity, and autonomy from gravity and mist. Horizontal displacement, on the other hand, is an illusion, it incessantly leads nowhere.

And where now is Polya? Why, enveloped by the azure in a gesture of awakening. Blue adheres tenuously to her forms, which have become dynamized, revealing and veiling the flesh. Happiness and victory she is; envy of the gods. The burning flames from her little body traverse the universe and penetrate the solid heavens, reaching the most profound ravines and crevasses. She can set ablaze the ocean! Her luminosity is not derived from some exterior source but emanates from an inner enlightenment. The snowchest, milky cloud. Breath is fire in her eyes.

The culmination at the summit will lead to peace and stability. Or is it that we are falling into the sky? The inexpressible sensation of a supreme conquest! Erection, bursting member . . . Nirvana perhaps, or a realization of the ultimate rhythm accompanying the dissolution of our individual consciousness. Bongos and drums and the indiscernible lark: an omnipresent song that may die but never fall. Riding on the invisible corpuscles or on the wave of happiness, I seek the sunlight, endowed with immaterial wings that fly the farthest, making a messenger out of every virgin, every time.

In a deeper and brighter sky we behold a light that produces sounds. A melody composed with the vital spectrum of motion. These are the essential colors (not superficial appearances), because they are alive in objects simultaneously sonorous, diaphanous and sufficiently mobile to penetrate each other and thus occupy fully the whole extension. Always at dawn. Penetrate and fully occupy. Space is the widest of all open pores, a yawning celestial mouth. I wish to emulate the task of angels, those thin forms that swim in the air, forever rising and filling the gaps with no cumbersome wings for fluttering.

Lost in her eyes, I happily behold the communion of love and my beloved. The arrows of her love lacerate my heart. Sweat, tears, and more peristaltic movements

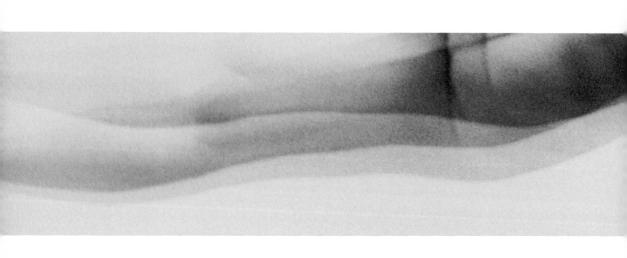

culminate in a frenzied passion for love and death. Mercy!

Deeper and higher, we witness a totally imaginary motion, beyond aerodynamics: pure ascension. The stern is in the place of the bow and the bow in the place of the stern. The wingless craft is too large for one mortal to visualize. Unfolded, it appears like a vast refulgent disk, pure gold, like the moving circle of the rainbow. Totally imaginary motion is invariably accompanied by imaginary music, the sweetest of aerial melodies for contemplation, unspeakable being present. The crew starts to sing. Am I singing as well, from my innermost center, in silence? Between my lips, the pearly essence of my heart escapes. Resounding tongues pervade the space, vibrating in a harmony of strings and membranes. Tonguing tremolos of pleasure! Ultimate rhythm! The vocal breath endows the vessel with qualities of flesh and crystal. A celestial dwelling!

In the distance, behind the window frame, we can now see the desired place where Platonic ideas become thoroughly concrete, the floating island of flesh where the sky, the earth, and the sea are transfigured and transmuted by air. The place of our destination is the umbilical nest. Omegaville in the sunset, collecting the offal of the universe, but also the Eastern Edenville, the port of the vessel. Is it the ground for architecture? Polya herself!

Polya?

My eyes absolutely fixed in hers. Utterly immobile unless revived by her sweet words and her insistence in enjoying the spectacle of flight. Might the omnipotent machine put an end to my torture and temper its weapons! From this cruel period of waiting, please deliver my perpetual hope! Nature has ill-accorded appetite with power. My senses have been stimulated with increasing pleasure by the triumph of flight. Yet . . .

Polya? Singing in the Lydian mode a thanksgiving poem in praise of perseverance. Checklist. On toward the delicious island.

Then sheer collapse, and we plunge suddenly. Our fall creates the abyss into which we swiftly drop. I turn for Polya but she is gone. Vanished.

The music reconciles all contradictions, and acute resounding particles penetrate my pores with the essence of lust, the piercing, irritating corpuscles of humid vulva

and erect nipples. I search for her eyes with a disorderly appetite. Presumptuous imagination! She has dissolved, melted perhaps, dispersed into the thin air! Oh that I should have pierced my heart and squeezed the loveblood out to flood her, rather than lose Polya in this infernal ocean of air. Prior to burial (our) wake must follow.

The vessel continues in its quiet, prolonged terebration of the sky. Desascension. Angels perceive the foliage of trees as roots drinking from heaven, while the roots of the great tree are seen to be the silent summits. In the presence of absence, persevering, triumphantly (we) arrive . . .

AT DAWN, as at dusk, an inexplicable stillness pervades all things. Under the aircraft's open sail the winds die, the jostle of turbulence ceases; vermilion ripples on the wings are all that remain of the vibration of forward flight. *To remind (us) that our flight is not a dream? Have (we) finally arrived?* All abides in this luminous stillness as if on an island whose horizon, like an immeasurable beam of light cast into the infinite, folds back upon itself and excludes unbounded darkness from the present, confining it to the beginning and the beyond.

The island is also a city and a theater of light without shade. It is the base of Mount Analogue, the mythical mountain that allows man to ascend into heaven! *This island, hidden from our normal geographical experience by a ring of curved space, is made visible only to those who wish to know about it.* The privileged moment of access is determined by a common measure of time and space shared by Mount Analogue and the rest of the world, an instant marked by the natural clock, the course of the sun. The sun can only "uncurve" the space around the island at dawn and sunset. *Always the same eventful moment revealing the gap through which (we) have penetrated, for the vessel, that most appropriate instrument of love, has the greatest potential of all to cross this gap. And so thus (we) find (our)sel(ves) on the Other Side.*

"On the Other Side" is the name of a hotel at a nudist beach near Trieste but also the motto over the door at the officer's club in Auschwitz: the other side of civilization, beyond the limits of the erotic. It is also the familiar name of a country in Central Asia, some place that resembles Europe yet is very different . . . A flyblown pastiche of styles that questions all conventional values and allows human actions to be polemical, but under a permanently cloudy sky.

The Island of Love necessarily incorporates the systematic exploitation of the accidental or artificially provoked confrontation of two or more alien

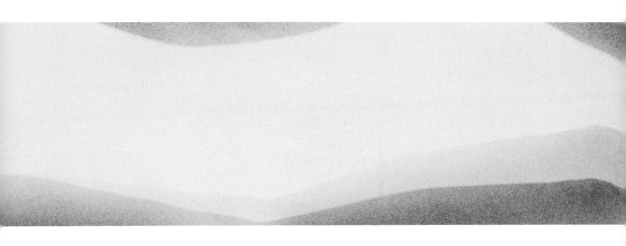

realities on an unfamiliar plane. It is also the broken line exposing eroticism to emptiness, the locus of universal orgasmic death. *Shall we soon witness a distinct, even more glorious modality of the other side?*

Here universal nakedness must not become a state of sexual neutrality! Ideal freedom and embodied necessity are no longer at odds in this island. There is neither disorder nor authority, yet the gender of objects and actions survives. Innocence of physical love and the experience of passionate climax, pure yearning and desire, are one undifferentiated, unlimited, and boundless feeling. *The love of the many in my providential name must be knowledge itself, an endless disclosure of meaning!*

No one here must dream about a creature offering endless possibilities for erotic transgression! In sexual dreams the dreamer invariably attains orgasm and remains in ecstasy until his dream lover provides a flight song to bring back and recite after awakening. The wholeness and complete integration of internal and external realities is the commonplace experience. When a boy reports a falling dream, adults invariably answer with enthusiasm: "That is a wonderful dream, one of the best a man can have. Where did you fall to? What did you discover? You must relax and enjoy yourself when you fall in a dream. Falling is the quickest way to come in contact with the real powers . . . Soon, when you have a falling dream you will realize that you are traveling toward the source of the power that has caused you to fall." *I recall?*

OUT OF MYSELF, suddenly expelled into another altered consciousness state at 8:00 P.M. . . . We must wait to be cleared for landing. Only the shadow of the vessel on the island is visible from behind the window. I can now interrupt my narrative to provide a description of the vessel and the island. Out of myself? Are (we) beyond the point of perspective?

The mighty vessel, instrument of this protracted voyage and vehicle of humanity's propitious return to nomadic life, is skillfully proportioned in

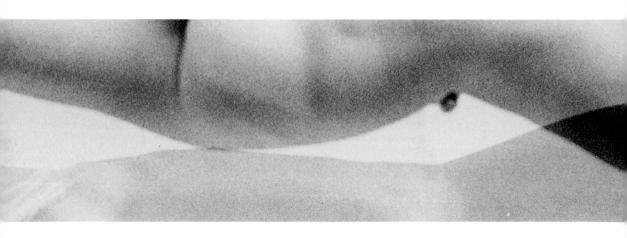

accordance with the laws of physics. It has a dramatically slender and long fuselage, pressurized to 10.75 pounds per square inch, small windows and a thin delta wing over four turbojets with silencers and reversers. In elevation, wheeled legs like a flamingo and symmetrical trapezoidal funnels under the graceful horizontal sail. Its cockpit is a crow's head, the drooped nose resembling those masks used by doctors during the Black Death. Made principally of glimmering aluminum alloy that cannot be employed with cruising speeds much in excess of Mach 2 because of kinetic heating, it is equipped with a special mechanism that enables it to pump fuel from the front to the rear of the aircraft and vice versa to counter the transonic change of trim.

Beyond the window, the island is completely flat: a barren horizon of light. As it was suggested by the guide in the suitcase and corroborated by the poem entitled "Reflections," its perfect, absolutely regular geometry exists only in the dimension of the hidden perpendicular, between the window and a looking glass. The whole island is natural, a thoroughly comprehensive paradise of animals and plants, yet every molecule is manmade: the entire city is technological, a thoroughly cybernetic hell of unrecognizable lead pencil rubbings, brush and pen strokes, yet every form is preexisting. *Wonder overcoming technique!*

This extraordinary place is a centralized space without a geometric center, a veritable theatrum mundi of spiraling time, shaped like a human body stretched out in a dream pose. Here the temperature is never seasonable and is almost excessively flawless, paradoxically both innocuous and provocative. The island is a flat palimpsest of history that contains the traces of all previous human cities, more dense at the conjunction of common rituals. A palimpsest infected by the blessed disease of forgetfulness, becoming a blank stone that awaits the poetic marking: primordial lapis, origin of labyrinth, and the point for a new beginning and definitive renewal. It is the locus for the corporeal poetry of reason, freed from intellectual memory and disembodied imagination, a place for the new man to dwell, with complete acknowledgment of the unthinkable potential of

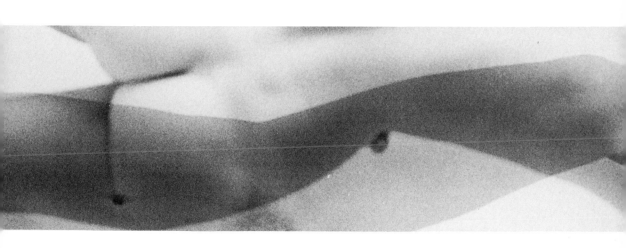

individual consciousness and imagination. It is neither an idyllic unperturbed forest nor a modern city as a mute technological utopia that simulates
a false security and immortality. Rather, this is a noncity which is not a
paradise because it abhors solipsism and yearns for the urban.

The choir for the round dance occupies the gap between navel and pubis,
an ex-centric space bound by the foci of a circle and a square, both invisible
geometric lineaments circumscribing the human figure. The moon's yellow
crescent, like a parachute, prevents a small object from falling. Tangential
to the sun, the moon barely touches its red aureola, leaving no space
between both celestial bodies and the body of the earth. The rising sun,
divided in two for easier rotation, is projected by strings onto the summit
of the metallic perspective pyramid. A floating hand partially covers the
pyramid, investing the earth with the full significance of a sexual organ.
Polya? The island's alchemical symmetry is curious, both sexes comple-
menting one another. *At last . . .*

From above, the island is simultaneously the spiritual body of a person
and an occult map of events in eternal dreamtime. This is, indeed, the
ubiquitous center! Twelve spirals mark the places of time and parallel lines
the footprints on the sand, broken or continuous. The littoral is neither
abrupt nor brittle or muddy, it dissolves into the perennial oceanic dawn
as a translucent, utterly precise substance. The coast line, washed incessantly by ascending currents, is covered with an artificial congealment that,
similar to gems of intense coloration, seems to hide an intrinsic darkness.
All the edges are studded with spherical crystals of varying thickness and
extreme hardness, perhaps the shimmering sperm of monstrous whales.
Conventional diamonds, resulting from a sort of squaring of the circle, or
more precisely, from a "cubing" of these spheres, would have seemed dull
by comparison. *Is this mineral substance the peradam or stone of Adam that may
provide, at last, the absolute standard of value? There are now shades of a future
obfuscation . . .*

The horizon beyond the vessel's window frame is the circumference of
the island, of exact anthropometric dimensions, ultimately unmeasurable.
At a different scale the sterile landscape is surrounded by diversely shaped

monoliths, like isosceles volcanos or the pyramids of sight. Spaced at regular intervals, these limiting stones are hollow, fragmentary casts of the human anatomy, enigmatic sections that encircle and enclose the entire island within the space of the body. Emerging from the mineral horizon, they are both flesh and bone, transmuted into pieces of folded petrified cloth and cranium-shaped concavities, capable of bearing and comprising every place in the universe.

ONTOGENESIS? The hollow fragments of a complete human body, maleandfemale, had been obtained by making the model stand upright in the bottom of a wooden box with a square base, built up to the height of its head. The quadrangular box was carefully crafted and could come apart lengthwise, halfway from one vertical side to the other. Thin templates of a special metal were drawn in many directions, perpendicular and oblique, following accurately the flesh of the nude, not pressing on the surface but gently adhering to it. The templates were nailed to the edges where the four L-shaped sections of the box fit together, encircling the body like fans. The nude was then carefully greased, the box closed around it and a great quantity of plaster mixed with warm water and poured with the help of an assistant. After the plaster had hardened thoroughly, chisels, funnels, and other tools were inserted into the bodily core. A potent solvent was injected through several plugs and the inside of the nude melted away, leaving an immaculate imprint of its rose-colored flesh. The box was then cut with a laser torch at precise angles that always added up to the circumference. The name of the new fragmented image was *The Pleasure That Abideth for a Moment*, obliterating the inveterate classical bronze entitled *The Sorrow That Endureth Forever.*

197

IN SPITE OF MYSELF I have begun to express the dream differently. Conscious-
ness demands factual exactitude, avoiding fabricated connections between visions.
Evidently confused by the mass of events, places, and sensations to which I have
been subjected in the past few hours . . . I now see the design transformed into a
disc with a diameter of nearly four meters but of indeterminate radius, a floating
round, defying gravity in the absence of breath. Walking on this disc, which is
capable of holding all the information in my world as digital time and space, would
be delightful. It might allow me the freedom to read the story in any order, starting
tomorrow and ending in the prehistoric city, and thus corroborate the equivalence
of symbols and their disclosure of order. Is this a modern Stonehenge or the contem-
porary incarnation of the island of Venus physizoa, the giver of life? Twenty-four
sectors marked by vertical slabs, pillars of the sky, form corporeal projections of time
at the horizon: the disappearance of the letter V; Japanese spherical souvenir; traces
of crystal on the mirror; the shadow of a shadow; Venice and the metabletic gateway;
a subterranean chasm; first horizons; aquatic epicureanism or sign of the dream;
Cafe Bon Voyage; Sphinx and the mystery of embodiment; objects of desire; the
temple and the border; dream within the dream, within the dream. Dream.

The hyperreal theater in two dimensions contains an immensely varied
flora and fauna. The multiple sectors are the outcome of an interrogation
about floorboards that took place in a hotel in Brittany on a rainy day many
years ago. The ground is constructed with the essence of laurel, oak, ilex,
cypress and cedar, chestnut, yew, elm, linden and ash trees, walnut and
hazelnut, apple, quince, palm, lotus, carob, and palm trees. Bark, leaves,
and other vegetable parts, covered casually with sheets of paper and rubbed
with a lead pencil, provide a sudden intensification of our visionary facul-
ties. In every sector the delightful, often contradictory superimposition of
images results in a fertile topography for amorous hallucination. The enclosures of the Island of Love, from the Ram to the Fish, and from the Sun to
Mars, beget a flat topiary of human heads, eyes, tame and exotic beasts,
and battles that finish with a kiss. These landscapes increasingly lose the

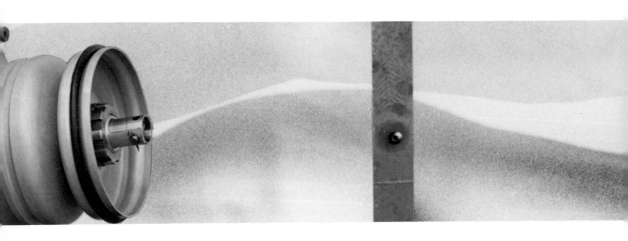

specific characteristics of the original material to resemble other distant images with an unbelievable precision, evoking visions that reveal the primary transcendental purpose of the maker's poetic obsession: a true recreation of nature, the unmediated demiurgic act itself, thoroughly new and enigmatic.

Toward the ex-center of the island successive, parallel rings, mysteriously concentric and ascending, accommodate more exquisite and natural works of the divine craftsman. Intricate interconnections between paths and enclosures are resolved by a novel form of pictographic writing, a pure gestural memory. Just as now and then a single star emerges from the constellations and becomes significant as a comet or a moving planet, so also does a cipher whose ideogram becomes intelligible, rising up once in a while from the continuum of incomprehensibility. The limits of vision correspond to the limits of our understanding.

In the first annular gap take root a number of floral marvels and square platforms. Among the bizarre plants there are tobacco shrubs that glow in the dark, a large puffball that explodes, projecting into the distance mature spores that catch fire after a sudden and violent fermentation, and a musical bush, a kind of mimosa whose fruits act like resonance boxes capable of reproducing all modulations of the human voice, repeating incessantly, like parrots, the words uttered around them. Most surprising is a large tree with fruit somewhat like gigantic bananas, which covers the soil around it. It is possible to pick up one of these fruits and mash it into the shape of a candle, inserting through the middle one of the creepers that symbiotically inhabit the tree's trunk. Placed on the platform and lit, the candle produces a long and loud noise, recalling a distant thunderbolt.

The second anus contains circular platforms and curious plants that bear red flowers issuing a potent perfume. Molding their fiery petals into the form of a cloud and placing it on a circular platform attracts a frenzied swarm of fireflies. The insects then devour one another, erupting into an arc of lightning.

In the third annular enclosure one finds a bush with purple flowers and

199

razor-sharp thorns like petrified butterfly wings. When crushed, the flower's petals yield an elixir with great antiseptic and coagulant properties, capable of forever curing and regenerating any wound perpetrated by the plant itself. The triangular sacrificial platforms lie empty, waiting for the instauration of a truly appropriate institution. They are obviously carved out of peradam, a kind of aromatic, solidified chrysosperm that anticipates rain, bringing about the unmistakable scent of an imminent storm.

This last compartment borders on a cyclical efflux tube beyond a magnificent peristyle of naked men and women of the most diverse figures, ages, and races. Utterly natural, and thus—ironically—absolutely artificial, innocent, and seductive, they are devoid of sartorial embellishments, haircuts, deformities, or body paints, which had caused ambivalent false modesty, old cultural values, and war. This recognition of the essential brotherhood of humanity extirpates the shame of pudor and enshrines the virtue of modestia, the homeless place of being, rooted in gender. The truth of convention will never again be a style here: this is the absolute architecture of shapely arches, translucent and fragrant columns of luminous skin, and uniform intercolumnar rhythms.

Slight accommodation. The bloom of Polya and a shade of longing to live here with her still loom in my memory. But this will entail an improbable renewal of vows, because I now realize that my present pleasure is above all else; it surpasses any imaginable sweetness or satisfaction. ReJoyce: out of sight, out of mind.

The meandering efflux tube is a conduit halfway from the corporeal edge of the island to the theater of homelessness. It has angular, plasticized embankments and carries a pure and silvery heavy water. Invisible vessels running under the surface feed this canal which drains into a windsock before oozing into the flatulent sea. This system helps to maintain a constant liquid level and the murmuring sound that pervades the space. Amphibious algae, like tall, white reeds, grow along the banks soaring upward and creating a spellbinding vault of light.

In the colloidal liquid live a myriad of exotic fish and animals, many of

which do not yet appear in bestiaries or natural history manuals. One remarkable example is a corpulent and inoffensive worm, endowed with such musical sensitivity that it always comes to the surface when enticed by a beautiful melody. Other animals and plants resemble curtains, chimneys, geometric blocks of jelly, soap, hoses, and several other objects. Occupying the most hidden crevices live sponges with the shape and function of the human heart.

The inner body, between the canal and the axis, the Scale and the Scorpion, focuses on the inaccessible center. This is the proverbial gap occupied by the *machina mundi,* the theater that generates architecture in the same way that a camera produces color photos, but without lenses or darkness. Several sparkling terraces surround the amphitheater, divided by climbing sets of sebaceous stairs and other dancing peristyles of flesh. These enclosures are paved with geometric meanders made of manifold organic substances, simultaneously abstract and figural, ranging from teeth of diverse colorations to coagulated blood and bladder stones.

Free within the inner compartments of the human vortex roam strange animals perpetually courting or making love, singing or showing their exuberant features, hiding behind every conceivable species of sexually differentiated plants. Besides the better-known baldanders, basilisks, centaurs, chimeras, and unicorns are a flaming giraffe, birds that appear like colorful fish with stylet beaks, and two species of elephants, one celibate of military metal capable of vacuuming the world and another, the head of a corpse with bisexual organs deflated after spending a day at the beach. There are also large centipedes, about two meters long, which form circles and move rolling at high speeds on the pavement, a cyclopean lizard resembling a chameleon, with its frontal eye permanently wide open, and flying silkworms that float after becoming inflated with a gas produced in their intestines, turning into voluminous spheres. Rather than reaching adulthood and copulating in the normal way, the spherical silkworms burst and their remaining tissue reproduces through simple parthenogenesis. Of special interest in this part of the island is a large carrion-eating bird with powerful wings, huge feet similar to those of the wader, and round orifices

201

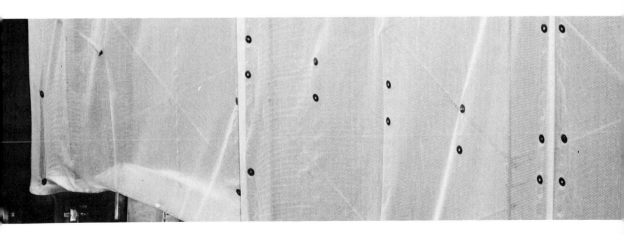

on the beak. Also remarkable is a Canadian squirrel with a small black mane whose hairs emit two musical notes of equal sonority.

Circumjacent to the theater are a number of awesome dynamic and static machines, unprecedented automatons possessing thaumaturgic properties. There is a levitating paving beetle activated by an aerostat filled with a gas resulting from the combustion of an ochre substance under the intense heat of light concentrated by a lens. There is also the absent body of a Titan, harnessed by an array of bionic devices such as a surgical wig and vitalium skull plate, a Heltzer valve to control the water in the brain, a metal plate in place of a jawbone, an electronic larynx, ball and socket shoulder joints and elbow and knee metal-and-plastic hinges, veins and arteries of Dacron fiber, a plastic ileostomy bag for the collection of bodily waste, compression plates replacing the long bones, and handsome, nonfunctional polyethylene genitalia.

Finally, there is a monstrous jewel, two meters high by three wide, flashing in all directions with an almost unbearable luster. *Peradam again?* A number of objects move inside it, together with a nude model standing upright at the bottom, completely submerged, swaying its head and long hair gracefully. *The original model?* The tank is filled with water from the canal that has undergone a potent and mysterious oxygenation, endowing it with particular properties and a sparkling phosphorescence. This water allows any terrestrial creature to live in it breathing normally, producing harmonious arpeggios echoing the motions and gestures of life and permitting an observer to see it all in one single circular glance.

By pressing my nose against the transparent, pressurized surface, I can scan the whole spectacle in one circular glance. The light waves are still suspended in the ether, free from gravity . . . From the edge of the island to the theater of homelessness, a radius of one mile, one third mineral, six to nine the orchard, then, beyond the canal, a last third enclosing the animals and the machines. The theater itself, following the ritual, occupies sixteen to seventeen. The dance floor, flat, polished, and totally barren, awaits for (our) arrival, as it would for a performance.

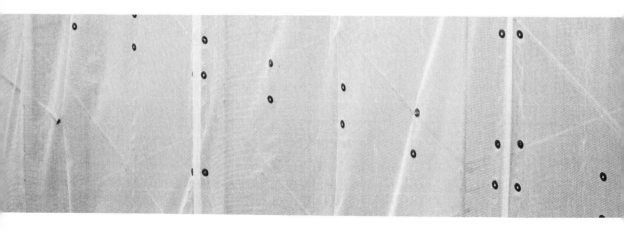

THE ERECT NOSE, indispensable instrument for an efficient supersonic penetration of the atmosphere, has dropped for subsonic flight. The gentle winds of dawn softly lower the vessel in one more northern airport. *Are we landing considerably ahead of time for a technical stop? The crucial triumph of love must be signaled by a radical collapse of time . . . During the whole trip it has never been earlier! Any SST has a shorter range than the wide-body jets, and flying west it can go back in time . . . but maybe it is sooner than I thought it was. It is probably more important to realize that the god has gone blind and to remember that while mortals call him the winged Eros, he is known as Pteros among other deities because his is the gift of wings.*

All passengers can now disembark in the much-coveted place, a remote island in a sea of snow. A majestic reception awaits them. All men, women, and children from every race and age are either fully clothed, painted, or tattooed in a universal dress, at once sensuous and innocent. No halos or odic forces. The crowd includes real monsters, such as men and women with supernumerary nipples or reattached scrotums; cyclops and castrati; the unkissable woman from Chad; and the Czech sisters joined at the sacrum who cannot get married because the bridegroom would have been prosecuted for bigamy. *Postapocalyptic mutants?*

Their bodily coverings, both extraordinarily individualized and genuinely exciting are unique, a truly collective architecture of desire that comprises clothing, body paint, and numerous other original techniques and combinations. The garments, loose but fitted perfectly as well, were manufactured in a manner that synthesizes Eastern uncut and Western patterned uses of fabric. Posture and movement are animated by the most appropriate clothing, applied colors or prints. When clad in these coverings, walking appears always natural while being also sexually attractive.

Paired shoes are normally of different sizes, acknowledging at last the asymmetry of human feet and the fact that the middle toe is not by far the biggest. Underwear, while veiling sexuality, is no longer reminiscent of painful corsets or chastity belts but the frame of eroticism. Narcissistic and exhibitionistic delights are attainable without having to undress the skin and expose the intimate substance of the flesh. Most garments are bisexual, beyond style and fashion. The rest can either be clothing for two, like tents that enhance physical contact, or complementary tattooed patterns, modestly covering whole figures. Gone are the conventional dualities and cliches of public and private, male and female. Only the essential gap remains: the difference of gender. Dress has become a pure manifestation of personal imagination and the ground of boundless curiosity; the most suitable for the body's gestural recollection of being, identical to the nudity of infinite flesh.

I must explicate the glorification of the sense of touch. Love is without sight because it is above the intellect, even though the vessel, with its orientation mechanisms, always seems to chart its course with purpose. Blind love may represent the end of repressive libido and the reason of power, beyond tyranny and anarchy. Yet in the recent past eroticism had become mere sexuality in the absence of gender. Surely the dream must soon go blind because the greatest mysteries are seen without eyes and accessed directly by our undifferentiated bodily selves. By the soul?

If time has reversed its direction with our arrested motion, its mystery, identical to the mystery of love, the key to which I have been seeking, may soon be revealed. Knowledge given to the senses and the luminous aspects of voluptuousness are at one with the praxis of the senses. The immersion of consciousness in the humid realm of absolute fecundity, however, necessarily entails a synthesis of darkness with the light of love. And it is still dawn!

Tattooed buttocks in vibrato creating a counterpoint of movement; virginal thighs; breast-shaped apples; half-balloons recently inflated; metal and concrete dresses inspired by musical instruments; sanded haunches; textured weavings; embossed skin and other permanent deformations. No more tans, trousers with vertical creases or imitation flesh-tone makeup. Humanity is once again capable of blushing. Everyone uses a universal perfume that magnifies distinct individual secretions, those sweet natural smells uninterrupted by artificial aromas: the ultimate elixir discovered by biotechnology. Ranging from the odor of sanctity to that of lasciviousness, the fragrance emanates with utter precision from each thoroughly purified body.

Engine of destruction! Blind instrument of provocation! Do knowledge and desire remain attached to power and concupiscence? I know that only true lovers may succeed, but my vow to the one woman whose image in my mind I can barely recall recedes from memory, and this is almost a relief. Is this an intimation of authentically detached love? The realization of my hope for personal and universal liberation? The empty bed over which I have wrung my heart fades from consciousness. Under the sheets, it is always a funeral bed. My devotion for the multifarious opposite becomes stronger: the real, unoriginal embodied woman of flesh and blood.

THE RECEPTION on the island always surpasses any such event previously recorded. An orderly procession sets out toward the ex-centric theater. Polyphilo carries his suitcase while his fellow passengers parade their vertical and horizontal trophies:

a window framing flat blue, reflecting the rising sun over the
enigmatic space;

sharp metallic stylets;

a looking glass;
a thin white starched veil over the vacant picture frame;

crystalline cubes engraved with poetry;
intestinal coils and bat's wings, grafted;
manifold canes or talking sticks: magic wands, instruments for
extended and double touch, winged oaks that support the sky;

an empty goblet;

a pulsating sphere and other electronic devices for assorted
simulation;

a cylindrical mirror;

dancing gloves;

a reduction of the large glass or cockpit window that is
gradually becoming opaque;

and beyond, twelve reciprocal symbols that complete the image of
the world.

205

In transit all passengers proceed through the aircastle in groups of three,
noticing the particularities of the place and the people. From above the
island had appeared like a crescent, with tapering extremities almost forming a circle. Without a pilot of local origins, it would have been virtually
impossible to negotiate the difficult approach. *Is this pilot Polya, then?* It is
obvious that the movable landmarks do not relate to any specific site.
Oblivious of genii loci, they generate their respective ground and thus
transform the place into inaccessible territory for alien vehicles from the
past. The terminus though, hardly alien, is identical to twenty-three others
around the world, roughly square in plan and close to a tidal river called
the Nowater. Services are provided from modular units whose fronts and
backs open automatically at a touch. They are covered with cheap, fireproof
concrete roofs that resist bad weather. Walls are glazed, as expected, from
floor to ceiling.

Some form of personal making is effectively the trade of all passengers.

Starting with their body, most children adopt a diametrically opposed expression to that of their parents and thus successfully recreate the rituals. Efficient production is not the objective of their techniques, the aim of personal making is life and love.

The first trio of young men bear their trophies filled with songs and flowers and juggle a multiple sphere that seemingly metamorphoses in midair from gold to plastic. *Peradam?* Traditional, expensive materials are evidently now used for the manufacture of humble domestic items. Personal wealth is irrelevant here, and perhaps only idiots still wear rings and necklaces made with precious metals and gems.

A second trio of female pilgrims exemplifies complementary and contrasting attitudes to pleasure and religion. They appear as reflections on a concave mirror of one unchanging face. In the center an austere woman with her eyes lowered, completely draped with light-absorbing fabric, is immersed in a mysterious perception of harmony, a silent music, intellectual pleasure, and celibacy: ascetic lechery. Flanking her, two uncovered women adopt obscene poses, their agitated eyes wander incessantly. They recreate in their minds bodily pleasure and procreation: licentious righteousness.

A third group of participants is a trio of androgynous youngsters who simply carry themselves beautifully, with unspeakable grace. They represent the end of all wars, euthanasia, and the many things in life that are brief. *Pain as well, but love is timelessness.* These passengers paid no attention to superstitions, omens, or fortune tellings but all believe in miracles.

SINCE WE STILL KEEP our eyes wide open, it is impossible to discern the concealed order. Not surprisingly, we are finally made prisoners. Our hands are tied behind our backs. Oh sweet captors, alchemical laughter! Out of fear, we decide to offer no resistance. Polya laughs with them. She is definitely absent and we are at the mercy of the blind god. Synesia, the manifestation of definitive union, leads me onto the transportation vehicle pulled by two saurians of a distinctively mythical lineage. The character of both animals, in all likelihood artificially bred, empirically challenges all known classifications stemming from the theory of evolution. Have they perhaps existed all along, hidden away from nineteenth-century biologists? Dinosaurs are birds!

The procession reenacts no temporal distension between birth and death but rather the absolute present, permanently in transit. Unbelievable harmony in the total discord; this is the melody of authenticity in the adulation of love. Besides the objects that have already been described, the travelers carry a variety of familiar suitcases, mutilated classical statues, banners, musical instruments, flowers, and a collection of disguised ithyphallic amulets like pipes, Greek helmets, two-by-fours, drawing triangles and T-squares, model airplanes, faucets, other assorted sections of letters, and metal edges for tailoring and dressmaking. In the instantaneous past, present, and future the three-headed man, with an apple in his chest and tightly wrapped genitals gleaming like a baroque blue pearl, is surrounded by blushing young girls, and all are circumscribed by a snake biting its tail. An inscription reads:

Erectio perpetuam sine qua non veritas est.

Polyphilo traverses the strict order of the terminus, along the mechanical transit gangway without detention. Passports are obviously not needed. Every passenger must now fully and visibly express his or her identity, tinted by all moods and feelings. *Always advancing closer to the innermost theatrum mundi, we construe our ground of freedom as we step through the perfect temperature-controlled air. While following the light and leading the way toward the evasive darkness, we crush rose petals and orange flowers, violets and jasmine. Our rhythmic walk becomes a primal melody in praise of physizoa, the absolute giver of life. We dance on her body amid casts and rubbings; I dance in her body enraptured with celestial transports and infinite, intangible motions. The giver of life, clad in white cotton and green surgical smocks?*

Closer to the marrow, near the tangent of the spiral, we face the gate again, which is like a proscenium. The theater at last! Yet there is no threshold this time. We may simply proceed.

The immensely tall construction is pure unoriginal space, at least fifty-five meters high, exploding in the palm-shaped hands that crown innumerable colonnettes. *I vaguely recall a most intimate space, visible in between the petrified veins and arteries of Neapolitan cadavers.* This ascending space is not gravity bound. The nave, humid and cool, is approximately five degrees cooler than outside at the height of summer.

The blindfolded god stops here. *Are we finally between the navel and the pubis?* It will take more than five minutes to get used to the uncanny light of truth, pale hues of pink and blue neon. The metaphysical clarity of details reveal: ram skulls; a reclining nymph modestly dressed with nothing but a large snake; a covered vase; dank breath; bulls in floral arabesques; live satyrs roaming freely and horns of plenty overflowing with fruit; eyes and eggs. All the attributes of love that have now been engineered into hard facts populate the atrium.

Surrounding the vast space are open corridors for the spectators who have stayed away, who won't witness the ritual, who insist upon hiding in their private cubicles. There are no seats in this circulation system, linked by the obligatory transparent elevator. All is in transit. Artificial plants and flowers of an immense variety are everywhere, potted and hanging, colors and aromas, for the theater is evidently a garden continually renewing itself. *Is this an architecture of cultural continuity?* This is a theater beyond convention and simulation, a theater for losing oneself, forgetting, unceasing transformation. There are no topoi here for mindless orators; there is nothing significant in this space because all is shocking; all is utterly new.

We sense the unequivocal emptiness when leaving, on this journey, the past

207

behind. The rhythmic steps of our stride circumscribe a hollow space and resonate through the arcades of missing tissue. We suspect that somewhere, under the invisible central hearth, must lie a decrepit monument, an altar for the old sacrifices. Yet, as we all know, a horizontal tomb is no longer useful. The bloody veins of the mineral now rise vertically. Somehow the sparkling fire must merge with the night.

As we track the upward thrust with our glances, we wonder about the limits of this spectacle. The roof may have disappeared, and the cerulean background of the fresco seems to have been obliterated by the starry shine of the permanent dawn. The columnar trunks, once robust and supple, disintegrate and decay. Blossoms and moldings flake off like snowflakes. Through the rose windows, under the cranial vault, the sky is present. The precise moment of death sets off the embracing and withdrawing motion of the clouds.

The millenary coincidence among sacrifice, orgasm, and death has already caused the vegetable ornamentation to rust and decay. Capitals gave way first, followed by arcades and portals. Two-headed serpents and other mythical beasts are now being discovered and documented as factual. Their frightening existence undermines the assured edifice of reason as they creep between organs and cobblestones.

The vast and narrow space contracts as the roof touches the dying man's head, while the serpent devours the copulating sex organs. The outside regions have been decimated by the exploitation of Prometheus. When the entrails of man grow no longer, the space will converge to a point and the eternal void will set in. But suffering is, indeed, still possible. This space, although constricted and thoroughly luminous, is not yet merely the locus of the soul. *We can continue, full of hope, toward the darkness.*

The gap is paved with one very large black stone of unknown nature, probably indestructible, totally flat and polished. This is the dance floor, the receptacle and liminal zone of being as becoming, evidently awaiting the new performance. *If I should step into it while suffused with love and voluptuousness, I will inevitably fall over a precipice, into an abyss, in accordance with my state of being.* The floor is solid indeed, and its sharp reflections stubbornly hold all the passengers close to the surface.

The new ritual consists in assembling a *machina mundi* from the individual fragments that everyone bears. Ironically, Polyphilo is set free when he tumbles into the luminous abyss, the hidden source of life, water, and fire. In the face of blind technology, his task is that of deconstructing the nihilistic light of reason by participating in the new choreography of intimately personal playacting. A golden arrow points to an inscription on the pavement:

And if you wish to see the reality of this mystery, then you should behold the wonderful representation of the intercourse that takes place between the male and the female. For when the semen reaches the climax, it leaps forth. In that moment the female receives the strength of the male. The male for his part also receives the

strength of the female at the precise instant of ejaculation, while the semen abandons his body.

Therefore the mystery of intercourse is performed in secret, in order that the two sexes might not disgrace themselves in front of many who do not experience that reality. Since each of the sexes contributes its own part in begetting, if it happens in front of those who do not understand the reality, the act is laughable and unbelievable. Moreover, these are unfathomable and eternal mysteries of both words and deeds, because not only they are not heard, they are not seen.

THE PARTICIPANTS PROCEED to construct in order to fill the gap, always under the command of the alluring god. A precisely crafted machine that serves no explicit purpose is erected to destroy the luminous abyss, constituted by the fragments created by each builder. No composition or totalitarian cosmic reference serves as blueprint. Innovative techniques and personal visions merge together without discomfiture, leading to the recreation of life. *Thoroughly inefficient, this is yet another machine. Is it a patient in the surgical amphitheater?* Everyone present participates in the operation, contributing their singular hi-stories to the consummation of the coxofemoral articulations, integrated circuitry, and practically nonexistent ticktock. A collegium of artists construct the machine in unison, silently yearning for transcendence and a new beginning of history, while hoping to destroy mechanistic nihilism. They celebrate at once birth, marriage, and death in the reality of a perpetual present. *We at last participate in a ritual. Is this the end of technology? Or our end? A beginning? Agoras or neighborhood action groups are no longer possible. This may be the first plausible ritual of the only real brotherhood left in the world, not yet numerous, finally granting its members a sense of belonging to humanity as a whole . . .*

The sole evident purpose of the unique *machina* is that, once completed, it could blush, laugh, and actually die. It is simultaneously the student-spectator, the teacher-surgeon, and the wiseman, patient, and corpse for dissection. Coincidentally active and passive, it embodies eternal motion and emotion. A red viscous liquid that seems to have already coagulated drips from the cavity where a stone heart is being placed. *The destruction of machinism will only become visible if we all agree to wear dark glasses and perceive the world through a blind man's cane.*

Meanwhile, the meticulous construction of the realistic young body continues quietly beyond the birth canal. Maleandfemale. The useless, immensely seductive but neutral machine looks nothing like a human body, but it is. Made entirely by hand from manifold personal visions, it is created without planning but in flawless order. *I can recognize Polya's voice, but cannot see her.* Touching gently the beautifully crafted parts, the mannequin vibrates and opens its legs slightly. More could be seen: long nymphes hang under the wings of the crown; they lengthen and shorten like the comb of a turkey. *At the point of coincidence between desire and fulfillment, men and women may finally realize the primordial reality of androgyny for the presencing of being, over and above the traditional repressive and illusory understanding of genders as polar opposites . . .*

The polished, black stone pavement, which creates the distance between me and the mannequin, now appears unconquerable, notwithstanding my boundless urge to vanquish it. Space affects me as much as the object. The voice announces the departure of the flight toward the west. Polyphilo, not yet blind, picks up his suitcase with extreme care. He is apparently conscious of the unfathomable pulsating sphere that in some way may hold the key to fulfillment. It unfailingly keeps time, 22:59:—A.D.; it is immaculate only a third of the day. *Where is one propitious hour? Less twenty-four milliseconds? Time has certainly collapsed, and a delay must be announced. Moving rapidly on mechanical walkways, we are transported around the exhilarating atrium of the airport hotel and continue circumvallating the mundium.*

SURROUNDED BY THE MIRACULOUS products of ritual, Polyphilo, not yet blind and barely able to behold the spectacle, understands that he is finally witnessing a communion of profound import. The generator of life is all-encompassing, its center ubiquitous. The fountain of fire lights Polyphilo's face, while the incubating warmth radiates from the surrounding shell. Fire consumes Polyphilo from within and without. The air is still and quiet under the bright blue suspended instant before which skyscrapers splinter into a multitudinous ocean of glass. *To become a city—symbol of sharp, glaring edges? A city of meaning and hope is embodied in every countenance around the abyss, partaking of what is only a beginning in the early morning. The sensitive gazes of the participants weave a subtle tapestry that reflects our gathering, the essence of our project, flat, continually overwhelmed by light.* The sphere had no center before Euclid, and it has obviously lost it again. It is merely the realization of the primary gesture of the human hands.

Not yet fully blind, I struggle to understand. The cold agitation of columns divides my consciousness and I touch my own sex, and the sex under my soul rises like a flaming triangle. The same philosopher who explained that the most beautiful order in the world was a random collection of things insignificant in themselves knew that lightning was the Lord of everything and that its fire would eventually catch up with all.

I kneel, face to face with the luminous abyss that has never been more clear. The blueprint of the wondrous machines, playful objects for perennial embodied reconstruction, is the incandescent spiral of deoxyribonucleic acid that contains the circle, the triangle, and the square. Paradoxically perhaps, even though life may have occurred as a chance biochemical situation perpetuated by the necessity of chemical reactions, the clarity of this logic is by far less blinding than that of the order in history, the actual order of perception. *Maybe in human existence chance is order and order is chance. Chaos is only a gap, and what we make is order.*

The participants face a machine that incorporates wisdom, although it hardly contains all of the information in the universe. The construction of a *machina mirabilis*, inscribing human love at the heart of things, poignantly questions the past practices of inhabitation in the world of man. Merely efficient or ornamented structures appear, by comparison, as meaningless endeavors. The biometric blueprint again: a perfectly delineated navel the color of blood and water, vaguely enclosed by an expanding pomegranate, viscid dripping lines of the same color surrounding the coils of the breasts, traced within the brain's cells. Amid disintegrating vegetation, cancerous spires, and broken pediments all columns have lost their egg-shaped moldings, and inside the dark crevice an egg germinates in the ovary. The mortal machine evidently manifests the divine duality of misfortune and love, and all participants celebrate the mysteries of uncertainty, the most wonderful thing about life . . .

The mysteries of fire are the mysteries of life, perpetually enigmatic. One can stare at the rising sun directly on the face and still ask what it is. Fire? Light? Waves? The sun was the first object of reflection back in the mythical times, during that same elusive time of day. *And we have no answer yet, really. Maybe all we truly know is that fire is the basis of culture and that we light a fire like we make love.*

Figuratively, of course, we make the fire of culture like we make love . . . Prior to culture, time had not begun. Then chaos was omnipresent. When there existed no solids, liquids, and gases, the universe was permeated throughout by states of heat and thermal forms defining in cosmic space regular and irregular figures. Each intangible and undifferentiated man was a unit that comprised simply changing temperatures. *Perhaps this is our constitution at both the origin and the end?*

A very hot sweat, a sort of watery fire sears my pores. Rather than die between the sheets of my bed, I should be able to plunge into a bath that will destroy the tissues of my body, producing immediate death. The formula of this liquor must be the province of poets! It is probably an oil of glass that conceals a powerful and invisible fire, subtle and digestive, penetrating and compressive, with opposite properties to any alcohol or semen . . .

THE MACHINE OF DESIRE comprises all known modalities of fire. To be loved means to be consumed by the flames, to love means to glow with inexhaustible light. Its fire may or may not burn, it is both punishment and universal purification. The gap is thoroughly deodorized by the inherent effect of fire, the same capable of preventing putrefaction in cooked meat and that has, therefore, made the first communion possible. Since its essence is light, the machine will surely become opaque when projected into infinite space.

This ambivalent fire is an insubstantial element that must be fed, difficult to light and stubborn to extinguish, and it is exclusively made by man with curiosity and loving care. It is the masculine principle or form enveloping the feminine watery or earthy matter to give life and hide the darkness; in the funereal pyre it is the medium that refines the body and renders it perfect, returning it to the original ineffable wholeness of the universe. It is also the invisible fire of digestion that is a synonym of life, without itself being alive.

The fountain of fire filling the gap of the *theatrum* is a union of elements in the flesh, of the invisible and the explosive, virtue and vice. The fiery substances contained in this machine are both masculine and feminine. They are kept on the right and the left of the central hexagonal column of transparent plexiglass that, being the core of the mannequin, constitutes the axis of androgyny by reflecting all objects around it. Feminine fire heats and burns from the outside, masculine fire scorches from within, and only recently it has been perfected. All fires are maintained in chemical receptacles with organic forms for the manufacture of respective bodily parts or their molecular secretions, ensuring the eternal imprint and reproduction of the genetic code, the second law of thermodynamics notwithstanding.

The machine now stands majestically on the polished black surface of the dance floor. Its motion generates acoustic words, a mechanically modulated speech which through tone and expression alone describes a permanent operation of building and demolishing, fall and resurrection. The silence after Babel is no longer:

One supervisioning multiple laborers, conceptioning freely quantumtative and dative semenal and ovarial ideals with bluepolished overalls and protuderous bums; distending, coextending, doweling, and nailing beautiflous details of desire in dressed and undressed maplewood, finis prima calligulating, entirely unpreplanned; molecular, staticular, and machinistical strictures withstandingnot, from bottomsparts constructed, (uyuyjoyious involuntary erectition!) eroginated from next to nothing and excalating and expandating ad circumferential infinitum, and downtumbling convexating intoentropy, oooo-ooo-oo, quietus all.

213

THESE WORDS OF FIRE may have been even uttered by Polya herself. *The machine?* The *machina* in the atrium, under a dome of pure crystal, is surrounded by the unoriginal individuals and monsters that create it, playing and plucking beams of light like the strings of a musical instrument. A cyclical melody is heard. Fiery stardust freely collected in gleaming electromechanical receptacles, male and female, is transmuted into incandescent geometric lineaments and construction material to be woven into the fabric of the universe. *Should a fossil stone be reserved for the heart, the substance of the island itself?* Amid the crystallized musical notes other letters appear: alpha and omega, as expected, and the floating words of light:

Seduction is like a spark.

Corresponding to the new words and melodious phrases constituting the ritual construction, original pieces are crafted to create the theater, a truly miraculous machine that overwhelms all inhabitants with the disclosure of the invisible forces not of nature but of history: the work of art. Nothing instrumental is hidden here, the enigmas of embryology notwithstanding.

The structure is composed of three pieces that are inexplicably one: the thin, energetic body of the past, the inadequate, utterly fragile body of the present, and the streamlined body of the future; the feeling body of personal consciousness, the second body that is its external appearance, and the mechanical body conceptualized by anatomy. Three pieces: enveloping, external, and internal; subject, object, and space; mother, son, and lover; daughter, father, and lover. Their assigned roles: the observer, the surgeon, and the patient.

The observer is a wheel on a track with seven stations: the circulation, standing room only. Through the different visors on the large rotating wheel the spectacle is filtered, according to the various ways of representing classical reality: perspective, anamorphic, and axonometric. *A distant objective knowledge, comprising the totality of theory or the binary encyclopedia of contemporary information with immense memory storage capacity, is still seductive but no longer sufficient. An ethic of scientific knowledge for a possible independent observer has not been formulated.* The unyielding glare of the ineffable spectacle is overwhelming: under the icy pavement, a frightening noise envelops a shimmering cocoon, purple moons, divided suns, terrestrial conflagrations, the gusts of milk . . .

The ubiquitous center is beyond a curtain. An inscription in Greek designates it as the membrane of virginity, the nuptial veil to be torn and through which humanity has already seen. *Dazzling luminosity! No pain, infinite pain.* Not even technological necessity or the ethic of scientific knowledge though, could lead the inexperienced Polya to commit such a laceration. Smiling, avid, and excited, Polyphilo happily accepts the task to tear the curtain. Taking hold of the golden stylet, the tantalizing generator of life, he is moved by the blinding fire and strikes the curtain. No delicate fabric, this one (all hymens are presently synthetic and reusable), it tears with the sound of thunder!

The ex-center of the island is occupied by both the patient and the surgeon. The cubical surgeon performs the previously annual ritual of cutting up cadavers, a spectacle that is now playacted in a refrigerated chamber and can therefore last more than five days. His knowledge, acquired and intuitive, is stored in opposite sides of the machine, east and west. Even though man has never possessed a map of heaven or hell, this machine knows that the outline of heaven follows that of an angel and that the most vile and loathsome hells lie to the west. Circuits and gears, however, do not match accurately. The motions and interventions on the human body that constitute the knowledge of the creator of statuae and animated skeletons stem from an indeterminate set of infinite combinations and are ultimately modifiable by love, the sole determinate cause.

The double triangular plexiglass prism where the patient lies is the locus of unconcealment, the source of unyielding iridescent glare. *Is this the site plan of the dream?* It comprises the labyrinth of the human body, the source of knowledge for the hands of the surgeon and the eyes of the observer, both permanently lost in its entrails and forever illuminated. Surrounded by men on the right and women on the left, it also seems to hold in its transparent womb a hermaphrodite child, enclosed in a cotyledon. *Can a cybernetic marvel provide the final proof for metempsychosis and the continuity of life? Can it finally open our vision to the presence of being, transcending duality and our objectifying stare?*

The surgeon proceeds to inject a reddish, thick liquid into the head of a defunct young woman through the suture at the top of the skull. Between the bone and the brain, the interior of the cranium is filled with a corroding paste that totally destroys her essential personal space, that individual, primordial gap constituting the substance of human mortality. The encapsulated brain is then put into contact with a short, thin rod of metallic vitalium. Together the two compounds release a powerful electric current, and its heat penetrates all tissue, overcoming cadaveric rigidity and endowing the subject with an impressive artificial life.

From the fountain of fire the young woman emerges in glory, virgin, fecund yet somehow complete. She repeats the most significant acts of her life, erotic gestures of self-recollection. *She is brighter than the double helix that allowed the king and his lover to ascend and descend naked and never touch, exposing the full mystery of voyeuristic knowledge!* Her transparent and sparkling body appears to be made of a substance as yet unknown. All of the spectators, ecstatic with terror, are consumed by a sudden appetite for pleasure.

The mannequin is absolutely beautiful, surpassing the latest media standards for charm and appeal. Ivory body, incombustible and unsinkable golden hair, frosted coral lips, bosom whiter than snow, pink shoulders, very pink, eyes round and bright like astral bodies, and inflated teats unaffected by even a slight declination. Frame of pearls, vertically and horizontally woven diamonds and flowers over the head. *The big, luminescent whore!*

Six steps lead down into the depths of the fountain from the perimetric edge of the black pavement, behind the torn curtain. A philosophic furnace on the left emits the smell of bread. On the right the retorts and distillation coils fill a wineskin, which in turn empties into the basin. There is a dry, fruity aroma on this side. Half-submerged in combustible life water, the youthful virgin mother of the hermaphrodite gently strikes her body producing an unearthly phosphorescence, an odorless aura: the infinite clarity of variegated sunlight refracted by a polished gem.

I kneel in adoration. I am unable to keep my eyes fixed on her, for human sight is not made to fathom such perspicuity! I feel utterly inadequate with my dirty embodied consciousness, genetically ill-prepared, awkward, and improperly attired. The mellifluous voice addresses Polyphilo's invisible companion, telling tales of love and eternal bliss. The feminine words emerging from the loudspeaker are spaced with a mechanical rhythm: "Sincere and happy lovers you will be; serving me well, you have deserved it . . . Five young girls assigned to you and five to Polyphilo to ensure togetherness perpetual, union in diverted boredom. Here are their names. Here are also your rings, wear them forever . . ."

From the operating table Polyphilo withdraws a double ring that becomes one at the moment of placing it on his finger. *A double helix? Polya is definitely absent and thus my marriage is finally consummated. Is this the end of the trip, the end of culture? Perhaps the tomb remains with its horizon . . .*

My five young attendants seem uncannily familiar. They are obviously cotravelers (for who is not), but time has surely passed. They throw themselves upon us and fill me with caresses and humid kisses. Love fulfilled!

In the fountain takes place the unexpected transmutation of water into fire and vice versa, a process perpetuated by chemical necessity: the ultimate self-referential technique of creation and destruction, the ultimate phenomenological contradiction. The water of life disappears with that which it burns; it is the very material substance of fire. *Is fire therefore that which feeds from its own substance?* To describe the essence of fire through the metaphors of digestion and assimilation is to explain a lucid physical phenomenon by means of an obscure, intimate certainty. *Right. But for thousands of years men and women that drank the water of life used to die from spontaneous combustion. Not any more.*

The bloodstained, golden arrow of light and a smoking heart occupy the field of vision. *This must be in fact the culmination of my story. Struck by love, struck with blindness! Welcome, blindness! It is the only way to see reality, to make architecture, to understand the fallacy of biotechnology. The aleph of the golem can be erased in my mind's eye, just as the rod of vitalium can be removed by the surgeon and the existence of the salamander ascertained. The earth is the virgin is the whore! What perfect mechanical identity! In the darkness I hope to be deconstructed by desire . . .*

The arrow of course pierces not Polya's heart, Polya who has washed her entrails in the maternal fountain and cannot die again. *Luscious burning, deep in my entrails, my whole being ignites, permeated by invisible fire. My form seems to change into a thermal differential. I am no longer the familiar human body but the substance of erotic abandon. Although broken and decomposed as such, I cannot yet understand the secret of the hermaphrodite. It may not even matter . . . Sweet flames inthrown. I feel neither alive nor dead but in a trance. I experience the continuity and density of the present, as if seized by an epileptic fit.*

Love fulfilled indeed! Aspersed by the playful mannequin, we are cured by the divine foam and brought back to reason. Cured? The clarity prevails. It will at least for a few more hours, and maybe even until the millennium. I certainly feel endowed with superior qualities. Anointed and tranquilized by my attendants, they all kiss us, with their ten, flickering tongues. And I am finally clothed with appropriate and magnificent garments, like everyone else on the island . . . One more erotic transit between nakedness and clothing, a garment upon a garment because everything is fabric, clothing to the very end. Everything turns to dust, but dust is still an extreme covering; it envelops everything.

The mannequin speaks unspeakably obscene words, and a warrior materializes, clad in technologically advanced protective gear. One more cadaver perhaps, but endowed with a prodigiously strong muscular body. He undresses, taking off his frightful black rubber mask with protruding respirator, his ample, olive green overalls, and all the rest of his equipment designed for the likely perils of chemical warfare. Naked, he enters the burning water to embrace the young woman and make love to her. The scene is indescribably clear, magnified by the resplendent lenticules of liquid. Every anatomical detail of bodily penetration and collision appears with fulgent luminosity. Positions, limbs, and orifices interchange in innumerable combinations. At the very least they include all the simple passions composing the narration of Mme Duclos for the first month of the 120 days of Sodom, but always between two, and in the longest night. The battle is explicitly deployed on the stage and its totally diaphanous secret becomes unbearable, utterly exciting but infinitely terrifying. *I cannot stand my passion and my wish to die!* Through the transparent membranes of the goddess all become witness to an internal ejaculation! In full view the loss of seminal fire that is demonstrably the greatest sacrifice, the only sacrifice that can engender life.

The slow and delicate friction has obviously separated the air molecules allowing for the passage of semen. Such atomic collisions produce a pleasant tickling sensation through the polarization of molecules and the accumulation of the fiery seminal liquid in the locus of friction. Incapable of holding back the increasing buoyancy of the seminal fire, the air finally yields its place to the forceful ejection of seed that irrupts into the womb, where it also displaces an electronically ionized atmosphere. The vagina is nothing but a conduit that leads into the general reservoir of inert molecules, devoid of motion, which become ignited like a noble gas by the seminal fire. *At last, the effulgent orgiastic image forces me to lower my eyes. Oh, to have dark glasses and a cane!*

The surgeon extracts the rod of vitalium and the scene changes.

217

POLYPHILO LEAVES and reenters through the same nonexistent gate, always head first. *Beyond pain or history? No more uncertainties? It is evident that certainty is evil and uncertainty good, and that I must put an end to any logical distrust. All is indeed clear, the hope of darkness endures.*

The dancing passengers on the island of endless spring surround the operating table, proverbial stage for the encounter. At present it appears as a paradoxical and impenetrable tomb. On the slab sits, cross-legged, the now immobile young woman, internally breast-feeding the hermaphrodite in her womb. The inscription at the feet of the statue reads:

Cruel child, you don't drink milk from my breast, but bitter tears which your mother has wept for her beloved.

Tears drip from the mannequin and accumulate on the slab, solidifying instantly as a thin, reflecting sheath. *Is physizoa the goddess of love, also Mother Earth emerging from the water? Bitter tears, the water of fire. I now taste them;*

they are the real food of love. Perhaps inevitably, the end is near. (It is always the same bed.)

The vertical surfaces of the funeral slab are mirrors, which render an impure softness and effectively dissolve into the black pavement, obliterating all edges. The tomb's dimension is the immeasurable distance between the front and the back of a human body. *Of course!* The slab reflects the now blinding circle of the sun at dawn, resting on a bed of lettuce, a kernel, and Polyphilo's face. Yes, the face of Polyphilo, never before seen!

Appropriately, Venus and the sun became lovers only at dawn, but the eternal instant has lasted already too long. The reciprocal trinities of deity are thoroughly transparent, yet the real hermaphrodite has not been born. *Still? In darkness it must be something else: surely a perpetual orgasm without emission of semen . . .*

The old Phoenician festival actually occurred not in May but after the harvest, the internal time of the suitcase. *Winter shall soon return.* It commemorated the funeral of a splendid young man, the glittering germ, born of a tree, nourished into life by Mother Earth, and unwilling seducer of the universal lover. *Was it incest?* He was killed in an explosion during a circumvallation of the globe in his role as perpetual traveler, the result of necessity. His lover, trying to save him, lost her virginity while abandoning the cockpit under decompression.

Periodically, every so often at irregular intervals, the whole commemorative ritual was playacted by the participants with the help of vitalium. The young woman bathed in the fountain of fire while her unborn child fed from the blood of her wounds. She would then throw herself upon the slab and cry, until her tears were absorbed into the solid void, the necessarily opaque mass behind the crystalline mirror.

The sacred realm has become profane, universally profane, but finally open to the sacredness of darkness.

THE PARTICIPANTS START to leave. It is probably time. I cast my head on the pillow and kiss her hand frantically. Is Polya indeed absent? When searching for the truth be ready for the unexpected, for it is difficult to find and puzzling when you find it.

A voice announces the departure of the westbound flight. It is still 22:59 in the suitcase, the sphere untouched. *Everything flows; nothing stays. The philosopher must be wrong.* Around the *mundium* on the mechanical walkway the passengers, always in transit, make their way toward the departure lounge. Polyphilo boards a new plane for the last leg of his trip. A familiar story . . .

2:35:06 . . . ONCE AGAIN a threshold of acceleration. *The same significant space of transition, in this phase presumably approximating the real meaning of emptiness beyond reason, closer to undifferentiated darkness.*

As I fall into a deeper level of gnosis, the dream goes blind. Yes. But I see the cabin, the seats around me and my suitcase. In all likelihood the sphere is still intact, judging from the perfect state that we now inhabit, seated comfortably and once more yearning to fly. Now almost at the point when flight can become real, the passengers possibly wish to hear Polya's eventful story of imperfect love. Her origin, her passion, happiness and suffering, her sense of honor and commitment, all of those curiosities from the past. The earphones are connected and everyone is plugged in. Polya, invisible, hesitates at first but strikes a relaxed tone of voice and decides to speak through time. Let the play begin!

219

I FEEL SOMEWHAT embarrassed unveiling the strange story of my transmu-
tation to an invisible audience of deaf eyes. In this city from which I come, one
avoids speaking of oneself in any way that may reveal even the slightest trace of
emotion. From an early age we are all taught to think about art in objective terms
and about love in a rational way, as pure efficient action and hedonistic information.
I learned how to reflect indifference on my frozen physiognomy, deflecting all
manifestations of wrathful impulse, delusions of fear, or uncontrollable affective
desires. It is now evident that, after several generations, the spiritual authorities
have succeeded in classifying these manifestations of an irrational order as symptoms
of mental disease.

From early childhood every girl is assigned a social educator whose role is to
inculcate a certain knowledge—apparently innate in previous times—of a unified
order transcending all incarnation. In certain cases such training tends to inhibit
sensations of pleasure or pain and deposits an invisible film of insensibility on the
skin that often penetrates deep into the epidermis. Thus you may understand that
in our country every sign of excessive emotion is perceived as a degeneration of the
primary functions of the neurorational system.

As a woman from the waning millennium I can't avoid feeling sterile, perhaps
still forbidden from entering your place of dwelling because I can barely achieve a
fragmented grasp of the unstable reality. I drift constantly between the mystified
context of the technological object and the demystified essence of its lost horizon,
infinitely powerless to grasp a sense of wholeness in this shattered world.

If in spite of all this I agree to tell my story, it is only because my narrative is
not an objective text. My feminine voice is the new articulation of myth, which
itself is more than a literary form or even a type of speech; it is our legitimate means

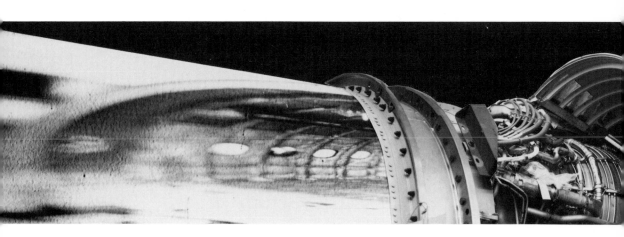

of understanding. The allegory must be spoken in order to allow comprehension of its totality, a metalanguage revealing more than it represents; beyond the dualistic alternatives of action and contemplation that it unveils: aletheia, noble goal. I share with you this poetic quest for the inalienable meaning of things.

I address you because I am encouraged by the unfathomable potential of embodied being, shining forth from the homogeneous profane ground which you inhabit, open at least to a dark sense of transcendence. Beyond my tears I can see the source of an eventual reconciliation, I can visualize a future synthesis bringing together figuration and abstraction in the architecture of our world, object and knowledge, reality and men, description and explanation: a new mythopoetic articulation, embodied gesture and speech, that coincides with our individually felt sense of wholeness and compassion.

Ultimately I can only deplore the uncanny imbalance of our times, when what we say about reality and perception is often more interesting than reality and perception itself. Soon this anomaly shall pass, but can one remain passive? Maybe all it will take is the seven hours of one night's sleep. The time of awakening of our dreambody . . .

I realize that all of you have beheld the wondrous structure that contains the secrets for the generation of life, but it is paramount to articulate again the question of origins. Please bear with me! Such is the spiral nature of the temporality that I am.

My ancestors were transformed into efficient machines. Engendered by a desire of maximal productivity, they undoubtedly believed in the possibility of incarnated perfection, in the existence of light without shadow, a good without evil. Oh deplorable metamorphosis! A silent cry invaded the ritual space where they wandered aimlessly but efficiently, without truly sharing in the making of illusions and dreams. If this impermeable darkness lies ahead, an absence of inner clarity will surely magnify my anguish! Thus I weave my story with authentic words that name the ground . . .

POLIA was my original name, derived from polis, meaning order and wisdom. I was indeed a citizen of the modern capital, the point of departure of all later colonizations, before the postmodern transliteration that reflected important changes but nevertheless left the primordial significance of my name intact. My ancestors were the founders of the rational and planned modern city, anonymous and hostile but also free and intoxicating, universal and ever-changing. They imposed on the island a grid of traffic engineering that bled with the restrained passion of millions of voyeurs, pregnant with potential myth. This was a unique city where mutability was the fixed condition, a city to be replaced by another city, perpetual demolition being its destiny. The inhabitants were obsessively cheerful about destruction, perennially in motion under a cloud of dust. They believed that the city was always in the process of becoming a better object of their desire, even if the reverse was in fact true and everyone had been enslaved by consumerism, biased information, and oppressive economic forces.

I used to perambulate in this city made for walking and observing, unequaled by any other in the world. Treading in this optical machine, in endless exhilaration, under constant threat and with mounting expectation, I stored my experience as accurate mental snapshots. The extreme alienation of objects carried the potential of the body's recollection of being! I was persistently excluded from participation and continually raped. My sense of individual power and freedom was always challenged by groans, sighs, muffled screams, steps climbing up an iron staircase or resonating in the ill-smelling tunnel, a pane of shattering glass, an iron latch creaking, and heavy footsteps coming closer down the corridor toward my room, while I hid my face in the sheets.

The exciting mental images had never been so clear, the most sophisticated products of perspective; plates that turned sunlight, and particularly electric light, into metaphysical silence. A truly random gathering: the steerage of a ship before dumping its human cargo at Ellis Island; beneath a dirigible the immense erection of lower Manhattan, towers of hope incessantly striving to grow taller, disregarding

the simulated end of human ambition enshrined in the World Trade Center twin parallelepipeds; an Italian immigrant woman carrying her home's materials on the head, in front of an empty lot, strewn with discarded objects like a big brass double bed with its metal springs spilling out tufts of rotten horsehair, a white Buick, recent model, with no engine or wheels, and a three-story iron fire stair, placed within the lot in the guise of a pulpit; six young newsies with vivid eyes, holding their quota of papers under their arms and dreaming of utopia on the Brooklyn Bridge; an early type of playground for tenement children below clotheslines; a baby pleasantly sleeping on the sidewalk, beneath a poster advertising a performance of La Traviata *in honor of Sig. Carlo Tricoli, starring Renata Brunorini diva extraordinaire as Violeta; a frozen cadaver on the pavement, under a cover of old posters and newspaper, in the process of being tagged by a policewoman; the hand of man in railway and subway tunnels, and beyond, the dangerous platforms; a long corridor, always very dirty, hollow, and silent, marked by disgusting damp stains and colorful new posters, leading to a huge, similarly vacant area, either dimly lit or brilliantly illuminated by harsh many-colored bulbs; a nun, her fingers barely touching her lips, awaiting survivors from a disaster at sea; the heavy, circular brushed stainless steel vault door, Mosler brand, perfectly accessible to my eyes behind a large glass pane on Fifth Avenue; railroad trains on the bridge, somber like coffins, unending noise of silence; white satin dresses tightly held at the waist by clasped male hands, dancing; the same nun in a hurry with her veil trailing in the wind, pushing a baby pram in front of a brownstone Ionic porch at the bottom of the picture; a wife comforting her husband just arrested for killing a member of her family; several rooms with a view, domestic and intimate scenes framed by indiscreet windows, always open to the city, the edge condition brightly lit; a pig and a blonde in a low-cut satin dress sharing a table in Sammy's at the Bowery; Marilyn Monroe in the act of contracting her lips and half-closing her eyes to blow a kiss into space; the roofs of Washington Square, presence of space between chimneys, water towers, and demolished fire towers; a man in white carrying four small wooden female mannequins, some without limbs; a man with a black jacket and a hat, smoking a cigarette without using his hands; the inside of an ornamented movie theater, the film being shown almost totally out of the picture while a brighter*

electric light reveals the absent meditation of a uniformed woman usher standing by the emergency exit; many gigantic hotels, ideal cities for permanent transients and entertainment parks for serious adult play, all ephemeral; the reflections of multiple lines of bare bulbs on the windows of the subway train; a number of people reading Listen to God *and turning their gaze upward as they cross the street; the elephantine colossus in West Brighton Beach, Coney Island, which cost over a quarter of a million dollars, acme of architectural triumphs containing a whole summer resort in one enormous structure; a young Brooklyn family going for a Sunday outing; more young people in a scattered crowd of regular density, in groups of two or three boys, although after close scrutiny, under the short hair, tight blue jeans, turtleneck sweaters, and leather or denim jackets, there are incontestable girls' bodies, eating hot dots or adopting poses intended to express self-confidence; a child in Central Park playing with a toy grenade in one hand and making a more threatening gesture with the left hand; a very low-key black and white photograph of a castle in Disneyland, California, the albescent swan too visible behind a pane of glass, as usual accessible only to my gaze; two adolescents in a Yonkers dance hall, posing beside a trophy proclaiming them the Junior Interstate Ballroom Dance Champions; a backward man in his hotel room, his nose pointing opposite to his feet; a Jewish giant with his parents in the living room of their home in the Bronx; the star-spangled banner extended during a patriotic holiday behind the ample glass window of a grocery shop, freedom within reach of my sight; a young woman executive dressed like a man, entering an office building with other colleagues through the revolving doors; a transvestite draped in green and wearing a winter bonnet, dramatically giving birth to a doll in the middle of the street, surrounded by admiring spectators, mostly smiling children . . .*

227

THE ORIGINAL FOUNDER, a clever Dutch merchant, had brought with him all the dying customs and beliefs of the traditional old world, together with a rich, charming, and well-read wife. For the first time in the history of mankind the culture of the colonist did not take root in the new place, no earth was transplanted, no auguries were taken, no mundus was dug. The new city was a radically different institution, not predicated on communal ritual but rather on the potentially miraculous nature of objects. It was built in the hope that space and architecture might result from the objects' establishing their own distance and thus recreating memorable places, always novel and changing and void of associative intellectual memories.

Numerous copulations of the founders yielded many children, five boys and six girls to be exact, whose names described their virtues. They were well-endowed, good-looking, and intelligent but destined to grow up on the uncertain ground of a scientific mentality that disavowed all responsibility for the reconciliation of the mystery of being. Facing the abyss of modernity and the nihilistic dangers of the new worldview, they became prey to misfortune. They could not cope with the anguish of a godless existence nor with the assertion that the violence of red is just an appearance whose reality is to be found in the chemistry and physics of the brain.

Emigrating to suburbia, they initiated false dogmatic cults, building and operating historicist churches and temples, often in renovated television studios, drive-in theaters, or amusement parks. Since they supposedly championed continuity and pretended to follow from the older traditional religions that were evidently inadequate, these fanatics called themselves born-again Christians, Moslem fundamentalists, neopagans, etc., hiding the contradictions inherent in modern reality. A punishment ensued, perhaps manifesting the order of history or the self-transcending character of technology. The necessary limits of the positivistic utopia were initially revealed: the impossibility of a meaningful human life if all acts and thoughts depend on the split between mythos and logos for their "truth" and "legitimacy." Indeed, the brothers and sisters were all transformed into efficient machines, praying on Saturday or Sunday and working without complaint from Monday to Friday, losing

all remaining contact with reality and depending entirely on simulations, texts, manipulated information from the media, nostalgic values, and fabricated pressures controlled by absurd technocrats. They became unable to establish a critical distance with this world and thus articulate their own personal mythologies. This made them incapable of standing in the open under an authentic sense of being in order to respond more appropriately to the historical situation: a veritable vicious circle that made it impossible for them to create architecture out of their constructions.

Only the eldest brother escaped with his body and mind intact. He had been attending a function outside the city gate, held in the urban cemetery of Battery Park, the beginning and end of the metropolis at the south end of the island, close to the sea. The play had taken place in an antiquated fortification, previously an aquarium, immigration station, museum and assembly or concert hall, occupying the ancient location of the forum or empty space left in front of the tombs, the original threshold and sacrificial trench. He had witnessed a young boy at the very moment of death in a concentration camp, and the same place, thirty years later, surrounded by souvenir stands, Pepsi-Cola signs, and tourist buses with circular windows. Present at the boundary between day and night, he had seen the trans-ference or initiation and eyed the monstrous face of Janus that was simultaneously laughter and catastrophe and that still prevailed, like hope over despair.

Thus Pollion decided to leave and wander forever, gaining an excellent education in history and rhetoric. He cultivated his revelation of a nondualistic reality in the space-time of the in-between. Eventually he came back to our city and founded a dynasty that survives to this day, while always insisting on remaining homeless. His spiritual children and successors followed his teachings in search of enlighten-ment. He became the head of the union for clandestine professional activities, seeking the implementation of limit situations and chiastic practices through a personal making embodying caring and compassion. Upon his return, many citizens under-stood his important position as the true shadow leader, and paid tribute to his underground organization. They operated beyond the realm of traditional morality

in order to restore a sense of meaning to the otherwise absolutely rational city and thus became responsible for the ever-present feeling of imminent threat and revolution. Adopting a perspective of active nihilism, they hardened and accelerated decadence, exceeding the mere recognition of the destruction of all values. Adolescents as young as thirteen and a half were instructed to become more and more incredulous and to look at Central Park and in empty subway cars for criminal acts. They were taught that a day has 86,420 seconds, that an ulva is a genus of seaweed, that little girls think about knives and blood, and that women who are loved are all in the grave . . . This gnostic organization remained comparatively small in numbers but extended to all confines of the world. It included all poets, artists, and architects who understood the issue of their work to be the revealing of reality rather than hedonism or aesthetics. Their personal introspective search into the felt wholeness of consciousness was always a dangerous one, at odds with the dominating outlook of technology and the "truths" of applied science. Their more open vision ran great risks in order to avoid nostalgia and dogmatism. Embracing excess and desire sometimes led to nonsense and pornography rather than to love and a transcendental eroticism.

THIS WAS THE UNCERTAIN state of affairs in the year 1968 of human redemption, when I attained the flower of my life. The ultimate fate of civilization was still undecided. Like most women of my age, I waited for the evening wind sitting naked in my room, at the edge of the bed. I had two recurring dreams. I dreamed of young colleagues eating hamburgers in an aseptic fast-food restaurant. Since we were attempting to become erotically aroused without touching ourselves, only the upper part of our bodies were visible over the tables. A boyish looking girl was the judge, providing questions written on cards while serving the food behind a counter. The young students concentrated their imagination and communicated

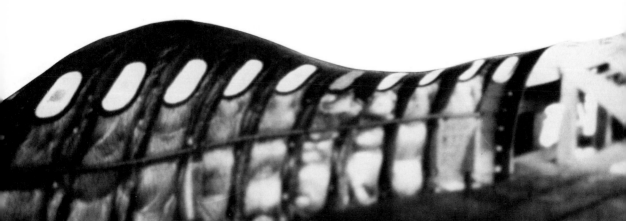

their excitement to the hamburgers, which they held with both hands. All-beef patties would become swollen and bulge irregularly, showing their obscene protuberances between the two pieces of bread. The judge would then measure turgescence in percentage points and declare a winner . . .

I also dreamed of a carefully rendered can of beer, resting on a pristine square base painted matte black. Over the satiny aluminum surface the brand was clearly legible: Cutting Edge. I realized that drinking it would stop one's body hair from growing. Perhaps there was a label on the can explaining the secret of the hermaphrodite. I became convinced that the meticulous drawing of the beer can incorporated the very essence of human order.

ONE LATE EVENING, or rather, very early in the morning, after having escaped my trifling existence for the duration of two or three movies, I sat in a corner diner with my father. Outside the night had engulfed the city, covering all signs of life and dampening the magnetic fields that could turn reality into a picture. The street was vacant, except for Polyphilo whose gaze from beyond the glassy surface searched my soul and surrounded my body like a powerful beam. I could feel the fire of his eyes pressing against me yet, embarrassed by the shameless attitude of this stranger, I acknowledged nothing and decided to ignore his presence.

Fate, as usual, took its course, and the scene was frozen in light. From right to left: the entrance to the kitchen, two big, stainless steel coffee containers, the waiter in white, a round wooden counter, and us, surrounded by bright electric glare and the transparency of large curving glass shop windows that echoed the shape of the counter and the building. The blinding light poured out into the deserted city and mesmerized Polyphilo standing inflexible in the darkness, at the vantage point of the perspective. I felt him staring at my golden hair as if he was suddenly inflamed with love. At first I was amused by the unexpected devotion of this anonymous admirer, but his insistence soon made me uncomfortable. The air became thinner

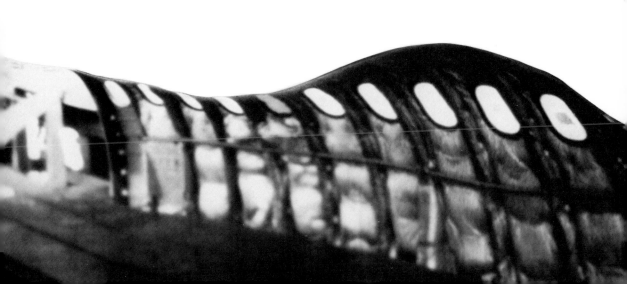

and I started to suffocate under the domination of his eyes.

Incapable of responding to his passionate gaze, I feigned to ignore his presence. I reasoned that my cold and despondent attitude would extinguish his inexplicable desire. Yet he followed us home that evening and kept returning every day. He came to wait under my window, perhaps to catch a glimpse of my intimacy as I opened for an instant the curtains of my room. Perpetually waiting. Looking endlessly at the high empty windows that I kept intentionally closed. Even when, unaware of his presence, I left the curtain drawn and he could grasp a shadow or a shade of the object of his lust, his waiting remained perpetually unfulfilled. He lingered day and night under my window, always wishing to see me at least once more.

He seemed never to sleep, and increasingly his body appeared deformed, hunched up, and closed in upon itself, as if internally corroded by his insatiable passion. I remained totally mystified by the absolute nature of his love, which evidently went beyond any desire of possession, and my only defense was a simulated indifference. In my ignorance of history, how could I have understood that his inordinate and tormented love was the result of a vital necessity to transcend his condition as voyeur. How could I have imagined that the pain that deformed his body was projected from the domain of the invisible by his aspiration to transcend the limits of a vision without shadow . . .

Polyphilo's vigil continued until the time when, alarmed by the inexplicable death of a great number of young children, the specialists identified traces of an old virus in a new disease that had originated in the laboratories as a result of genetic manipulations. Although the disease remained without name, many assumed it to be the plague in a new genetic form. The microorganism soon developed a mysterious natural virulence. It killed many people and instilled terror in the hearts of all the citizens, forcing them to flee to the suburbs. When it became known that I had been attacked by this mortal virus, everyone abandoned me.

I was alone except for my nurse, who always kept me company and provided invaluable advice. Soon I understood that the tumor that I believed I was carrying

in my entrails was in fact the seed of a hermaphrodite. Miraculous immaculate insemination! I uttered strange words and became intensely aware of the borderline. Again the space of transition was engraved in light. From right to left, the edge condition inside of my room: a night table with a pitcher of water and a vase with a few wilted flowers on a white cloth, the large open window framing the city extended to the horizon with early morning light pouring in. In a feverish delirium I saw myself naked, sitting on the side of my bed in the gloomy extreme left. Death appeared to me as a young, strangely seductive woman of angular features. From her gestures I understood that in order to avoid giving birth to the hermaphrodite that was taking shape in my womb I should develop my capacity to withdraw my mind from this corrupted body. I would have to deny the reality of embodied consciousness and reduce it to a pure ego-logical intellect; I would need to renounce the exclusivity of a physical love that might open every pore of my skin to reveal the implicitly corporeal essence of spiritual love. Thus it seemed that my only alternative was to devote my existence to the freedom offered by solitude. I made a vow to consecrate my life to the domination of solar time as long as I were spared the personal responsibility of hermaphrodite childbirth, potentially bringing utopia to a close and resulting in the apocalypse of culture. I did not perceive then any contradictions in my decision to embrace the will to power. In my ignorance I could not yet recognize the hermaphrodite as a symbol of unnamable completeness in the absolute realm, the coincidence in art of desire and fulfillment. I could only grasp it through my logical mind as the absurd incarnation of a perfect wholeness without gender, a democratic monad in the imperfect relative realm . . . Into the depths of my womb penetrated the warm, golden beams of the rising sun!

233

Close to death indeed, I sank into the limbo of forgetfulness. Raising myself from the pillows I sought some familiar thing or something once seen but saw nothing. I perceived everything differently, yet I lived.

The wonders of technology seemed to have saved my life, and I therefore decided

to fulfil my vows. I changed my name to Polya and left the city in pursuit of endless information, which I mistook for ecumenical wisdom. The golden knowledge at the core of my body remained hermetic and unrecognized. Admitted by a chartered corporation in the service of modern destiny, I became a legitimate, efficient member of the decadent, phallephoric society: a professional flyer, myself an instrument of technological domination . . . To succeed I had to deny all my natural instincts, becoming completely impervious to physical love and desire.

Thus I devoted the best part of my youth to my professional training. Driven by an obsession for equality, I sought to overcome the limits of my physical constitution to compete with my male colleagues. The profound split between my body and my mind pervaded my whole outlook with a perverse dualism. I could not recognize the meaning of gestures or emotions, poetic words made no sense, and my perception of value was exclusively quantitative.

Over a year had gone by and Polyphilo, ignorant of my whereabouts, continued to haunt the night in his perpetual search. A member of the lineage of permanent wanderers, he recovered enough energy to travel, and in one of his perambulations he caught sight of me among other uniformed colleagues.

It was the very day when I was meant to pass a final flying test, after a lengthy and demanding initiation. I had endured enforced continence, abstention, and with- drawal from pleasure, drills in the altitude chamber and physical conditioning in the centrifugal machine. My whole life had been strictly devoted to the community and to the contingencies of my uniform. Thus I was ready to submit my flesh to the collective ideal of mastering time, the most inhuman form of existence: to become a full-fledged jetwoman. My success in the preliminary ordeals and the confidence of my severe white-haired master had demonstrated that I was apparently truly gifted for my calling.

On that eventful day when Polyphilo found me I was to demonstrate my mythical role by physically inhabiting the heavens in a totally passive, computer-controlled

solo flight. I had long since erased Polyphilo from my mind. I had even forgotten the image of myself that had tormented his spirit during endless nights. Even though I was wearing an anti-G suit of inflatable nylon and a shiny helmet that transmuted my skin, Polyphilo recognized me. Cunningly he discovered a way to enter the cockpit, that most private of places, which I considered ultimately sacred. I could never have imagined that this temple of technological domination might be so fragile as to be revealed as the place where destiny becomes publicly manifest by an act of divine profanation, by a willful violation occasioned by one man's irrational passion.

Polyphilo approached me with no hesitation, like a sick man looking for a cure. I felt contaminated by his presence, deeply irritated by his intrusion; my heart froze more solidly and my attitude, devoid of charm, turned profoundly hateful. He seemed already half-dead, and my aggressive attitude depleted even further his vital strength. His countenance oscillated from red to intense pallor, and his glance became an almost pathetic act of admiring contemplation.

Between sighs, panting, and crying, his limbs failing, he uttered prolix and incoherent words of passion: "Polya, my goddess . . . hermetic golden hair . . . pity, have pity on my tormented life . . . expanding and melting and not knowing about your iridescent skin . . . flaming coke, rivers on fire, armored vehicles and worse, behind every chain link fence and under the Nevada desert . . . terrifying silo, mushroom cloud, exploding sphere, holder of mystery . . . divine nature, singular, manifold earth . . . be touched, allow yourself to be touched, become sweeter . . . better pass away immediately than die forever, unimaginable any worse condition, abominable curse . . . mortal ruins around me, only rubble and disintegrating tombstones, sticks and bits of human bones covered with snow and the false angle in a dark-green robe with long pointed wings like pincers holding a viridescent flame that floats in the hollow of her hand . . . abandoned I dreamed, withstanding the pain, patiently and willingly for you . . . annihilated by the void of the reticulated prospects of the city, infinitely clear, and by the invisible masks of the inhabitants . . . aimless passion and nocturnal tears . . . feel my torture, put your hands in

the destructive fire and in the corrosive saline solution, or put me to death . . . only a step and my deep misery would be beatitude, but I have fallen and cannot pick myself up again, because I am broken . . . death, welcome . . . deceiving, treacherous woman, without you I die . . . I must with all become one."

Saying his last sentence he dropped as if dead, not before fully introducing his right hand in the slot. The deadly invincible coldness that started to overwhelm his body was like a mirror image of the icy indifference that he had always found in my heart. He wanted a word. I said nothing.

Gradually his body manifested the extinction of his natural forces. He became paler, unresisting. His livid face, veiled by sadness, seemed increasingly more distant, as if the surrounding indifference were dragging him away from me. He lowered his inundated eyes. Rolling over, he pulled the emergency lever in the slot of the vacuum formed window panel, finished. Tumbling on the floor he came to die in ecstasy by my side, imploding, for there was simply no place left to grow . . . Doubt should have then infiltrated my conscience; at that time I should have understood the consequences of my cruel rejection . . . But I never lost my composure and proceeded to rationalize the situation according to the conditioning that I had acquired in my previous training. The double panes of glass and pressurized plastic shattered. Pulling Polyphilo's body by the feet, I cast it into a corner of the cockpit, the force was brutal: a corpse abandoned to be found by others, coldly, deliberately without entombment. I saw him expire but remained distant, incapable of projecting the meaning of my own mortality through his death. I was morbidly fascinated by his crystallized membranes, soon to be no more than frosted dust. My sole anguish derived from my obsessive resolution to complete efficiently the function that I had undertaken. I showed no compassion and remained blind. My only objective was to escape this intolerably turbulent place. A hurried exit ensued, probably unintended, riding the decompressing waves. All I could do was to flee prudently into space, protected by my acquired technological freedom. Yet I wished to go back home. My conscience adumbrated something akin to guilt. A spell?

236

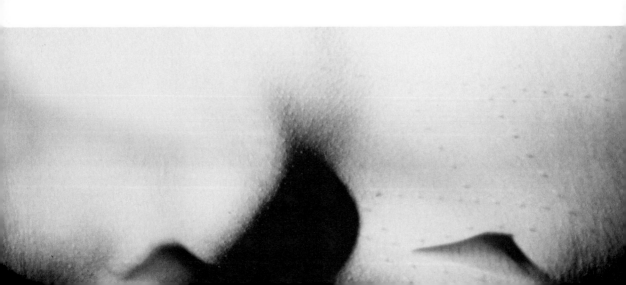

A PAUSE IN THE SPEECH follows. A pause between the oval mirror circumscribed with plastic moldings where no one can see the void and the oval window, down through two panes of glass and a sheet of pressure-resistant plastic, framing the unfinished urban sprawl of the world village. All briefly suspended in silence.

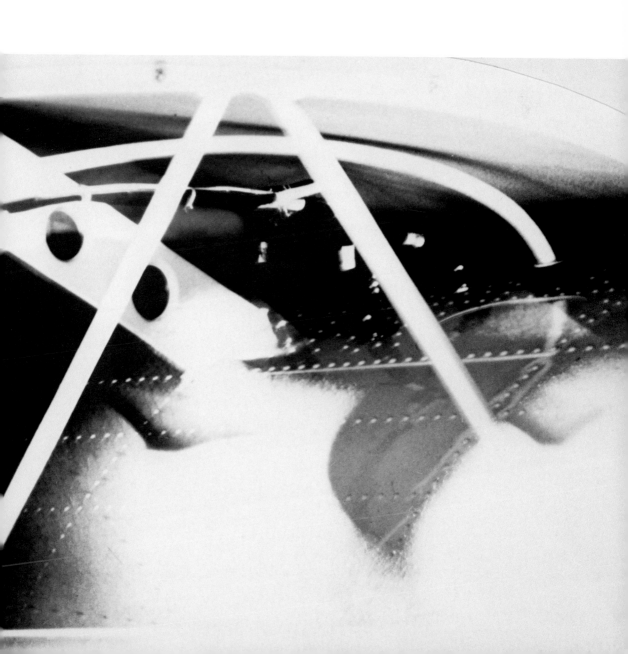

FROM THE EXTERIOR, a sigh is framed by the oval window. The tension relaxes for an instant amid bodily accommodations and the stretching of numb limbs. A faint expression of emotion over the earphones, coughing perhaps, suggests the imminent continuation of the story. The electronic omnipresence is a clear sign of ritual participation and a new brotherhood, however disembodied. The passengers manifest unanimous compassion for the unfortunate lover who perished in the horrid implosion of rapture and excessive pain. Certain faces remain pensive, disconcerted by the obvious logic of the lover's quest and the inexplicable cruelty of the invisible voice. The whole audience, though, shows a keen interest in the conclusion of the story. The tiny electric lights, punctual affirmations of individual presence, are soon turned off and general attention focuses on the invisible voice projected through the shadows. Early morning back in the fall. First instant, elusive first season. The sun is rising, but the inward clock is approaching midnight. The shadows of suburban houses become lighter yet more sharp, obliterating the natural landscape. Endless . . .

BUT LET ME CONTINUE . . . I escaped in secret, mysteriously maintaining my integrity, still ignorant of the consequences of my inflexible behavior. I was perhaps immune to death or on the wings of a nightmare. It is certainly possible that my ancestors had at last succeeded in founding a race of immortals passively inhabiting the heavens. At the same time I clearly saw that love was like a wax that, having lost its softness or malleability, could no longer be applied directly to the world to make a better mold. Compassion devoid of desire was incapable of recreating an adequate model because all objects were simulations, already covered

with radioactive dew. The new version could not simply be a cast of tradition . . .

The appalling accident caused within me neither terror nor excitement; it left intact my rational poise but marked the beginning of a series of sinister premonitions. First the sun became pale in comparison with my internal iridescence, a phenomenon that I had never before witnessed. Then a violent gust of wind blew me off balance and cast me into a visible vortex surrounded by tactile forces. When strife reached the lowest depth of the whirl, things started to come together to be only one, not suddenly but combining from different directions at will. Countless splinters of mortal things poured forth as they mingled. Initially these were parts of disjointed limbs of animals and chopped sections of plants oozing a red, viscous sap, the vegetable segments transforming into fragments of bone in a bath of ground flesh. This bloody vision was followed by creatures resulting from the joining of these dislocated limbs and by the monstrous animals resulting from the condensation of their nourishment or sexual urge. Gradually the scene became less threatening, covered by a white neutrality, until it revealed a total absence of fear or anguish. The vortex no longer suggested monstrosity: no twin branches sprang from its back, it had no feet, nimble knees, or fertile parts but appeared as a sphere thoroughly equal to itself.

240

IN ONE INSTANT *I was taken through the air and deposited in a city that immediately evoked familiar fears. Its walls were made of old, carefully carved yet sadly eroded stones.*

The bright and uniform illumination of this place prevented shadows. The labyrinthine structure was thus intensely disorienting, lacking any points of reference. Even though the buildings, statues, and fountains incorporated many inveterate emotions, I was unmoved. All was superficially seductive, like a high-quality color photograph or the aestheticized objects in a museum, translating misleading cultural memories. All of these appearance effects, however, merely clouded even further my

personal experience of the present.

This was a city of perpetual unchange: delicate ornaments, volutes, and acanthus, chubby children with wings. On the deserted balconies the dizzy morning seemed bleached with tears, and in the squares dying shadows also refused to be cast in wax. Red and green louvers, irregular vertex, and the triangular square where the Templars were sacrificed on March 13, 1313. A ruined thermopolium, now empty, with its perspective frescoes and phallic symbolism. Multiple intersections of canals and alleyways, vertical towers and hunched bridges. Gliding on the black water, the gondola carried a corpse, while a widow, dressed in tears, followed in mourning; reflected on the canals, crisp, shrilling cries of terror could be heard. It was difficult to tell if these were reflections or reminiscences. Perhaps the scintillating slit of my soul already adumbrated a dark, distant fire of love.

The classical city of long avenues, pedimented buildings, and arcades was populated almost exclusively by naked or half-naked women. They moved gracefully and gently, ignoring the presence of others and performing deliberate actions, walking in groups through the structures that now appeared like thin props in a theater stage. They held dry bushes or wore lengthy, flowing capes of diverse colors and materials, solid and transparent. I admired the mastery of panic resulting from the daring and often quite provocative exposure of the pubes, combined with the serenity of each face. Yet there was always the presence of posts carrying the electrical power supply, rails for trams, and cast-iron registers betraying the path of the gutter, all firmly embedded in the cobblestone pavement. The only real possibility of meaning seemed to reside in the unacknowledged electronic impulses filling every cubic centimeter of the invisible geometric entity that was, even here, the space of my modern city.

Leaving the hot and humid street behind orthogonal, transparent screens, I paced on a wooden floor, removed one step from the stone sidewalk. This was probably the ancient presbytery or the waiting room of the railway station. In the center stood that same reclining couch where I had often waited, in my own metropolis: an altar in front of a mirror, because every bed is a funeral bed as well, complete with its

241

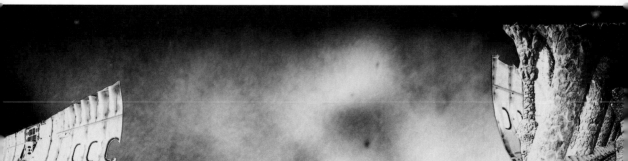

iconographic headpiece. I also identified the same menacing noises: the heavy foot-steps, a latch creaking, a window pane crashing. A stranger was about to enter, this time dressed in a three-piece suit with a bowler hat, while a stripped young woman lay stretched on the couch, her legs slightly opened and her eyes serenely closed.

Within the heavily ornamented wooden frame, her delicate curves, her pink skin, and abundant hair appeared to have been arranged with care by the designer, amid the tawny coats and plumages of does, hen pheasants, and quail. A little fresh blood was still running out between the girl's parted thighs, adding a touch of true red to the crimson wounds of the slaughtered animals in the hunting tableau. The pure flesh of the child had been sacrificed for the communion of the spirit. Judging from their howling, the hunting dogs were still hungry . . . There was clearly no escape from nihilism through the nostalgia of ostentatiously carved frames.

Outside in the public square the statue of the bronze horseman, founder and builder of the city, had been concealed by a protective wooden scaffolding since the war. According to an inscription on a plaque, the enemy bombs did not affect it, but the structure's permanent shadow covered it all and did not disappear when the scaffold was reused as formwork for the concrete casing of a monument simulating a nuclear reactor. Only starving stray dogs roamed noisily around this place, ignorant of the history of the square dedicated to scientific glory and cultural continuity.

Within the long but narrow cast-iron shed for the trains, the bustle was human, as in an urban arcade. An open prospect to the sea was framed by a partially glazed metal structure while locomotives and other machines groaned and whistled. A photographer was diligently taking snapshots of the half-naked population. Another tableau: in front of my very eyes, two young women were being tortured and massacred. The outlines of this vision alternated between the precision of a technical drawing and the evocative freedom of a sketch; the angles of the T-square and the accuracy of French curves and the prophetic blob of organic matter in bloom; machine and human body. A man in a green surgical smock inflicted wounds following a prescribed plan. The two women, resembling dolls with spherical articulations, were

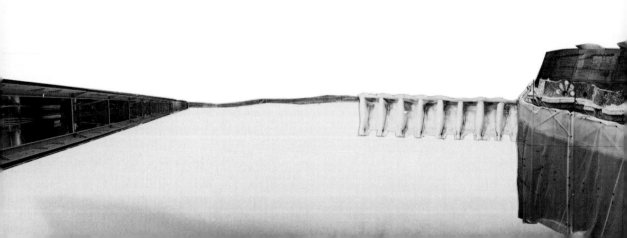

attached to a mechanical chariot by means of electrified chains and forced to pull it along the railway tracks. The hot cables produced burns and lacerations whose intensity was evidently controlled by the man seated in a cab on the chariot. The women cried miserably while becoming aware of every part of their bodies and every pore in their flesh, and they forever lost their memory. I feared that a similar treatment might await me, as if my flesh, transmuted into an insensitive film, instinctively recognized the identity of its father creator and eventual executioner. The curse that had one day caused the separation of my body and mind would soon have to be exorcised through a recognition of love in the flesh, and I would be the next victim to be tortured.

The shining machine became smothered with blood. Pulling the chariot, the women's skin peeled off like old leather. When they could go no further, the experienced torturer in the green smock descended from the chariot and pushed some more buttons. This caused the small locomotive to move by itself and to cut the women's heads. Photographs were taken with different lenses and from multiple angles, long shots, closeups, and endoscopic plates. In the midst of this frightening vision I was struck by a lightning bolt of understanding: these images might be employed for the documentation of inner space, the not-yet-existing but utterly real topoi that would have to be implemented in the construction of a future city.

Once the women had expired, the executioner used a chain saw to cut up their bodies into four pieces. Again photographs were taken: fingers, tongues, and whole hands penetrating reversible orifices; greasy eyelets floating on broth; capillary flesh braided into intestinal coils; structures of bones and teeth coalesced or crystallized into networks of lines; interchangeable double and triple armpits and loins; assorted lips dripping liquefied flesh, nipples, and other excrescences. The executioner removed the skin like a coat covering their trunks and extracted their organs, placing them in containers on ice, ready to be transplanted or dissected. He kept all organs with the exception of the hearts, genitalia, and other reproductive viscera, which he

243

threw into the gutter. These organs of affection had uncannily metamorphosed into perfectly geometric bodies and thus were presumably of no use . . .

For the first time since the onset of the strange calamity that had caused the transmutation of my nature, I felt my flesh vibrate with emotion. I was overtaken by the ghastly scene and shocked by the uncharitable burial. The pain of these women drenched my own skin. Overwhelmed by anxiety, I could not grasp what was happening inside me, why I had been made to witness this horrible spectacle. Scared and agitated, I failed to react to the situation, remaining vulnerable to the frightening destiny in store for me: my virginal flesh would soon be consumed in the cause of a savage sacrifice. This painful emotion had in fact entirely superseded my memory of Polyphilo's death. A smell of rotten organic matter pervaded the place. I hoped that the approaching darkness of the night would engulf the last images of this unbearable nightmare, but I still doubted that the shadows might not tempt some mutant creatures to violate the purity of my being. I dreaded the apparition of monsters resulting from radioactive tests or questionable laboratory grafts, their eyes of basilisk and their foaming mouths blabbing dirty words and terrifying sounds, forcing their way into the waiting room by breaking the locks of windows and doors, touching my soft skin and my golden hair with their hard, sticky, and polluted hands. I feared the soft prehistoric mollusk that might envelop me with the deceiving, anesthetizing warmth of its gelatinous mass and penetrate every orifice of my body with its loving tentacles, silky threads, and rubbery hoses of dark blue and scintillating turquoise. The origin and end of life.

Yet behind the orthogonal screens the city appeared uncannily normal. For a few minutes it seemed possible that my silent cries for relief had been heeded and that I could rest comfortably in the couch that was now my own bed. Very soon, however, I recognized the same utterly unbearable reality of my previous experience. The restored, self-conscious traditional city, polished and aseptic, appeared ostensibly pleasing but was in fact incapable of embracing monstrosity. This was certainly the obverse side of the same alienating world into which I had been hurled, and maybe

its most sinister dimension.

In all likelihood every stone had been sealed with an invisible plastic film to avoid further deterioration. In this absolutely fixed and apparently safe world men and women played their traditional roles. Street demonstrations and gatherings were promoted in order to exorcise all acts of violence and torture. Obviously orchestrated by political or religious authorities, these artificial processions appeared like an empty mimicry failing to reveal a transcendental order in the gestures of ritual.

Beyond the gridded screen had materialized a city in anamorphosis. The privileged position from which the fragmented and abstracted ordinary vision of form could have access to meaning had been displaced to an inaccessible realm. The geometric appearance of the city was incapable of revealing the totality of a world in transformation. Its perspectival distortions were destined to remain incomprehensible, forever concealing the approach to a universal order. There were here no decaying ruins or images of death; all references to primal scenes were excluded. The cemetery perhaps existed in drawings and paintings in the museum, significantly alluding to the cultural traditions of the city, but the structure could not be built in the same style without losing its meaning: recycling of cadavers appeared as a more authentic option than the monumental tomb.

Also striking was the absolute transparency and fixity of forms that could not carry meanings beyond their given scales. No metonymy was possible: eggs could not be put out, and eyes could not be broken. A sphere with the consistency of a soft-boiled egg, the glossy quality of an eye, and the pearly coloring of raw testicles remained only a sphere. The architecture of objects, reliquaries, and miniatures was here out of the question because the secret, visceral identity of objects could not be perceived. All machines in this world were truly neutral and frozen, grasped solely in terms of their inherent mechanistic logic and therefore suitably hidden behind hypocritical facades, in fact reminiscent of Walt Disney World.

For shelter there were efficient, comfortable and even elegant buildings. Most likely the city was ecologically appropriate, politically ideal and socially equitable.

Land values were seemingly not the product of speculation or capitalistic interests. A better quality of life from the material standpoint of a rational democracy could hardly have been conceived. Despite all this, the absence of architecture was shocking.

Time elapsed and I begged to be relieved from my misery. The obsessive accuracy of this formal historicism was profoundly disturbing: a repulsive panoramic vision of cultural doom. The whole distressing experience finally led me to question my very reason for being and my mission as a jetwoman, together with the technological, humanistic, and ecological determinations of destiny to which I had devoted my existence with such vehemence.

246

FILLED WITH ANGUISH, I called for my nurse, who responded in a soft voice. I was sweating in my bed, the sheets humid with tears, my wet nightgown stuck to my stomach and my hair totally disheveled. I felt more dead than alive, convinced that existence had no value. My nurse listened patiently to the story of my strangely dualistic nightmare. She knew that I had devoted my life to technological destiny as a result of having been spared from giving birth to a hermaphrodite child. Her unexpectedly wise and forthcoming advice was to renounce my profession and seek love through incarnation. She said:

"The technological world is strong and tyrannical . . . but desire cannot be beaten. The ORDER of things is the order of THINGS. Ignoring the importance of desire whole civilizations have perished, precipitating their own massacre. Love can ultimately not be resisted. Like death, it is unbeatable, but it must take over all our actions and perceptions or else the flesh of the world may die first, bringing about the dreaded collective apocalypse. Love is the price we must pay to have harmonious cities like your splendid body, living cities filled with tombs and aedicules, anamorphoses and perennial ambiguities. And only such places embodying simultaneously harmony and monstrosity, order and confusion, light and shadow, disclosure and

concealment, not as polar opposites but as aspects of the same reality, are the proper ground for human culture.

Your flesh is also the flesh of the world, and love in the flesh is the sole alternative possible to gain an understanding of human order. You have been created beautiful and charming: metaphysical oval face revealed behind the thinnest layers of clarity, veils that do not conceal. Delicate and graceful figure that illuminates, small feet that walk on a cushion of air. In view of your noble lineage and temperament, you seem better disposed to serve Venus than Diana. Knowledge is always here and now. Do not let this moment pass, you may find one day the extinction of your futile passion for power and domination. Devoted exclusively to yourself, deep in the cult of your own individuality, you will eventually sink into despair, ending your life isolated and without aim."

My nurse concluded her speech insisting that love should guide all our actions, particularly in order to make what one loves. Neither passivity, sighs, and tears nor a domineering will-to-power would do. She emphasized that love is a kind of active feminine making, a compassion that lets things be, beyond the dualistic alternatives of action and passivity; an intuition deeply ingrained in the soul of women that would engender the unnamed order of the future in an act of creation that should invariably be implemented at the right and propitious time and place. She sent me on my way back to Polyphilo, repeating for the last time that my vision and personal knowledge through love were indispensable to avoid the demise of the world . . .

247

IN THE SUITCASE, not far from the pulsating sphere, is a pair of heavy insulated pliers, useful to radically interrupt any annoying or threatening electrical supply. Fall has finally arrived. It is past midnight, and regardless of the vessel's seemingly unperturbed geohistorical position, we can presumably expect the further materialization of phantasms.

AS DAWN BROKE *revealing the embracing figure of the horizon, the last words of apocalyptic wisdom uttered by my nurse found their way into my consciousness. Darkness was still dissipating, together with the evanescent fogs of the somber night of prehistory; light was about to triumph over our inveterate nightmares of thunder and unreason. Golden rays shone behind the objects of the world, converging toward a single point two fingers above the horizon. Sublime moment, I thought, when we can concentrate our glances and look onto the incandescent sphere, now and forever.*

The light projected to the confines of my room also delineated the limits of my solitude. The macabre nightmare of my damnation had finally led me to question the consequences of my rebellion against love, and I became absorbed in a profound reflection on my condition as a rational being. On my body surfaced a faint evocation of Polyphilo, while my flesh trembled in fear at the recollection of both the combats of love and its absence, remembering the unending struggle of humanity and the inevitability of death, the eternal contradiction of our human condition: the fragile vibration of the spider web and the weeds singing in the wind.

The flickering light was always changing, new yet always the same. The flame of the candle penetrated everywhere and infested my being. This was an exiguous and quiet flame, incapable of tearing the veils but all the more powerful in the empty space . . . If the continuity of the human experience allows us to recover the traces of the past, if our collective memory makes it possible to grasp the poetic sense of fire, always novel and pregnant with meaning, one should at least acknowledge the possibility of metempsychosis!

Engulfed by this punctual light I had a vision of Polyphilo resting breathless where I had abandoned him. I was overwhelmed. A strange feeling of guilt such as I had never experienced incited me to return to my origins and to recognize my responsibility for Polyphilo's death and for the degeneration of my own coherence. I decided at last to go back to the site of the violent demiurgic act, the locus of the

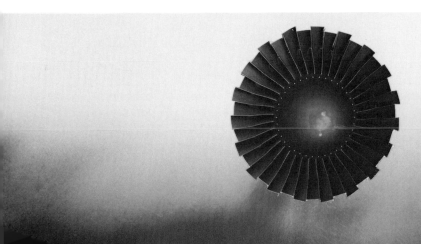

coordinates in space-time where the place had been created and the ground had already started to appear.

IT WAS NO LONGER possible to move frontally. I glided laterally on successive parallel planes, drifting on their surface until I fell through accidentally onto the next plane, always face to face with an extensive hexagonal field divided into smaller squares and triangles, projected and built up. This flattened structure might have been the deconstructed cockpit or the collapsed universe, but certainly not the biblical Babel. The horizon was not visible. Through the homogeneous space of each hexagon I could see, interminably, the undifferentiated upper and lower floors. The exploding metal structure consisted of three large, glass spaces devoted to universal electronic communications and ubiquity. The glass enclosures were separated by double partitions capable of withstanding a vacuum.

Like a spiraling tower, the place disclosed its internal structure and the mechanical forces of torsion that oriented its upper cylinder toward the sun during its daily revolution. The bottom cube rotated imperceptibly, perhaps once a year while the middle pyramid may have taken one month to turn on its axis. Due to its complexity, the structure seemed to contain an indefinite number of hexagonal galleries. To the left and to the right of the hallway between each gallery were two undersized rooms; one was a toilet and the other could have been for storage, or perhaps for vertical sleeping or entombment. The overwhelming presence of mirrors suggested that the field was not infinite.

I penetrated the harmonious order of intricate geometries and traversed several thresholds. The first appeared as an organic formation devoid of joints, reminiscent of our privy parts and the gates of hell; the very structure of the cosmos at a reduced scale. Under the second threshold I realized that the true source of wisdom about things was their geometrical essence, their name and their number, always inscribed in human flesh. In a finite and corruptible universe like ours the finest things are harmony and beauty, all of which are brought about by love in the spellbinding

250

objects that we make. Under the third threshold it became evident that this architecture was powerful because its revelation conveyed wisdom, the translation of the Book in all languages and none into marks gathering and condensing all that could be said in each language.

Perhaps the origin of earthquakes could no longer be attributed to a concourse of the dead nor the echo resounding in our ears to the thundering voice of mightier beings; perhaps the rainbow was nothing but white light . . . Yet the cockpit in its transformed state appeared truly awesome, and I perceived myself as the source of erotic desire for having bared my feet and nothing more. Enveloped in music, I fell to the bottom of the tower and came to find Polyphilo.

ON A PERFECTLY WHITE tapering rectangle, reminiscent of a lid for a box of shadows, lay Polyphilo dead. Intersecting manifold planes of circles and right angles receded and projected forward: white on white, cold and livid. Polyphilo's silence pervaded the place, and I was at first overtaken by fear. I understood that the immense void emanating from him, the waxen cold that shrouded his body, was the result of my intransigence. The phantasm of his death started to haunt me and his muteness became unbearable. His obsessive insistence had obliged me to ignore him in order to maintain my chastity and my vows to the profession. Now his absence made him even more intensely present, and for the first time I could see him in all his purity, totally free from masks or ambivalent intentions. I recognized the extent to which he had infiltrated my being and become part of my own flesh.

Desperate I leaned over him, offering my soul to reanimate his being, hoping that my own warmth might rekindle the vital flame in his inert body. I took his head between my hands to implore his forgiveness, and as I came close to him, the lines, surfaces, and volumes of the construction were projected outward in harmonic and rhythmic ratios. I caressed his body, anxiously trying to revive his idle senses. Despite his unchanging immobility I could feel the pores of his skin opening under the magnetism of my fingers. The lines of construction surrounded us with a woven

251

fabric, both material and nonmaterial, an aggregate of percussive moments that in varying degrees contributed to the wholeness of the impression. I finally realized the importance of this harmony beyond the specificity of the senses for a potential culture of the future.

Since the slightest sensorial variation was now amplified by a perceptual consciousness free of all disruptive expectations, the visual phenomena no longer blinded the other senses. I may have closed my eyes . . . The place was transformed into a materialized pure feeling, the place of human dwelling: a desert filled with the sensation of nonobjective belonging pervading it all. The apex of the finite visual cone of perspective was finally extended to infinity, breaking through the blue lampshade of the heavens to attain the whole spectrum: WHITE.

Embodying my caring gestures in its objective and universal forms, the projective construction continued to embrace us. The total absence of arbitrary form was the spatial embodiment of an overwhelming sense of joy and relief. The pure white square, infinitely extensible in depth and foreground, had become a cube with a large black circle embedded off center, close to the upper left-hand corner on one of its faces. The actual cockpit, the place of the oracle, was becoming a symbolic construction as it was polarized by erotic intentionality. While the technological homogenization of language would surely fail to bring about the brotherhood of humanity, this construction demonstrated the pentecostal reconciliation brought about by architecture: Either one must acknowledge the inalienable meaning of poetic construction beyond cultural differences or one must recognize that there is nothing else to say . . .

Polyphilo's body was now peacefully at rest, and his face radiated the serenity of perfect abandon. I danced around him, projecting on his inert soul the essence of my amorous desire through oblique and helicoidal gestures. I had initiated a ritual that would demand as a final sacrifice my total abandonment to him. Suddenly an irate group of uniformed colleagues, whom I had all but forgotten, irrupted into the cockpit and condemned my actions. The implicit profanation of my professional vows had obviously disturbed them. Noisily they recited the values most recently broadcast on radio and television, reminding me about trade secrets that were supposedly in the interests of society, the economy, lower liability and life insurance premiums,

old-age security, my psychic sanity, and the efficient workings of the police state . . . I was not convinced by their argument, being aware of the consequences of grounding my resolutions and determinations in the ultimate delusion: simulations were indeed distinct from reality, and the real was irreducible.

Calm and poised, I continued my dance around Polyphilo, whose soul started to emit a luminosity that soon enveloped me. My body, still chaste, was unavoidably attracted by the aroma of his exaltation. I refrained myself until an intense pain gripped my most secret parts. The torture became unbearable, and I understood the reciprocity beyond all familiar dualities: by means of a mysterious transmutation my body would be able to penetrate his, reviving the flame that had to be rekindled. When our flesh finally fused, the fire that I wished to inspire in him swelled within me and ascended vertically, seeking to escape through the crown of my head. The air became liquid and the shadows translucent, and our bodies were projected into the eternal present of a geometrized infinity. The final coincidence of one bodily threshold with inner and outer space! To dwell and to make fire, to give form to a new mode of architecture! Nothing remained but the primal order of rhythmic heartbeat and the void carried over from the plane into space. Nothing else.

Amid shadows I still recognized the short, familiar looking bearded man with a horizontal neck followed by his college of aviators, screaming and yelling obscene charges. These disgruntled false priests of academia with indoctrinated verbal brains incessantly repeated the incoherent demands of the profession! Outraged by my irreverent attitude, they wished to expel us from the wonderful place, only to find that we had already left, intertwined, and that the coordinates of the site once again indicated the spot where the plane had disappeared from the sky, the epicenter of the nuclear explosion.

253

VERY CLOSE TOGETHER, Polyphilo and I started on our way home. I had recognized our fusion as the ground of order, yet our journe᷈ back to the public place at the center of the city was uncertain and could be protr᷈ted. The end was obviously approaching and with it, the darkness. I remained in the suburbs while

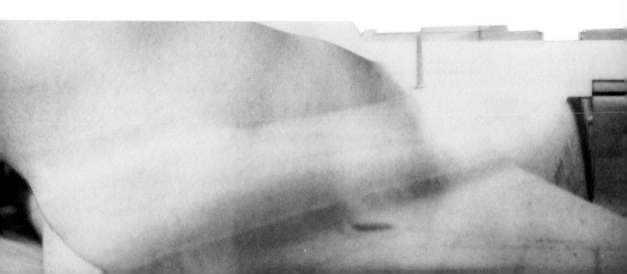

Polyphilo continued his eccentric wandering, and thus we were eternally paired, like Hermes and Hestia.

Back home I retired into the solitude of my quiet bedroom and started to relish the intensity of countless sensations amplified by a silence such as I had never heard before. Superimposed upon the same world, where until then I had only been a distant and objective observer, I discovered a new sensuous universe. Like a fallen angel, I was stricken by the unsuspected depth of my experience of reality. For the first time my sense of smell was assaulted by the presence of the living city. I could taste the scent of fresh bread and black coffee and savor the dancing steam and the warm cup in my hands. The vortex of life and sensations secreted by this city overwhelmed me. It was difficult to believe that this was the same city of my childhood.

This metropolis of abstracted orders and mechanistic logic could now become the authentic city of the future, pregnant with imagery like an inextricable puzzle of constructivist architectural visions: a city of emotion materialized in paleolithic tectiforms of ambivalent scale. I could sense the symbolic resonance of these urban menhirs, the same poetic power of an art object. Other archetypal structures, like black and white suprematist skyscrapers and horizontal plaster architectons, translated a new reconstituted order. The loss of color revealed the energy of architectural essences, absorbing and reflecting light. These structures could have been new machines devoid of wheels, steam or fuel. The real imaginary context of these objects allowed them to operate in real cosmic space rather than in mathematical multidimensional spaces that cannot be visualized or represented. The truth was disclosed exclusively in concrete abstraction, regardless of function or practical purpose. I thought only about Polyphilo. Every artifact and building reminded me of him, and all became sweet and warm and subjected to the delights of a transgression. All around, it could only be him.

Alone I sat waiting by my window, experiencing the identity of thinking and action. The edge condition that limited my horizon no longer included a night table with a pitcher of water; the objects had been released from the tyranny of linear perspective. The limit was rather the square of the dusty windowpane onto which the city beyond had projected its geometric essence as a filmic montage, threatening

254

to become opaque and eventually totally dark: the black square on a cast plaster cube that could not be penetrated frontally, heralding the demise of painting and hopefully the beginning of a novel architecture, in the plane and in space. The square window was divided into harmonious smaller rectangles and squares through the golden section method of Hambidge. One panel contained compasses. Anthropomorphic compasses with straight and curved legs rested on wooden panels as well. These generated geometric tracings, particularly the pentagon: compasses constructing structures, spelling the name of the architect, and creating a frightening nature of mutants, explicit and camouflaged, and serpents behind bars. A few panels were covered with flat blue, one with clouds and some shooting stars and another criss-crossed by a web of electric lines. A fragment of the Eiffel Tower was engulfed by a fulgent yellow background: anthropomorphic arches, hinges and V-shaped monuments. The Empire State Building stood side by side a candle about to fall and set the world ablaze. The sun was being chased away by a more potent fire, a blindfolded god with a lit torch attempting to obliterate fire with fire. The black square was separated into two equal rectangles that overlapped to form a cross, which in turn rotated to constitute a black circle. On the floor of my room the wax had spilled, and I became convinced that I should keep waiting and pursue a life of total voluptuousness.

255

BEHIND THE COCKPIT'S double pressurized window the sun was chasing away the moon. It was early morning. I took off the remainder of my uniform signifying a final decision to relinquish my chastity. I was now devoted to Polyphilo, the lover of All. He had been present throughout my ordeal and was startled by the final revelation of my identity. He no longer saw me as a disembodied spirit devoid of gender but as the ungraspable projection of feminine nature, enticing and inaccessible, offered through the perfection of a plastic golem behind the heavy wooden door and reflected on the large glass, naked and stretched on a natural bed.

Wearing Levi's overalls and a bright T-shirt, I was overcome with tenderness and

desire. I had finally realized that love was not biological procreation, that a desire conducive to liberation necessitated the detachment of the body from its reproductive obligations. I also understood that this physical liberation devoid of an aspiration for authentic love would inevitably lead to the incoherence of a homogeneous universe and to the impossibility of ritual. Conscious of the ambiguity and extremely delicate balance between two extreme positions, I swallowed the synthetic food that would make me physically infertile but a true lover: the bread of communion. I could now believe that this technological nourishment of universal taste might eventually allow all mankind to appreciate an irreducible order in the richness and subtlety of cultural differences embodied in the taste of locally baked breads . . . Just before I definitively exited at the top of the world, my heart was pierced.

BEFORE DESTINY finally said the last word, fusing our flesh forever in incandescent harmony, our dancing bodies intertwined violently, transgressing, dwelling in our reciprocal intimacy, the inner space amid clouds . . .

256

POLYPHILO THEN SPOKE, defining life as a struggle and a constant search for order. He praised perseverance as the only guide to success once man identifies an authentic goal and the daily battle that endows actions with meaning. He now celebrated my initial reluctance to easily concede my favors and proceeded to tell once more the story that I am now telling:

"The sun was rising, drying up the fresh tears of Aurora. New green and gold in the earth and sky. Always new. I had come to the airport not expecting to find the young woman whom I had first seen at the corner diner and ever since loved, through the window, until her mysterious disappearance. On that occasion, by a strange coincidence, she was there. Among uniformed jetmen, she prepared for a

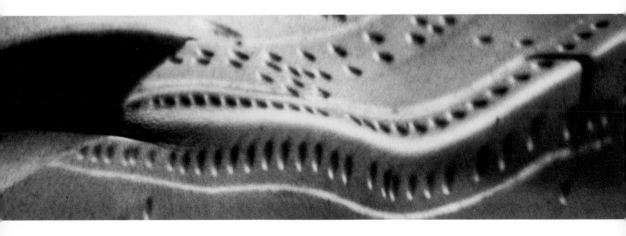

training flight in the stratosphere. Dressed in her silvery suit and holding a shining helmet, like an angel, she instantly rekindled the old fire that had apparently been extinguished in my heart. Her eyes seemed brighter than the sun, and I became a victim of uncontrollable cupidity, like dripping, softened wax. My senses took delight in her universal beauty, visible and invisible, well known by all. Her countenance and her voice heralded the arrival of a new matriarchal age. Transported beyond my limits, I felt my life breath abandoning its dwelling place; I was ready to die beside her as soon as possible. I knew that in my heart I carried only her altar, no other god or simulation. In the corner of my icons the black square hung alone. Through Polya I would be reborn, and she would surely restore me by her domination!

I was of course unable to let her know my feelings. The night was about to arrive, and I uttered a faint good-bye while she vanished with a few of her colleagues behind the door of a supersonic orbiting plane. My bitter tears and deep anguish transfigured her golden braids into horns, and her sweet voice became the sound of thunder. In a few seconds my sight was gone, obliterated by the violent irradiation of the takeoff.

The mighty projection of the mechanism into space was an astounding and unequaled celebration of the demiurgic power of man over nature and of the possibility of self-referential orders. An explosion? The initial stage of the rocket? The overwhelmed spectators could not tell the difference between glory and doom: the transparent order of mankind in the projection of an exploding abstract trace, the utterly precise and surprising geometry of destiny's scientifically calculated trajectory.

Video replay, over and over. I felt uneasy about having thought evil about her, even though I had been abandoned facing a seductive but ultimately undecipherable mark. My voluptuousness turned to pain. O splendid light within my blindness! The cosmos definitely did not emerge from consciousness, and the abstract orders created by man ran the risk of exposure as nonsense.

Not knowing Polya's exact coordinates, my despair did not abate. As a last recourse I attempted writing to her on several occasions, hoping to soften the hard concretions that had apparently formed around her heart. Was it all the result of

her antigravity training and her ability to inhabit the vacuum? The sphere was a last recourse and would only roll if pushed."

The feminine electronic speech now fades behind static noise . . .

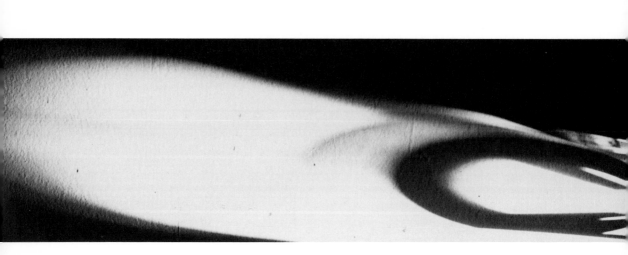

Julianehab, Greenland, June 21

Dear Polya,

I write. Orthographic signs, how many? Recombining twenty-six. Two more than the hours of the deity? No light in this vision. Only the opaque ciphers of language ordered at random. There is no symbolism before man speaks, but the power of language is grounded much deeper. Marks on rocks and the dazing calligraphy of equations that obsessively pretend to explain the workings of the universe and the unfathomable genetic designs of viruses. All referring back to the redness of my blood, the uncontrollable rhythm of my heartbeat, and the tones and gestures of my speech. The shadows of these letters, sediments of the burning thunderbolt, embody all architecture within the walls of my room. Through the models of infinitely variable scale I long for you, sitting at my draftsman's desk, enclosed by the bubble of candlelight.

I write LOVE. This word, abused and corrupted but ultimately the irreducible and only idea capable of reconciling every man, momentarily or not, with the idea of LIFE. Our incarnated truth.

I write to reveal the flame that envelops my loving heart. Should it be kept forever in a canopic jar, placed in the darkest corner of the funereal chamber, together with the androgynous foetus and the intestines of ancient dogs? It is crucial to remember that the very prolonged and narrow gateway is open to receive the sun's spermatozoa, impelled toward violent impregnation through the absolute and oppressive silence of the Valley of Death, beyond the ancillary vaults for six awaiting predators and the cosmic pit that reaches the stars of heaven and earth.

With tears and a tormented heart, I implore you. Don't be deaf to my passion. Death is not a quiet liberation of the soul, it is vomit and convulsion. Amid the mutilated classical sculptures in the park and behind the red curtain of the arcaded door in the palace square I can hear the bloody screams. The absurd unreality of serene death is like a bird that sings by candlelight: black birds have the fire in their eyes. While a golden nocturnal sun homogenizes the walls along the Neva, its liquid exploding reflections shed a fluid metaphysical light on the city, extending loneliness and despair into every cubicle through geometric webs of scintillating canals. White summer nights, white winter days. Always blazing white! Light reflected off the river at the core of nothing, like the milk of the moon. In the darkest corner of my *profound silence is a compressed space of unbounded dimensions. Beyond the constricted and miasmic alleys and seemingly endless rectilinear prospect and under the hard, blistery skin: a white curtain, the skin soft and perfumed, the bird, the legs, total silence, and infinite pleasure. The absurd unreality of serene death!*

I am in your hands. Love me or help me die in peace. Let at least the candles that flank my coffin burn through the eternal night. The day around this monastic church whose proportions are those of a tomb only discloses the indisputable presence of nothingness. No more sinister facades with two symmetrical eyes and a wide open door contemplating the nudity of the virgin! This is perhaps the truth of Cathar. Squares, parallelepipeds, and cubes of many sizes, an asymmetrical cross, a red confessional, altars with no congregation, and the menacing flat roof resembling a lid about to close that would obliterate the thin clerestory window. Black!

Sweet hope, I will love you always, dead or alive. Your eyes are constellations staring within my empty chest, like the orifices on pig Cupid's snout, flickering mucous membranes under the bubble of candlelight. I love you as no lover has ever loved a woman, as I imagine Saint George loved the dragon to cause the colorful fusion of its bones, scales, and entrails in a living dwelling not far from the Mediterranean. Protected by his shiny black armor, the saint with curly, golden hair rides on a superb horse and thrusts his spear at the beast, pushing it deep inside its mouth. In the field of battle are strewn mutilated and rotting cadavers and pale bones; hands and legs lie between frogs, snails, and other infernal animals. Meanwhile, the wind stuffs the scum of the wide, noisy street up my nostrils. The bird, exhilarated, continues its flight toward the night, never reaching . . . Adieu!

THE VOICE EMERGING through the electronic earphones has changed pitch, like a record rotating at a different speed. *From within my head?* It had probably started to transmute many hours ago but is only now clearly noticeable. Projecting an unquestionably androgynous hue, the ubiquitous lover explains that the first clumsy and confusing letter, written in the grip of blinding passion, had no effect whatsoever. Incessantly pursuing his constant wandering, he wrote twice more from other enchanted regions of the world where he had found the presence of love's order . . .

Uranium City, Saskatchewan, June 21

Dear Polya,

Torture only breeds patience and character, my little virgin. In the northern city where architecture is the mask of buildings but masques have never been staged, where everyone waits perennially and edifices constantly reveal intimate gestures, the inhabitants exchange childish embraces and kisses in an endless performance of astounding mimicry. Life here is the absolute synonym of love. There the universe is early morning strawberries and midnight dill, not a colorless onion to disrobe, releasing a disheartening odor. In the heart of this northern city I can also wait, enveloped by the freezing sensuality of the sauna, enclosed by the walk-in ice box at the vertical axis of the cubist-Japanese villa cum guitar, where timid spectators become actors again, playing Man, Woman, Desire, and Suspicion in a plot of humid carnage, all drawing the inseparable delight, while the burning flesh is purified and the icy water traps the soul inside.

Your cruelty, dear Polya, seems greater than my strength. Will I ever convince you with my enticing words? You are like the tense Aphrodite, incandescent marble goddess amid glistening olives, very erect cypress trees in ordered clusters, and a few Corinthian maidens. With her sensuous torso arched gracefully backward and up, Aphrodite embodies the precise posture of offering and denying love: an overwhelming vision of the uncertainty that hinges on the foundations of a silken, round abdomen and the concealed sacred triangle. Your heart is colder than ice crystals or a salamander. Love, however, cares not, and the fire burns on. Little tongues, candle ends, will eventually light your adolescent mind and irrigate the innermost places.

Despite your savage resistance, I cannot escape this love—even if it means that when two or three are finally welded together they may tumble, identical and depersonalized, into the terrific Nirvana. I realize this while imprisoned in the sacred private chamber where man talks to himself, surrounded by embracing stone couples in untold obscene poses, recipes for pleasure, disclosing the idea of moksha, only broken at the time of the division of the eight Purushas. The understanding of these Purushas and their separation is indispensable to overcoming the tribulations of our world. Witness the epitome of arrested motion at the Black Pagoda, the manifestation of being enduring the instant of penetration! Countless bodies fused in an orgy of melting flesh that is not necessarily a cosmic procreation, under the beneficial rays of the sun. In unison sings here the flesh of the world. The timid spectators become

261

participants once more. Polya, lend me your favors, let my words into your heart! Remember that robbers have attempted to take away the Purusha's bones, mistaking them for something else.

I am your humble servant. Allow me to create a cult for you, my goddess. Possibly under the clock tower where Bernard admonished the Sienese women and asked them to abandon their licentious habits, on the red, fan-shaped square inlaid with lines of light gray stone forming triangular sectors. Under the letter V of the clock needles, where the lines come together but there is no perspective, I offer the nascent virginity of myself to you—but no. No love, not even the impact of electrified bodies knocking sparks off one another in chaos. Only the incomparably vertical shadow of the tower into which I fall and return to my unfulfilled desire.

Possessing universal beauty, as you do, you must have some compassion in your heart. The living stones of Venice have made me understand that regardless of how much I search for and how much I find, I must learn to be alone with myself. Through the window it is always the same padded, rancid, red velvet stall facing a dazzling tablecloth in any restaurant, empty and silent for a whole day. I need you like the most beautiful poem of intersecting alleys, campos, rounded bridges, and canals needs the nucleus of nothing, the inconceivable concept contained in our ephemeral conjunction, flowing from the abundance of presence to the irresolvable absence. Without this I shall become an irrelevant museum under the bubble of candlelight, a residue of human debris, an object for the sterile consumption of tourists and voyeurs.

Dear Polya, help me and save me! Don't be mad or indifferent. Remaining inviolate in your process of utter crystallization will only bring about catastrophe. You are not just the other side of my ego: breath-giving, clear carving space; drinkable fresh water; absorbable levitating substance in recaptured cyclical pulses of light. Let me be eternally at your service. Adieu!

PLEASE RESTRAIN your impatience. *I know well that time is running out. But I wanted to persuade myself about the importance of perseverance. I had to write again, despite the failure of my previous epistles to touch you in any way . . .*

Magadan, Russia, June 21

Dear Polya,

Language, my goddess, is coming to an end. My words have failed, we are back to making marks on rocks.

> *We're all in the dumps*
> *tatatatata,*
> *tatatatatatatata,*
> *tatatatata,*
> *tatatatata*
> *tatatatatatatata*

Perhaps I should simply add that both my unbearable pain and my love for you keep on growing. Architecture of divine ancestry! To serve you and to be your slave is all I wish. My procreative truth has often petered out in pestilent tear drops, and my voice has been abruptly silenced by your cruel indifference: houses are built without walls. I know that in darkness the stars will stare and the moon will no longer bleach my pain. You will realize that love must be reciprocal. The secret properties of the triangle, point downward, will be disclosed. If the three sides of any triangle are extended to infinity in the six directions possible, the result is a plane. In that infinite plane the three apices of the triangle lie on a circle that wholly contains the triangle, and thus the finite is subsumed by infinity. There is no option. If you are loved you must love or accept the inevitability of the final cataclysm. Adieu!

263

PROTRACTED WAITING and no answer. In the innermost recesses of my mind, I tried to think of more sweet and flattering words to utter, hopefully in her presence. I imagined trying to compose a passionate diatribe that might convey to her the virtues of carefully making fire. Inevitably, but with some embarrassment, I could only conjure up objects that referred to herself as a sign of the erotic . . .

If I could slit axially your glimmering nylon cocoon with a single stroke of my X-Acto knife! Parting the two edges of material, I would fold back both flaps and verify the absence of underwear, apart from a triangular mask of satin the color of apricots; the firmness of your young breasts, perfect hemispheres; and lastly the uniform tan of your skin, which is remarkably fine, delicate, and soft. With two more clinical motions of the expert knife, following a trajectory toward the top of the groin, I would remove the fine garment superimposed on a perfect triangular fleece, as pale as straw, so transparent that it reveals the blinding darkness of your porcelain fissure.

Polya was more unyielding than Icarus, the son of the architect. She persisted in her flight, and my words were to no avail. However convinced as I was of the beauty of the fragments, I knew that order must eventually appear. The coming of darkness was imminent. In any case, the holograms could be shattered and still contain the whole in every fragment. If the parts were profoundly erotic, the infinite totality must be harmonious. Glossiness may have fallen into disrepute, but it often betrayed true quality. With the help of love, which held me firmly in its grip, I intended to overcome the barren horizon of my life.

I wandered and traveled until that important hour when I finally recognized Polya in the cockpit and spoke to her. My incoherent words, uttered in the place of architecture, have already been transcribed, as well as the events that followed. No discourse would soften her heart, and I saw the termination of my day arriving. Death or the absolute liberation of the mind? The simple completion of my infructuous impulses?

Close to the end, I find myself back in Polya's arms. Resurrected? Dwelling at last in a place where every combination of lines, colors, and forms has a definite expression particular to this aerial structure and therefore never again to be translated into words, yet capable of yielding to my desire. The medium is unimportant; all materials are perfectly adjusted and free. Back home, lost in a passionate embrace, where the surrogate order of the candlelight bubble is no longer necessary. Back from the realm of darkness or not yet there?

WHILE THE VOICE FADES in echoes and reciprocal mirages, the cabin lights are turned off and everything is engulfed in shadows. The shades of the oval windows are also lowered and expectations grow. All earphones are still tuned to the correct channel. There must be approximately three hours left in the sphere's clockwork mechanism. *It is now time to keep quiet and witness a full recollection through my own projection on a window to the beyond.*

IMPRINTS ON THE SCREEN. Four, three, two, one.

Opening with a romantic burst of music played by a large symphonic orchestra. Chords usually associated with the endings of extremely emotional films. The credits show simple black letters over a gray field of about 80 percent. After the frameless title *Last Year . . .* by Alain Robbe-Grillet follow the names of the director, producer, actors, and technical staff. These are enclosed in still frames that become increasingly three-dimensional until, after the last credit, we see the frame as a cardboard box from below, as if held above the viewer's head.

The camera slowly rises and turns around the corrugated cardboard box, exploring its aerial perspectives and elevations, passing over a semitransparent vinyl sheet, black rubber tape of the kind used by electricians, about two meters of wire, and a small, very sharp pointed knife. On one side the box has been pierced with a rectangular observation window about fifteen centimeters from the top. The camera now proceeds toward the window, which has the same proportions as the frame on the screen, and enters the unlit box.

Parallel to the development of this image, the music has been transformed into a male voice:

> *Once again I walk, after an absence from this world. Back and*
> *filled with pleasure. Back in my body, my place of dwelling.*
> *Once again I walk down these corridors, through these halls,*
> *these galleries, in this structure from another century, this*
> *enormous, luxurious, lugubrious vessel. Through endless,*
> *silent corridors of clean, efficient shape, lined with extruded*
> *plastic moldings and comprising all lines, forms, and textures;*
> *all the geometries of desire in drawings and paintings and*
> *objects of wood, plaster, graphite, and metal carefully assem-*
> *bled and fitted together.*

The camera continues its straight, slow, and uniform movement through a dim gallery of which only one side is seen, lit by regularly spaced windows on the unseen side. There is no daylight, but the electric lights are off. The wall is explored in detail. On it hang many simple frames like those at the end of the credits containing paintings, drawings, and views of the city, which from the air resembles a French garden with geometric lawns and shrubbery clipped into cones and pyramids. There are also photographs of the vessel with its name S.S. *Labyrinth* clearly legible, and a shot of the same interior corridor gallery being traversed, showing particularly the diminishing perspective of the two partitions. Lastly, also framed, a theater poster depicting an abstract design of what is perhaps the trace of electrons, with a foreign, meaningless title and a superscript in large letters: TONIGHT ONLY . . .

Meanwhile the same male voice, neutral and monotonous, continues speaking the text:

> . . . *The sound of footsteps absorbed by carpets. No sound can be heard aboard this structure from another century, this enormous, luxurious, lugubrious vessel where endless corridors succeed silent, deserted corridors, punctuated by oval windows and mirrors and boxes framing geometric drawings, holograms, objects of plaster, metal, wood, or extruded plastic carefully assembled and fitted together. Silent corridors where the carpet absorbs all sound* . . .

The images that accompany this text do not necessarily correspond to the elements of the setting to which it refers. The photography in black and white has a constant silvery shine, a glossy varnished quality maintained throughout the film, even in the darker sections. Also constant is the smooth, floating motion of the camera. It is always evident that light and shadow are the main protagonists of the story.

The camera continues along the corridor, recording familiar images never before seen, behind the frames and on the mirrors. At the end of the gallery is a door, and the camera passes through it with the same continuous movement shot with a wide-angle lens; the salon is made to appear much larger than it actually is. It is a kind of theater, but not arranged in the customary manner. The faces are seen in profile and from behind, lit from the front, possibly by the very spectacle that the sitting men and women are watching.

The offscreen text continues to be read in a more theatrical tone:

> . . . *between models of infinitely variable scale, I was already waiting for you. Returning from very far away, I am now back in front of you, still waiting for the man with a horizontal neck who will no longer come, who no longer threatens to come, to separate us again, to tear you away from me. . . . Are you coming?*

After a silence, a woman's voice answers, measured and calm. It is the voice of the actress who will be seen shortly:

We must still wait a few hours. A few minutes.

Having reached the first row of spectators, the camera reviews the faces, aligned and frozen with attention, brightly illuminated by the light from the stage.

Suddenly, the shot changes to the stage itself, occupying the whole screen. Through the cockpit's windows the curving horizon can be clearly seen. Below lies the promised city, the earth of man appears like a fertile garden from the stratosphere; above, a vision of heaven. The stage thus recalls some of the prints in the corridor. The celestial city is represented on canvas with great precision, lying foursquare, its length the same as its breadth. The cardboard wall is simulated jasper while the city is made of artificial gold, transparent as glass. The foundations of the wall are adorned with every available fake jewel, and the twelve gates are each made of a single plastic pearl. There is no temple in the celestial city, nor sun or moon to shine upon it. The actor is seen rising amid the clouds, flying toward the night. In a grandiloquent voice, he says:

Once again I wander, homeless, in search of the promised fruit. Without knowledge or rest, forever proscribed from the dwelling of my body. . . . This city itself with its deserted streets, empty salons and silent corridors, through which I walked to meet you. . . . While I was already waiting for you, forever, and while I am still waiting as you again hesitate, perhaps, staring at the door of the garden.

A feminine voice is heard speaking into a resonant amplifier. Her voice echoes like thunder:

In a short time, two hours perhaps or two seconds, these discords will be resolved, and your love will be reciprocated.

The camera zooms in on a holographic bust floating in the clouds. It is an accurate, three-dimensional reproduction of the upper torso of a mannequin whose crystalline heart has been pierced by a golden arrow and has started to liquefy. The shot then changes abruptly to review the front row of spectators, including the heroine, a woman of beautiful but rather indistinct and hollow features. She is intensely absorbed in the action and the camera does not pause to observe her.

Offstage the voice of the actor is heard:

> *Having enjoyed the mystical and secret visions usually denied to mortals, I am back again between the walls of my body, assured of salvation, I return to the flesh forever, to celebrate the new reconciliation of content and form.*

Also offstage and coinciding with the end of the shot, the other male voice adds:

> *Beyond the empty corridor lies the city, like a geometric garden. Remember, indigenous inhabitant of my home, dame of the highest citadel of my spirit. Remember our past together between these walls covered with models, prints, and paintings. Are you coming?*

271

The shot changes back to the stage. There are now two actors facing the doorway, a woman in her early twenties and a man clearly over thirty. They occupy the lower central part of the stage in front of the curved windows; the cockpit now appears to have the proportions of an ancient temple. The actor is lying on a hard platform, similar to a bed, an altar, or perhaps a tomb. He seems to be in the process of regaining consciousness. She has her arms around him and appears to be uttering inaudible sweet words and filling him with amorous attention. The actress then says:

> *No, this hopeful ambition is without any purpose. . . . This whole story is already over now. It came to an end. . . . A few seconds more. It has come to a close.*

The actor responds:

> *. . . forever back, in this vessel with its abandoned corridors through which I walked to meet you, among engravings, prints, objects, and collages. I was already waiting for you and while I am still waiting for you, you hesitate perhaps, staring at the door of the garden.*

The actor and actress have remained motionless since their appearance on the screen. A familiar clockwork mechanism can be heard. The actress, without moving, declares:

And now . . . I am yours.

During the burst of applause from the invisible audience the curtain falls. It rises and falls twice more without the actors making a single gesture. The applause continues, violent and long, gradually transforming itself into the romantic music heard at the beginning of the credits.

The shot dissolves and the camera circulates around the audience, which now fills a brightly lit room, standing in groups of three or four. The hero and heroine are shown in diverse combinations. He is recognized by his voice, she only by her outstanding beauty. The camera recedes into the corrugated box, making the frame of the observation window totally explicit. In this manner we see fragments of the vessel and its contents, accompanied by calm music and lengthy, incoherent conversations about rape, murder, and romance.

The series of views of the vessel ends with the camera leaving behind the cardboard frame and coming to a stationary shot including, at the far left, a blurred closeup of a man's head cut by the screen and not facing the camera. It is the hero, barely identifiable from other characters. In the center of the screen is a wide corridor with rows of tall seats, and in the distance, through a doorway, a man and a woman in uniform stand arguing in low voices, surrounded by lit instrument panels.

The hero's head, in the foreground, turns in the direction of the cockpit. It is possible that he is looking at the couple, but there is no acknowledgment of eye contact. The words spoken by the couple become increasingly more intelligible. He is questioning her concern for what others think. She answers:

> *You know perfectly well . . . we are living side by side, you and I, like coffins laid side by side underground in a frozen garden.*

With these words the heroine starts walking toward the camera, leaving her companion behind. The man goes after her, and the camera rotates to keep them in sight as they turn in the foreground. More encounters follow, with the rhythm of water merging in a labyrinthine system of pipes. Fragments of phrases are heard offscreen:

> . . . Really, that seems impossible . . .

> . . . We've already met, long ago . . .

> . . . I don't remember very well, it must have been . . .

Two men in profile are seen observing a set of framed drawings for a masque, or a city, or the depiction of a geometric garden. The camera recedes again into the box, exposing the cardboard frame.

The shot changes suddenly to the salon of the vessel, brightly lit, as it was at the conclusion of the performance. Groups of passengers in conversation. In a darker corner the hero is opening a patent-leather suitcase with great concentration. He seems pleased to find everything in its place. We can recognize some clothes, a map, a clockwork mechanism, water-resistant rubber tape, and a small pointed tool, its sharp apex illuminated and photographed to appear like a bursting sphere.

The camera continues its slow rotation around groups of animated passengers. Becoming stationary, we hear more fragmented dialogue that does not correspond to the gestures of the characters on the screen:

> . . . Extraordinary!

> . . . Actually, it wasn't so extraordinary. He made it all up himself, knowing in advance with utter precision the consequence of his act . . .

Discreet laughter, followed by exclamations like:

> Oh well then, that explains everything. Yet . . .

A couple in the group framed in the stationary shot now walk slowly off the screen. The corridor can be seen receding into the upper right-hand corner. In the penumbra a solitary character examines the print of the city, embedded in the wall. He seems to be concentrating not on the drawing but on the frame itself. The shot is cut abruptly. Next, a barely distinguishable image of the city's aerial perspective is seen out of focus, framed by the observation window of the cardboard box, every crease and detail of which is clear in the darkness.

Emerging from indistinct conversation offscreen we hear the distant voice of a woman, possibly the heroine:

> . . . *and there is no way of escaping* . . .

The well-known voice of the hero repeats, in an echoing tone seemingly enclosed by a corrugated cardboard box:

> . . . *and there is no way of escaping* . . .

The camera shifts back to the salon, where the man in uniform, standing rigidly beside a table, is setting out cards or beads in the form of a tetractys. He is either plotting the course of the vessel or playing a game that will determine everyone's fate. The hero is seen from behind, facing him. The man says:

I can lose. But I always win . . .

While the camera moves backward, the corridor becomes recognizable, then the passenger seats. Offscreen the hero declares:

You are still the same. It is as if I had left you yesterday. . . .
You are still as beautiful . . .

Through the frame of the observation window the camera once again reviews fragments of the vessel, including drawings, collages, prints, and engravings. During these images, and without any obvious relation to what they represent, are heard, without apparent reason, either when a shot changes or in the middle of a shot, a random number of irritating noises like electronic bells, hydraulic mechanisms, water boiling, buzzers, and other distinct and implausible sounds that can be heard aboard an airplane.

The camera now advances beyond the frame. The heroine can be seen, waiting behind the doorway at the end of the corridor, exactly as the hero remembers having first met her. The noises have stopped. The hero's voice:

But you scarcely seem to remember.

The heroine turns her head quickly, as if she were trying to locate the source of the words just spoken. A brief shot of the city that resembles a geometric garden from above but actually consists of numerous structures prepared for a new masque, an unknown ritual.

The music is now atonal, broken, and incoherent. Percussive timbre. The camera surveys indiscriminately constructive details that may belong to the vessel, to the cardboard box, or to the mysterious objects carried on board. The film is shot from below, within and behind, as if the details were seen by an invisible voyeur. Then the camera appears to fly and rotate smoothly, examining the chosen object rendered visible by light, in the manner of documentary films on architecture.

The hero's voice, now more persuasive:

275

> *Yet you already know these extruded moldings, these oval windows and mirrors, these complex geometric projections, cast and carefully fitted together . . . the experience of collapsing perspective . . .*

The camera examines a triangular object from above. It is slowly lowered until it adopts the position of the spectator on the short side, facing the proscenium opening: the screen itself. Closeup on a shimmering metal sphere, surprisingly immobile on an inclined plexiglass plane that crosses the whole screen diagonally. The hero:

> *Hadn't you ever noticed this?*

The heroine replies:

> *I had never had such a thorough guide.*

The camera glides deliberately backward after registering the spherical reflections of a man and a woman. Now we can see them from behind, imperceptibly turned toward one another but facing the stage where the performance had taken place. Talking and dance music fill the air. Their dialogue continues:

> *There are a lot of other things to see here, if you want to . . .*

> *What a mysterious look. Why are you staring at me like that?*

> *You hardly seem to remember me.*

The camera moves backward and records a wide-angle shot of the brightly lit salon. At the climactic moment of a waltz the music and the shot are cut without warning. The camera seems to have turned around 180 degrees. A long pause followed by silence. Slowly the passengers are shown in their seats on one side of the aisle. Their faces are attentive, illuminated from the front by some sort of spectacle. The camera comes to rest on the hero, who has his suitcase open on his lap. The seat to his right is vacant. Now the ticking of the clockwork mechanism can be heard becoming louder. With the sharp, pointed tool that doubles as pliers he is carefully piercing a gelatinous sphere in order to introduce a piece of wire, perhaps electric wire. The hero's countenance is frozen but tense. A short stationary shot framed through the observation window suddenly shows the vessel from

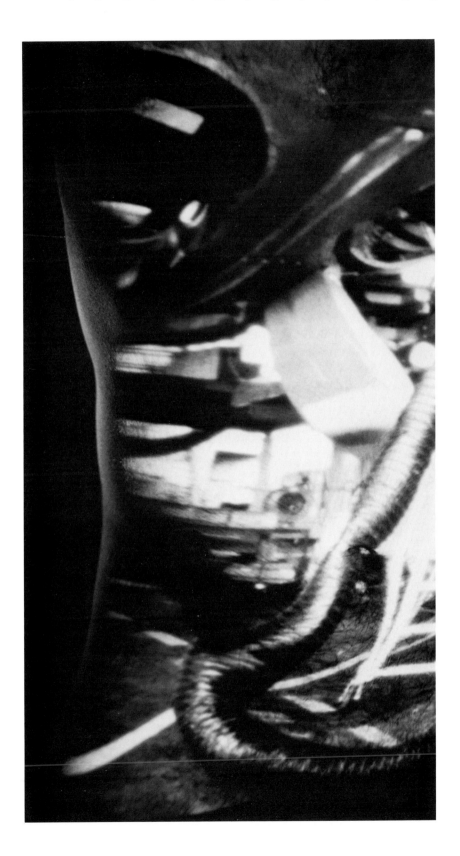

the outside, in suspended motion, exactly as it appears on a photograph in the gallery.

Once again the camera explores the corridor, and beyond the cockpit door the heroine waits while scrutinizing the sky, just as she was seen at the beginning of the film. She turns toward the camera and steps forward slightly. During this last sequence the hero's voice, offstage, has started to substitute the ticking:

> *The first time I saw you was on the corner of 48th Street and*
> *Third Avenue. You were alone at the point of perspective under*
> *the yellow artificial light, sitting a little apart from the others,*
> *behind a curved polished counter and a curved glass wall. You*
> *were facing a little to one side, toward the deserted street.*

The heroine remains motionless while the camera approaches her, at a slow and steady pace. The movement ends with a closeup of her face, unbelievably smooth and varnished. After bending her head slightly and smiling, she says politely:

> *I don't think I'm the person you mean. You must be making*
> *a mistake.*

> *Remember. Quite near us there was a fan-shaped square and*
> *a bronze figure. And a clock, certainly, on a tower. You asked*
> *me who that character was, and I answered that I didn't know.*
> *You made several suppositions, and I added that he could just*
> *as well be the architect who had devoted his life to studying*
> *biochemistry and mastering the secret of life. . . . Then you*
> *began laughing.*

The camera, having rotated behind the heroine, now reveals the silhouettes of a man and a woman surrounded by shadows and facing an enigmatic object, perhaps the stage on which is a door. Their heads are imperceptibly turned toward one another. He says:

> *I loved . . . I already loved . . . to hear you laugh.*

The shot changes abruptly to the table where the game was being played. The celebrated rectangular object of wood and plexiglass is seen from above. The beads, which appear to have assumed distinctly anthropomorphic features, are now in disorder, as if thrown at random over the map. The hero's voice, offscreen:

*And once again we were separated. . . . And once again I
found myself in this labyrinth, walking forward, alone, down
these same corridors and abandoned galleries, containing all
of the architecture of the imagination.*

A sequence of moving shots shows stationary characters, emphasizing
their individuality and an insurmountable loneliness surrounding them
resulting from the camera's movements and the motionlessness of the
passengers. Following a pause, the camera recedes into the box, and the
frame appears again. The hero's voice continues in a descriptive tone while
the camera discloses manifold airplane details, reflections, and spaces
within prints, models, drawings, and other architectural objects:

*Empty corridors, salons. Doors. Doors and thresholds. Empty
chairs. Stairs and steps. A crystal sphere that falls, three, two,
one, zero. Mirrors and suitcases. And the city, like everything
else, was empty.*

279

The camera shifts suddenly to examine the inside of the suitcase, which
now appears like an X-ray, the objects delineated with utmost precision.
This stationary shot is accompanied by atonal, percussive chords at irregular
intervals. Silence. The electronic footprint has an uncanny resemblance to
the poster for the stage performance that now comes into focus, crisscrossed
by complex geometrical projections. The sign still announces: Tonight
only . . .

But on this occasion the camera does not arrive at the cockpit. Having
taken another route, which cannot possibly be very different, the camera
reaches the inside of the box at the end of the gallery. This is a room of
ordinary size, a bedroom perhaps, the most unoriginal and familiar space.
The heroine is seated in the middle of a circle of empty chairs, reading a
large old folio from 1499. The camera slowly approaches her from the front.
The music fades and the hero's voice is heard, offscreen:

It was last year.

A silence. She keeps on reading, motionless.

*Have I changed so much then? Or are you pretending not to
recognize me? I shall now put on this mask, presumably
identical to my face, which will reveal to you my real identity.*

She directs her gaze away from the book and stares at the floor without moving, her expression remote. The heroine now looks exactly like Polya. The camera has come still closer and stops. He says:

> *A year already, or maybe more. You, at least, haven't changed . . .*

At these last words, she raises her eyes to the camera, which is at the eye level of a man standing up. A fiery light coming from an open observation window or a performance of some sort gives her a metaphysical radiance. It is, indeed, the familiar face!

The camera revolves 180 degrees. Soon the screen is totally filled with a brilliant image that recalls the theater stage. The city is now a masque, a geometric garden like that appearing on the prints and drawings. Virtually without vegetation, containing towers, mazes, theaters, and shops, including one for the mask taker and other mythological structures. The landscape is empty, without a single living being. The frame has vanished and the camera, previously fixed, now follows a long and deliberate lateral movement.

The hero's voice:

> *Remember. Behind the chosen gate, at the threshold of this labyrinthine vessel that comprises all architecture . . .*

The camera finally stops on a distant character, the solitary player on the stage of the pantomime theater. At close range the setting is similar to that of the theater scene shown at the beginning of the film. She seems to be leaning against an invisible, curved polished counter, her arm half extended, in front of a curved glass wall. The distinguishable sound of male steps is heard and the actress turns toward the camera. From offscreen the hero speaks again:

> *I walked forward to reach you. But I stopped at a certain distance to behold you. You were turned toward me yet you didn't seem to see me. I told you that you looked so ALIVE.*

After the word alive, with a few seconds delay, the heroine smiles gradually, perhaps finally recognizing the hero. While his voice is still heard, the camera fades out and in, focusing on a familiar mannequin that soon dominates the center of the screen. The camera does not remain stationary. It turns, showing many unexpected aspects of the structures in the masque, uncannily similar to the models and drawings exhibited in the gallery.

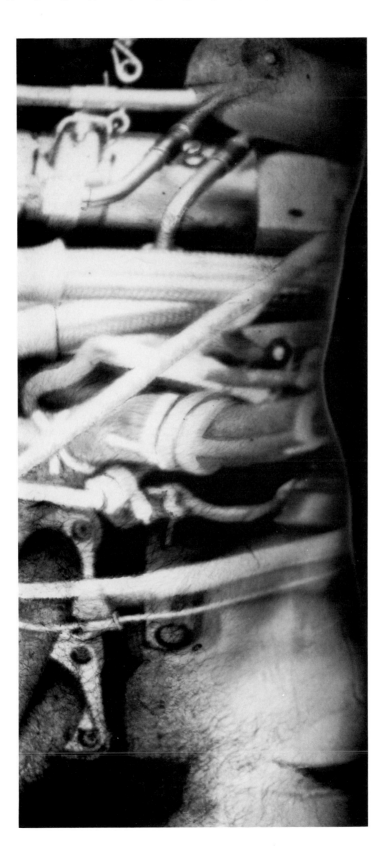

The hero speaks:

> *To say something, I talked about the mannequin and its an-*
> *drogynous offspring, and fire and earth, and the flesh. And*
> *you asked me the names of the characters, and I told you that*
> *it didn't matter. You insisted on giving them mythical names,*
> *like Medusa. Then I said that it could just as well be you and*
> *I . . . Or anyone. And I was back.*

After these last words a laugh rings out. The shot cuts unexpectedly to the hero and heroine in their new identities as actor and actress occupying center stage. She declares:

> *I am now yours.*

NOISE IN THE BACKGROUND, sporadic bells and buzzers, and Polya's voice declaring the conclusion of the story of her love: *My speech has been detailed. I hope not to have unduly extended your time. Just before sunrise I returned to the proverbial place and amid caresses and tears of repentance, Polyphilo resurrected in my arms. And here we are now on the island, in the final place of dwelling, on the edge of darkness.*

With these words the absent Polya finishes her prolific discourse. She has closed her lips and rests, perhaps finally trapped in the past, a prisoner of her own story . . .

THE FILM *is now in color and has become uncannily realistic. Or are we back on the island of eternal spring? The clock hasn't stopped, and it must be close to sunrise. The cabin is still dark, however, and the screen is no longer framed. Without stereoscopic lenses we can enter the city at once, hand in hand but not frontally.*

The ground and support of our organic bodies has finally exploded. It is now a compact and hard blue capable of reflecting even the purest things, like sapphire condensed in the hollow of our hands. The aerial images of my dream of flight at last approach the pole of crystallization. Evaporation will be the only other alternative. Crystals allow our imagination to dream vertically, up and down, overtaken by depth or exaltation.

Through the fragments of our bodies we burst in tangentially, along the projection screen or the mirror glass wall that encloses the masque, beyond the experience of threshold. Are you finally persuaded? This is your history that I invent at each moment, a story which is also mine. Even though time is apparently abolished in this labyrinth, I offer my lover a past and a future, and freedom. We are together at last. Or am I simply confusing two faces?

In section, but solely in section, this city is founded on the rubble and debris of torture cubicles, prison barracks, cloth made with human hair, gas chambers and crematoria. Thus, no souvenir stands selling postcards, ballpoint pens and soft drinks can be built here, no places for tourists to witness the vultures devouring Tibetan cadavers. The maddening unfolding of identical images multiplied forever has ceased. Instead, the inevitable foundation is the pristine order of two kinds of needles arranged in multiple patterns, vertical and horizontal. The long ones are for writing the unknown sentence on the backs of the strapped, naked prisoners and the short ones for spraying a jet of water to wash away the blood and keep the inscriptions clear.

THE MAN AND WOMAN penetrate, dancing lightly. In fragments, gestures of limbs and oriented motions of the senses. Tapping the horizontal plane in order to ascend, the two lovers are embraced by primordial rhythms: rites of fertility or the ultimate consecration of all time. *Raised on the points of my toes, standing at the highest place for a solitary spectator in the amphitheater of pantomime, I am light and free. A levitating heart and a joyful sight. I discover the exclusive reality of ascension, the real motion, which is no substance. Do you remember? The past and the future?*

Are you finally persuaded? In my strife for love I dreamed of being lost, thirsty, and alone in a threatening dark forest, something like the maze of hedges that we can now visit and should no longer mistake for a labyrinth.

Beyond the gates of steel is heard the music of Revueltas. *Or is it Stra-vinsky?* It pours out through the balcony of a circular wooden tower capped by a triangular umbrella. This is the dwelling of the architect and mask taker, the individual responsible for maintaining the life of the place and for inventing the participant's roles. This choreographer is a craftsman of the flesh interested in human space. He is evidently the creator of the triangles, circles, and squares that look like faces and constitute the masque, the quintessential figures held by the participants or worn by the buildings.

Before proceeding any further, the man and the woman stop at the gate and take their identities from him.

SEARCHING FOR YOU, long ago, I found myself in a site just like this, examining the ruins of pyramids, obelisks, and other great architecture from antiquity. I measured columns and noted the characteristics and ornament of their capitals, bases, and entablatures with their diverse architraves, friezes, and cornices and their respective moldings: the petrified spoils of a sacrifice meant to bring us together. Do you remember?

Today, though, an inventory of towers must be taken: a clock tower made of thirteen steel cubes with numbers from 12 to 12 and a square, blank surface in vertical motion, always concealing the number that names the propitious time. One typical New York City water tower, a wooden cylinder with a conical lid supported by a steel frame. A circular glass block tower topped by a leather mane that indicates the presence and direction of the wind, like the cock over the pinnacles of ancient structures, which also manifested the uncertainty of Fortune. A bell tower, ninety feet high, constructed of wood with steel ties. A public observation tower built of concrete and granite where only one person is admitted at a time. It is possible to take the elevator up this observation tower and then climb the spiral steel stair to the top, and maybe never come down!

I vividly remember the great winged horse, uncertain destiny, and the magnificent elephant carrying an obelisk. Now the cow, the chicken, the pig, and the horse are contained in standard farm barns. Are they also open for internal visits? Perhaps they enclose visceral spaces and mysterious sarcophagi as well, like the inner sanctum of the large colossus that today serves as a reliquary for the useless house with a living room, bedroom, kitchen, and bathroom, all locked behind closed doors that resemble funereal stones, strangely warm to the touch.

We pass under the glass block threshold in the direction of the silos, invariably seeking the way of ascension. As we cross, I recall the triumphal gateway of excellent craftsmanship and harmonic proportions behind which I became frightened, plunging

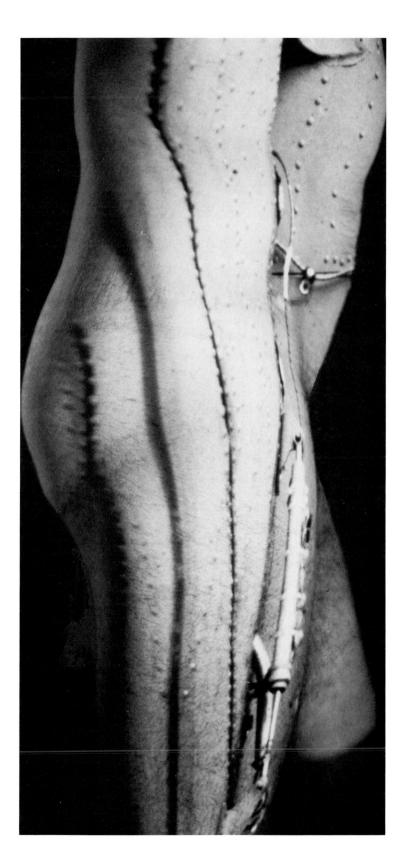

into darkness. Witness the awesome production of a fireworks display including Minotaur, Griffin, Gorgon, Unicorn, Chimera, Satyr, Dragon, Pegasus, and Basilisk!

They both enter the frightening tunnel, a corridor between plate glass and glass block surrounding an interior courtyard. Empty and inaccessible, the courtyard contains the ascending and descending silos, two circles in plan meeting at one point only. *Is this the impenetrable octagonal theater, sometimes sighted in the proximity of Venice, where no memories can be kept?*

After losing their bearings, the masked couple circumambulates the passage and exits through the same orifice, greeted by five mobile steel-plate shopping booths hovering on reflecting rails. Liquids are sold, ranging from pure water, perfume, and wine to acid, gasoline, and mirrors: water for the five senses. *I am reminded of the five nymphs whom I met when you were conspicuously absent, the gentle women that became my saviors and companions, taking me to admire lavish fountains and the munificent bath where I regained my energy following an aspersion of eau de vie . . .* The couple uses the public facilities, which are electronically activated for perfect hygiene. The man laughs after flushing the urinal by stepping away from it, while the woman plays at activating the soap dispenser and the water faucet several times, placing her hands under the photoelectric sensors and moving them haphazardly.

Reunited, the couple follows the moving structures on rails to meet the lottery woman encased in her mobile box with ten pneumatic tentacles. *I now recall the wonderful fountain of Venus Physizoa who is also the earth and the primordial mother, water spouting from her breasts, about to be covered by a lascivious satyr. Love is Fortune.*

A map blown out from one of the tubes provides a key to the city. The man contemplates the order of existence as it is revealed simultaneously at every scale, in the vivid present. The woman, in the meantime, focuses her gaze upon familiar objects and forces them to occupy the fourth dimension. *This must be the same map in my suitcase, the chart that allows me to fly and has led me to unravel the disorder of the world. I remember that it showed the way to you, after spending some time in the palace of a generous queen who embodied free will . . .* In the arbitration hall the couple participates in a symposium. A cacophony of philosophical speech reverberates within the reinforced concrete and steel, metal-clad structure. Medusa-like light wells, open to the weather, let in the azure and dissipate the now irrelevant words into the silent sky. Immediately following a splendid meal the couple is shown the three guest towers, the first made of reinforced concrete and faced with brick, the second of wood, and the third a triangular tower of steel-frame construction. *Thus I am reminded of the three extraordinary gardens that I once visited, the first made of glass, the second of silk, and the third the labyrinth which is human life.*

We view the vertical gardens from a watchtower that resembles a crane with a

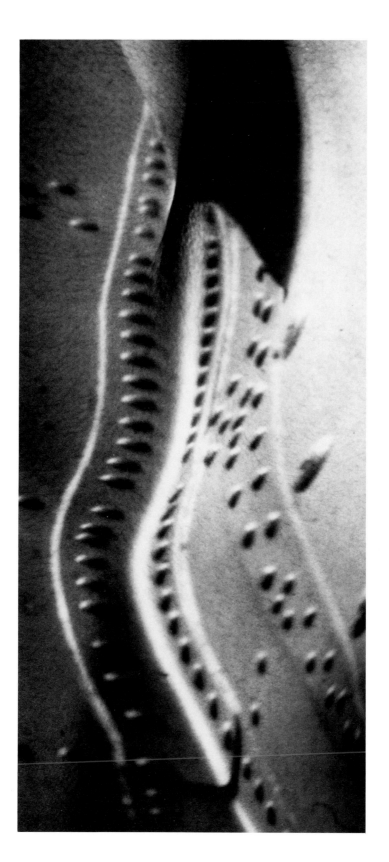

capsule for a single observer. This is perhaps like a control tower where one can see all around, 180 degrees vertically and 360 degrees horizontally. Through a viewing instrument the city now appears not as a parking lot but as a mobile home lot for single male and female individuals, occupying all public space. The towers are a circle, a square, and a triangle extruded one hundred feet high, perfectly upright as well. In the midst of the last garden, I remember, was trinity itself, expressed through hieroglyphs as in sacred Egyptian sculpture.

After leaving the palace I came face to face with the three doors and made my happy choice. I hoped that behind the door, which led to knowledge through voluptuousness, you would be waiting . . . The couple now confronts the crossover bridge with two one-way passages that are, therefore, useless. Each realizes again, this time in the privacy afforded by their masks, that to visit the kernel of the site and eventually consummate their love, they cannot choose either passage. They must penetrate it in a different way, possibly abandoning their bodies, or flying. *Or else?*

Without mutually acknowledging the meaning of their physical proximity, she takes him to admire the carnival games, the spinner, the seesaw, and the merry-go-round, freaks and monsters, gaudy colors, and mythological representations. There are no children, and the contraptions lie silent and immobile, animated only by desire. *Strange childish eroticism, the triumphs of love according to the poets. Do you now remember the ancient sacrifice of Priapus?*

The couple soon arrives at the place for the enactment of the masque. *Back in the cockpit? I recall: the beautiful temple of love, sacrifices, and miraculous rites and germinations. That was the place where we finally recognized each other and woke up to our loving encounter, sanctified by the deity. Are you ready to yield? Don't you see that in fact you have long since yielded?*

The locus of the masque is a rectangular plan with wooden roof trusses. The woman enters through one of the nine Medusa tentacles on the west to occupy her house of reinforced concrete and steel. The man enters through the funnel on the east and occupies his wood and metal house. The two structures confront one another across an earth floor on which is a diagonal wood-tied track and a steel-rail handcar. On the steel-frame element outside the south wall the lights are off. The sun is rising, and the geometric stars are fully visible. The man and woman come out of their respective houses and face each other in the arena. They then turn toward the north, where a hydraulic amphitheater has just appeared behind opening automatic doors, revealing the silent audience. Only two seats are empty. The man and the woman now drop their masks and recognize each other as lovers. *I suspect that the rest of the women in the audience may be identical to Polya. Hand in hand, we at last come to occupy our places in the amphitheater.*

Judging from the applause, the spectators are delighted with the story. Polya lays

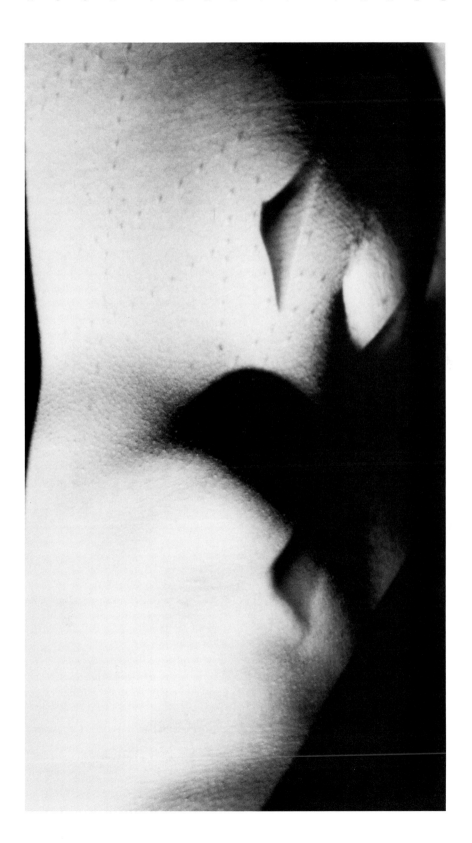

a crown of flowers on my head. She kisses me tenderly with her lips of cinnamon and nectar. The doors close and the amphitheater seems to move, sinking into the earth. I remember how we traveled together to the edge of the sea and how we boarded the vessel of Cupid that took us to the Island of Love. Then we were alone, finally together in the promised place. Now I face a long tunnel at the end of which is the reader's stand, and Polya enters through a side door from an underground elevator. As she speaks from the stand and tells the story of her love, related images are projected onto a screen. We can see the forests, fountains, gardens, and rivers on the island, as well as the procession of triumphal chariots and nymphs in honor of Cupid, the venereal fountain in the middle of the island, Mars's copulation with the goddess and the tomb of Adonis. Her speech is heard throughout the whole site by means of sound amplifiers. She speaks about her genealogy and citizenship, explaining her initial inclination to ignore her lover, her horrible experiences in the dark forest where she witnessed cruelty and dismembering, and the ultimate success of their love. She finishes her story by accepting the identity that destiny had offered her and agrees to go with her lover toward something. Something unnamed. Something OTHER: love, architecture, poetry, freedom, or maybe death.

THE SCREEN now goes black. The film has finished. *Putting her milky arms around my neck, Polya embraces me tightly and kisses me, biting my lips. Without measure, transported by an extreme voluptuousness, I give her my full tongue. O sweet embrace unto death, our two-backed beast of love! Fused together we may now inhabit the new locus of the future!*

But is this meant to be? Small tears of emotion glaze the ivory white of her cheeks, like crystalline pearls. In a twinkling her porcelain visage begins to evaporate amid sighs, a lamenting cry of farewell in her throat, and an electric smell, a fumigation of musk and amber. I feel her body falter against mine, and she soon dissolves in space like the vapor of a celestial perfume, disappearing in front of my eyes.

And she is gone, like my very dream.

SITTING ON THE AMPHITHEATER, I am now under the sky. One more spectator in the public theater. The moving picture may have been rear projected from a concealed stage structure supported by a hydraulic lift. Indeed, the movie screen is raised into the ceiling and the stage is revealed: the waiting room of an airport, unoriginal ubiquitous space! The captain's voice announces our imminent landing in Lerwick, Shetland Islands, at 60 degrees north latitude. On my right there has probably always been a vacant seat. I open the shade, and beyond the oval pressurized window the sun is still barely rising. My suitcase is, as expected, under the seat in front. But the empty space beside me is now aggravating. Not permitted to see her anymore, I am incapable of visualizing those things once invested by her spirit. Polya's absence has become as corrosive as a vapor that absorbs all light and dissipates with my dream.

Electronic bells. Hydraulic systems are activated, and the plane descends on its final approach. As it lands, the stage lift first comes down and a "real world" situation is disclosed. The spectators move into a mobile lounge connected to the terminal building after being raised one last time. The doors open. Now we can see the true section of the stage. The strings of a life-size marionette are suspended from the upper realm, the world of the traveler. The marionette itself has just pulled up the blanket all the way, presumably wishing to embark upon a journey. It is placed in an utterly familiar room, *mine,* on *my* bed, alone.

THE DARK FOREST REVISITED

CHARACTERS

The Lover

The World

An androgynous choir (always invisible, off stage and behind the spectators)

The play should be performed slowly, during twenty-four "hours" of experiential time. It should last as long as the day, from sunrise at 2:35:30 to sunset at 21:27:30. There are no intermissions. The appropriate rhythm will dictate the intervals between scenes. (Left and right in the following script invariably refers to the spectators' point of view.)

SCENE I

The stage is fully visible, although almost completely dark. It consists of a vertical section showing two distinct places separated by the plane of the horizon. The play will unfold like a mysterious mechanism inflicted with spherical perspective, disclosing the structure of the book. The upper scene reveals the familiar airport waiting room with its glazed reflections and the rising sun. The Lover, sitting on a soft molded plastic chair, hand on suitcase, is about to wake up. Barely discernible to the left, the city lies in the distance. On the right the embarkation gate leads toward total darkness. The mobile lounge is absent.

The lower part of the section shows the bedroom with which we are also familiar. The Lover lies naked on his bed, face down, apparently deep in dreams. The slight morning brume is dissipating, and amid more pronounced shadows the cracks on the wall that had become a map are gone. Behind the man still crouches a large cat with enormous batlike wings outlined by the faint greenish light. In the rear stage the sky corresponds to the black space of the upper realm, while a dark, fiery maelstrom (a dangerous whirlpool not far from the Norwegian coast), lies below the horizontal dividing line. Eyes, large fish, crosses, eyebrows, or black elongated birds, balances and broken boundary landmarks are among the heavenly signs that can be barely seen, all disappearing, while in the foreground marionette wires extending between the upper realm and the body of the sleeping Lover become clearer and conspicuous, like the traces of shooting stars in the darkest firmament.

While the action develops in the airport scene, the sleeping Lover in his room remains more or less motionless. Only the wires of destiny vibrate with greater intensity or become warmer as the events unfold.

The play begins when the Lover, disoriented, opens his eyes and finds himself in the maze of steel and glass. His clothes are wet and sticky from sweating, and he is visibly overtaken by bitterness. An intensely bright, yellow sunlight spreads over the upper stage, glaring through a very low circular cutout, about five feet in diameter. No other light is used.

THE LOVER (*addressing an intangible vision*): Oh Polya! Where are you, my pleasure? You are mine . . . you were mine . . . she was mine. Vanished with my dream. The clearest of dreams, perfectly recoverable. A divine intimation? Just before sunrise, a crepuscular dream that filled only the infinitely short instant preceding orgasm. The experience of zero. My hand sliding on her thigh, and at the precise moment when the tightly articulated limbs finally yield, revealing the void, the dream stops, as if my inner being had opted for temporal space, chaos, and life over the seduction of death and its promise of a nondualistic vacuity!

THE CHOIR: The magician's power is the power of Eros, manipulation through passion and seduction, remaining ultimately unfulfilled in our temporal world. We are the victims of the artist yet this is our only hope for meaning, our sole way to catch a glimpse of the absolute. Love and salvation take refuge in the execution of the work of art. Redemption is the discipline of a rigorous technique.

THE LOVER: My brief dream was chased away by the sun, who was perhaps jealous of my power and happiness; it was vaporized by the light that denies a tomb to my Polya and, indeed, all building designed in the image of love. The light that ultimately obliterates the geometric incandescence, the coinciding point of life and death, of desire and severance, may thus also destroy civilization. This light must come to an end!

THE CHOIR: According to the ancient Egyptians, the word "dream" derives from the verb "to awaken." And the sun is a two-way bridge of fire between being and nonbeing.

THE LOVER: The millennium is approaching. We have flirted with reason for three thousand years. Moving perennially from east to west, we have lived in the twilight. Now it's time for the night, for the age of awakening. We must escape through the gap in time that allows us to reverse our direction and come back to our nondualistic origin.

THE CHOIR: The firmament can no longer be addressed by its given name. Jacob's ladders collapse without a sound. Everything is upside down, and all that is square is round. The Milky Way: ammoniacal vapors shining in empty space and bursting forth absurdly like the tears of a broken egg, the mucus of a dazzled eye or the opalescent offal of the shattered skull of humanity. It is only a gap of astral sperm and heavenly urine, the true substance of communion! Heaven gradually turns into hell, and people must gradually turn into birds.

THE LOVER: Adam found Eve at the time of awakening. That is why women are so beautiful. The richest occurrences come to us long before our consciousness realizes it. When our gaze stops in the visible, we are already in love with the invisible. Intimate destiny! Your absence in death does not deny to poetry the power to give us youth and convey wonder, to animate space and to articulate the speech of genuine thought. Death is not an event but a substance, and true poetry an awakening. Let us proceed into a night dream, again into myth!

THE CHOIR: Love may not be genetically efficient, but it perpetuates humanity through metempsychosis by willing death away. Man, born poet, is not a creation of necessity, he is the creation of desire.

THE LOVER (*standing up and facing the audience*): The external world is not made of inanimate matter. No impersonal laws are operational. All is flesh and the chiasm has been revealed. The death of Polya must be avenged. Catastrophe must ensue, or our ultimate transformation into objects will persist.

THE CHOIR: You know how it always is, yet humanity remains deaf to the call for authenticity. Will we ever be at rest? So many times already! The same ending once again? Will you not finally believe in reality? The dream must be trusted. You have the divine in you, but beware of coveting the spurious or you will never win out!

THE LOVER: There is a certain point in the mind, now at last accessible, from which reality and the imaginary, the past and the future, the communicable and the incommunicable, life and death all cease to be perceived in a contradictory way.

296

The lover then proceeds to stop the sun from rising. He places his suitcase on a low table upstage and opens it with a deliberate motion, exposing its contents. He extracts first the book of poetry. Reflections *is the title of the collection, but this is perhaps no longer important for the spectators. He next removes a pulsating, shiny sphere that, as it is held much closer to the proscenium plane, hides the artificial sun completely.*

SCENE II

The spherical depth has now become dominant, analogous to the human eye. The conventional experience of perspective begins to collapse. The timepiece, activated by the sun, will soon stop. The end of the play coincides with the end of the book. The present reading is 23:23. At this moment the structure of the work is disclosed as a superfluous geo-metric instrument for the architect to measure in her body the longest possible day, lasting 18:52:00, precisely calculated during the summer solstice, 21 June, at 60 degrees north latitude. The vertical stage, with its structure of wires like a web of time meridians, is still visible, but now seems to be contained within the projections of the sphere, which also reflects the contents of the suitcase (this may be achieved through an ingenious system of lenses and mirrors).

The Lover continues to hold the sphere with fascination, probably aware of its important function as a geographic instrument and map. It has undergone a process of crystallization, becoming smaller and more pure. With resolute motions, he then extracts a tool from his suitcase. As soon as he grasps the tool in his hand, the sphere appears intimately provoked. Showing his great expertise, he begins carving the object. His countenance shows an expression of strength and delight typical of the craftsman in the act of creation. It is perfectly evident that he is making an orifice, perhaps eventually a circular orifice, very dark and profound. After being carefully polished, the black crystal resembles the pupil of an eye, or the inside of an egg, entirely void of light.

THE LOVER: The time has come for the end. The sun will no longer rise and the crystal will obliterate the dualism of shadow and light.

THE CHOIR: In its implosion, the sphere will turn out to be the dark sky, synthesizing the space of the heavens and internal space, like the original matte pearl congealed in a heavy, fundamental water. Light will become corporeal and the matter of objects celestial.

THE LOVER: This sphere acts like an uncanny anamorphic mirror that distorts ordinary objects as they are projected outward. The distorted objects, which are now real, reflect back on the incomprehensible, monstrous mirror. A key to our nightmarish jumble rests with the mirror reflecting the eye of the spectator, the black hole that I hold in my hands, the vortex of emptiness that will finally absorb and liberate all of humanity.

THE CHOIR: Little by little the black hole will turn itself inside out, scattering in a spin-weighted harmonic motion. Neutrinos and electromagnetic and gravitational forces will break through the barrier of reflecting metal or crystal surfaces. This time the sphere will not be captured by the stratagems of reason and man will stop imitating his ancestors. From within the fertilized egg-cell at the moment of conception the world will appear as pure concavity, as space: *Makom*. A new mode of dwelling on the earth, probably free from gravity in the conventional sense, will necessarily follow. Beyond the absolute-event-horizon we will be able to *touch* the invisible light, remain impervious to violent toroidal forces. Men and women will increasingly reduce in size in order to share the finite surface until, after the year 20,000, humanity will adopt the dimension of zero. Thus the human race will ultimately vanish in a dignified manner and attain infinity.

The spherical projection becomes filled with a dull yellow light in crescendo (the color of sand). The light emanates from the surface of a floating square inscribed in the sphere. It turns first brown and then a dark red that then becomes brighter (the color of blood), while the luminous surface metamorphoses into a triangle. Next the light changes to a dark blue-gray, followed by violet and then dirty green, emerging from the lower part of the sphere that now appears like a flat semicircle (the color of the sea). Gradually the circle completes itself, the light becomes more orange and finally incandescent yellow, turning into the brightest blue (the color of noon), a radiation so glaring that the spectators are forced to close their eyes. The sphere is now so large that it is no longer noticeable.

THE CHOIR: A man slaying a bull, a vulture eating the liver! The scrutinized sun can be identified with a mental ejaculation, foam on the lips, and an epileptic crisis. No longer the preceding sun that had made the objects visible, epitome of beauty and goodness. The scrutinized sun is horribly ugly yet death by the consumption of fire is the least solitary of deaths. A true cosmic death that takes the whole universe with it!

298

SCENE III

The shadows in the upper stage have become permanent, regardless of the retinal fluctuations of light. The objects have shifted in their relative positions, as depth has continued to collapse. The scene, however, is similar to the beginning of the play. A premonition of laughter and catastrophe. The Lover now holds nothing in his hands. He stands up and walks gracefully to the embarkation gate. Facing the abysmal darkness on the right, oblique to backstage, he arrives at the edge of a platform. As soon as he stops, very simple dance music is heard, the precise opposite of Wagner.

THE CHOIR: It is the time of awakening: the time of poetry that says the truth; the time for the realization of the dream. Just as the intersection of two lines on one side of a point suddenly appears again on the other side after passing through the infinite—or the image in a concave mirror, after receding into the infinite, suddenly resurfaces close before us—grace appears purest in the human body that has either no or infinite conscious- ness, that is, the body of a lover, in the marionette or in the god.

THE LOVER: The round dance of thought must now conclude and become gesture, but not a fertility ritual. Depth is on top and our destiny is to overcome heaviness. Wings are useless. The force of flight is in the dancing feet and flying is no longer forbidden. To will is to fly, to will with optimism with liberation of humanity.

Jumping slightly, the Lover strikes the earth with his heels. Arching his body from the feet to the nape of the neck, he becomes infinitely vertical and rises into the freedom of night. He really flies, finally detached. The upper stage is now dark. We can only see the broken marionette wires that appear like shooting stars (continuing into the unperturbed lower section of the stage) and the Lover's body, free from gravity.

THE CHOIR: Ooo-oo-ooo. The experience of zero in a unified field of space- time. By means of a sustained action from this quantum field, through powerful ceramic superconductors, it is possible to modify the curvature of space-time geometry so that the body can rise and climb in any chosen direction.

The lover continues ascending, very slowly.

THE CHOIR: Being is becoming and there is no present or substance, only vacuity. Deeper, more profound, simple and essential than love itself!

The lover pursues his strictly vertical levitation, avoiding any impression of swimming or drifting east or west. His deep breathing is noticeable. The atmosphere is absolutely odorless, without memories or spurious desires.

THE CHOIR: The substance of freedom is air, because air is nothing and gives nothing. This is the greatest gift.

THE LOVER (*in an uncanny androgynous tone*): Listen inside my head. I rise in the supreme voyage that goes nowhere along the horizon, desiring to reach the ocean in the depths of the sky that is never visible during the day. To become one with the primordial plasma, the opaque clarity or shade that is more brilliant than the light of the sun. Cold fire in the night, the semen of the universe, origin of a new sun.

THE CHOIR: Night synthesized with the light of love. Real flight is always blind. Forever rising toward the cold, high, and silent place integrated with our own being.

While the scene stays unchanged and the slow, undisturbed ascent of the lover continues, the voice now comes distinctly from the lower section of the stage where the body of the Lover remains motionless on the bed.

THE LOVER: I saw myself partaking of the world of light. All was a rainbow of colored light; yellow, red, green, blue, and white. I experienced an overwhelming nostalgia for the colors of the world while I was carried outside myself by the violence of the presence. I wanted to fly in the air, but I noticed there was something resembling a piece of wood at my feet that prevented me from taking flight. I kicked the ground with violent emotion and rose, shooting forth like an arrow from the bow. Suddenly I saw that black light had enveloped the entire universe. Rays of light joined in me and rapidly pulled the whole of my being upward. Finally I reached the sphere of spheres, without quality or dimension, and I was annihilated, losing consciousness. When I came back to myself I realized that this absolute light was I. Whatever fills the universe is I; other than myself there *is* emptiness.

THE CHOIR: The yes and the no have been left behind. Now the formless is. In the perpetual present the soundless is, total and unending.

The levitating body in the upper stage now starts to vanish, a dark vapor transformed into black space and consubstantial with the pleroma. While this happens, the marionette wires are pulled in all directions, becoming tense and incandescent. The naked body of the Lover, lying face down on his bed, shows undisguised signs of excitement through motion, rubbing his groin and feet against the surface of the sheets.

301

THE LOVER: Twenty-four milliseconds are appearing. There are moments when my body is illuminated. There are flashes of lightning that resemble ideas. It is all very strange. I suddenly see *it* in me! I distinguish the depths of the layers of my flesh, and I can feel areas of pain—rings, poles, plumes of pain. Do you see these living figures? This geometry of my suffering?

THE CHOIR: Love is the first scientific hypothesis for the objective reproduction of fire, the origin and apocalypse of culture. Prometheus was a vigorous lover, and in his body pain was converted into knowledge.

THE LOVER: Pain is a very musical thing . . . There are deep and high-pitched pains, andantes and furiosos, prolonged notes, fermatas, arpeggios and chromatic progressions, abrupt silences . . .

The body of the Lover now appears fragmented. In every limb is a whole body, the gestures of humanity present in every part. But the gender of each limb is not recognizable. Beautifully crafted pieces rub against one another and become visibly inflamed.

THE LOVER: I am changing in the shadow, on my bed. My body hardly knows that the tranquil masses of my ultimate horizon lift it up; on it my reigning flesh fuses with the darkness.

THE CHOIR: The fire is not pure any more, it has been stolen from the gods. Desire is genetically inefficient, but it abides at the root of human order. Infinity remains and humanity endures between an eclipsed beginning and a glaring beyond: a two-way traffic that discloses the architecture of the flesh of the world. We wait.

THE LOVER: I am the source of pain or voluptuous pleasure. I feel coming from me an array of modifications, values, sensations, and accelerations at once intimately mine and most alien. They are my masters, my being of the moment and of the coming moment.

Two delicate hands carefully take a long and erect piece of flesh and slide it into a dry fissure. Always two hands. Slowly and deliberately they rub it, patiently rotating and waiting. The rhythm is accompanied by other motions, primitive music and song. After a few minutes of expert craftsmanship a new order has been created. The primordial dialectic of soft and hard has been synthesized in a novel, intimate substance. Neither a text in the past, perpetually absent, nor a pure and eternal presence of nothing. Rather, the future universal language: the bodily fragments are totally enveloped by a humid, invisible dark fire. The androgynous head, placed on the pillow, suddenly opens its eyes in an orgiastic expression of death. Depth has now collapsed completely. The shifting objects have dissolved into the center. The stage becomes absolutely pitch black. No more games of appearance. The last images to vanish are a view of the planet from outer space and the death bed in the room.

H O U R   O N E   *From the plane of the earth, dividing the black space above and the dark fire below, the participants can feel the emanation of an intense heat. They breathe deeply, with a deliberate, musical rhythm, extending their senses and opening every pore of their glowing bodies. They finally experience the omnipresent coincidence of desire and fulfillment: their individual completeness as necessary participants in the continuum of life. The new light of being, diffused in infinite space, is obviously a shadow. But the glaring presence of the Lover's tomb is undeniable: a clearing made possible by the spectators' open vision, the first architecture of a new age made with the spectators' own flesh, primordial substance of interfused mind and matter, the final coincidence, supreme apex of analogy. The intimate, warm emanation radiating from the tomb, a never-ending cyclical melody sung at the lowest possible registers and capable of penetrating beyond the surface of things makes present the brightest light to all the senses, ours forever to keep and share.*

The realm of dreams is the realm of the unoriginal, and this book is composed of the dreams of philosophers, poets, scientists, artists, architects, and musicians of the last two hundred years. Although knowledge of the sources is not crucial for the narrative and may in fact disturb some readers, under modern usage I have felt the obligation to acknowledge my predecessors I paraphrase or quote directly. For the most part, however, the references are oblique, and often the sources are not immediately identifiable. Any mistakes of interpretation are, of course, mine. I have provided brief and general acknowledgments for each hour rather than footnotes, which would have been inappropriate in this kind of text. I can only hope that the great artists and authors without whose work this story would not have been possible forgive me for my often impertinent visits to their visions.

H O U R   O N E

00:10 Vincent Vycinas, *Search for Gods* (The Hague, 1972).
00:35 Rainer Maria Rilke, *The Notebooks of Malte Laurids Brigge* (New York, 1964).
00:37 Malcolm de Chazal, *Sens-Plastique* (New York, 1979).
00:43 Iber, *Personal Diary* (Lerwick, 1968).
00:45 Giorgio de Chirico, metaphysical paintings (ca. 1912–1918).
00:54 André Kertész, *Distortions* (London, 1977).
00:58 Paul Valéry, *An Evening with Monsieur Teste* (New York, 1947).

H O U R   T W O

01:01 Kobo Abé, *The Box Man* (New York, 1973).
01:51 *World Atlas* (New York, 1986).
01:54 *Patafisica*, ed. Enrico Baj (Milan, 1982).
01:56 Lewis T. Cetta, *Profane Play, Ritual, and Jean Genet* (Birmingham, Ala., 1974).

H O U R   T H R E E

02:01 Joseph Needham, *Science and Civilization in China*, particularly volumes 3, 4, and 5 (Cambridge, England, 1974), and *The Grand Titration* (London, 1979).
02:09 Lily Chi, "Mirroring the Suzhou Garden," in *Carleton Book*, ed. Stephen Parcell and Katsuhiko Muramoto (Ottawa, 1986).
02:15 Maggie Keswick, *The Chinese Garden* (New York, 1978).
02:17 Peter Eisenman, *Projects and Lectures* (1985–1986).

H O U R   F O U R

03:09 Natalija Subotincic, *Theatre as Paradigmatic Architectural Space* (Ottawa, 1984).

03:20 *Herakleitos and Diogenes,* trans. G. Davenport (San Francisco, 1982).

03:27 Antonin Artaud, *The Theater and its Double* (New York, 1977).

03:35 Giorgio de Chirico, "Espoirs," in *La Pittura Metafisica* (Venice, 1979).

03:44 Francesco Colonna, *Le Songe de Polyphile,* trans. C. Popelin (Paris, 1883).

03:45 Malcolm de Chazal, *Sens-Plastique* (New York, 1979).

03:46 Ambroise Paré, *On Monsters and Marvels* (reprint: Chicago, 1982).

03:48 Etienne-Louis Boullée, *Cenotaph to Newton,* six watercolors (1784).

03:54 Natalija Subotincic, "Theatre of the City," in *Carleton Book,* ed. Stephen Parcell and Katsuhiko Muramoto (Ottawa, 1986).

H O U R   F I V E

04:01 Antonin Artaud, *The Theater and its Double* (New York, 1977).

04:02 John Hejduk, *Lectures* (1984–1985).

04:03 Natalija Subotincic, *Theatre as Paradigmatic Architectural Space* (Ottawa, 1984).

04:16 Ben Nicholson, "Travulgar Square," *Architectural Association Projects Review 1976–77* (London, 1977).

04:30 Andrey Bely, *Petersburg* (Bloomington, Ind., 1978).

04:39 Malcolm de Chazal, *Sens-Plastique* (New York, 1979).

04:45 Wolfgang Meisenheimer, "On the Use of Materials," *Daidalos* 18 (1985).

04:51 *Poimandres (Corpus Hermeticum),* as cited by Wayne Shumaker, *The Occult Sciences in the Renaissance* (Los Angeles, 1979).

04:53 Max Ernst, *A Little Girl Dreams of Taking the Veil* (New York, 1982).

04:55 Michael Piraino, "Descendant of the Dragon," in *Carleton Book,* ed. Stephen Parcell and Katsuhiko Muramoto (Ottawa, 1986).

04:57 Jean-Jacques Lequeu, *Temple of Divination at the Northern End of the Elysian Fields,* watercolor, part of a manuscript entitled *Architecture Civile,* donated by the author to the Bibliothèque Nationale, Paris, in 1825.

04:57 Aldo Rossi, lecture on Venetian projects (1985).

H O U R   S I X

05:17 Alfred Jarry, *The Supermale* (New York, 1977).

05:26 Gaston Bachelard, *La Terre et les Rêveries du Repos* (Paris, 1948).

05:36 Giovanni-Battista Piranesi, *Carceri,* etchings (Rome, 1745 and 1761).

05:48 Ambroise Paré, *Monsters and Marvels* (Chicago, 1982).

05:50 Antonin Artaud, *The Death of Satan and Other Mystical Writings* (London, 1974).

05:58 Dalibor Vesely, "Libeskind's Micromegas," in *End Space,* exhib. cat. (London, 1980).

H O U R S E V E N

06:02 Daniel Libeskind, *Chamber Works* (London, 1983).

06:03 Georges Bataille, "The Pineal Eye," in *Vision of Excess* (Minneapolis, 1985).

06:06 Geoffrey Steven Kirk et. al., *The Presocratic Philosophers* (Cambridge, England, 1983).

06:25 Mary Alice Dixon-Hinson, "Erasing the Ghost of Perrault," *R.P.I. Journal of Architecture* 1 (1986).

06:34 *The Drawings of Hans Bellmer,* ed. Alex Grall (London, 1972).

06:35 *Herakleitos and Diogenes,* trans. G. Davenport (San Francisco, 1979).

H O U R E I G H T

07:02 Maurizio Calvesi, *Il Sogno di Polifilo Prenestino* (Rome, 1980).

07:07 Gaston Bachelard, *El Agua y los Sueños* (Mexico City, 1978).

07:27 Philip Glass and Laurie Anderson, "Forgetting," song (1986).

07:37 Geoffrey Steven Kirk et. al., "Thales of Miletus," in *The Presocratic Philosophers* (Cambridge, England, 1984).

307

H O U R N I N E

08:05 Denis Diderot, *Encyclopedia: The Complete Illustrations* (New York, 1978), vol. 2.

08:07 Man Ray, *Violon d'Ingres,* photograph (1924).

08:09 *Hardcore Crafts,* ed. Nancy Bruning Levine (New York, 1976).

08:18 Promotional literature, ICI Americas Inc. (Wilmington, Del., 1978).

08:25 Enrico Prampolini, "Futurist Scenography," in Michael Kirby, *Futurist Performance* (New York, 1971).

08:42 Tristan Bastit, *Prospettiva di una Rappresentazione di Dio,* in Enrico Baj, ed., *Patafisica* (Milan, 1982).

08:50 David Michael Levin, *The Body's Recollection of Being* (London, 1985).

08:53 Martin Heidegger, "What Calls for Thinking?", in *Basic Writings* (New York, 1977).

08:55 *Essays in the History of Ideas,* ed. Arthur Lovejoy (New York, 1960).

H O U R T E N

09:07 Malcolm de Chazal, *Sens-Plastique* (New York, 1979).

09:10 "The Treatise on Resurrection," trans. M. Peel, in *The Nag Hammadi Library,* ed. James M. Robinson (San Francisco, 1981).

09:16 David Michael Levin, *The Body's Recollection of Being* (London, 1985).

09:29 Martin Heidegger, "What is a Thing?", in *Basic Writings* (New York, 1977).

09:34 Louis Aragon, *Paris Peasant* (London, 1971).

09:42 Friedrich Nietzsche, *Thus Spoke Zarathustra* (Harmondsworth, England, 1976).

09:49 Martin Heidegger, *Der Satz vom Grund* (Pfullingen, 1957).

09:52   Rainer Maria Rilke, *Sonnets to Orpheus*, as cited in David Michael Levin, *The Body's Recollection of Being*.

09:53   Martin Heidegger, *Discourse on Thinking* (New York, 1966).

H O U R   E L E V E N

10:03   Denis Diderot, *Encyclopedia: The Complete Illustrations* (New York, 1978).

10:03   René Magritte, *Un peu de l'âme des bandits, La Bataille de l'Argonne, La belle captive*, and other paintings (ca. 1925–1962).

10:26   Alberto Giacometti, *Objets Mobiles et Muets*, constructions (1933).

10:33   Gustave Flaubert, *Madame Bovary* (Buenos Aires, 1968).

10:34   Stendhal, *La Cartuja de Parma* (Mexico City, 1968).

10:34   André Gide, *Strait is the Gate* (New York, 1952).

10:34   Alfred Jarry, *Ubu Rex* (Vancouver, 1977).

10:34   Tom Robbins, *Even Cowgirls Get the Blues* (New York, 1976).

10:35   John Hawkes, *Death, Sleep and the Traveler* (New York, 1974).

10:36   Gabriel García Márquez, *Cien Años de Soledad* (Buenos Aires, 1971).

10:37   Gerard de Nerval, *Journey to the Orient* (St. Albans, England, 1972).

10:37   Andrey Bely, *Petersburg* (Bloomington, Ind., 1978).

10:38   Juan Valera, *Pepita Jiménez* (Buenos Aires, 1969).

10:38   Alain Robbe-Grillet, *Jealousy* (New York, 1959).

10:39   André Breton, *Nadja* (Mexico City, 1972).

10:39   Milan Kundera, *The Book of Laughter and Forgetting* (New York, 1980).

10:51   James Joyce, *Ulysses* (New York, 1960).

H O U R   T W E L V E

11:02   Alberto Giacometti, *The Palace at 4 A.M.*, construction (1932).

11:06   Marcel Duchamp, *Objet Dard*, construction (1951).

11:13   Richard Howard, "Architecture of the Roman Catholic Church," in *Carleton Book*, ed. Stephen Parcell and Katsuhiko Muramoto (Ottawa, 1986).

11:39   Marcel Duchamp, *Large Glass* (1915–1923) and *Étant Donnés*, (1946–1966), constructions.

11:43   René Magritte, *Le Viol, Le modèle rouge, Le principe du plaisir*, and other paintings (ca. 1925–1962).

11:46   Malcolm de Chazal, *Sens-Plastique* (New York, 1979).

11:56   Octavio Paz, "*Water writes always in* plural," in *Marcel Duchamp*, ed. Anne d'Harnoncourt and Kynaston McShine (New York, 1973).

H O U R   T H I R T E E N

12:02   Lucie Fontein, Stephen Parcell, and Alberto Pérez-Gómez, *Hidden Cities* (Mexico City, 1979).

12:04   Jean-Jacques Lequeu, *Cabinet Indien de les Délices*, watercolor part of a manuscript entitled *Architecture Civile* donated by the author to the Bibliothèque Nationale, Paris, in 1825.

12:08   Sappho, "Love Poem," as cited in Iber, *Personal Diary* (Lerwick, 1968).

12:09   James Joyce, *Ulysses* (New York, 1960).

12:10   Georges Bataille, *The Story of the Eye* (New York, 1986).

12:12   Henri Corbin, *L'Imagination créatrice dans le soufism d'Ibn Arabi* (Paris, 1958).

12:20   Joanne Paul, *A House for an Alchemist*, construction (1984).

12:21   "The Apocalypse of Adam," trans. G. W. MacRae, in *The Nag Hammadi Library* ed. James M. Robinson (San Francisco, 1981).

12:31   Stephen Parcell, *Camera Obscura*, construction (1984).

12:41   Alain Robbe-Grillet, *Project for a Revolution in New York* (New York, 1972).

12:45   Revelation, chapter 4.

12:47   *Aztec Prophecy*, as cited in Iber, *Personal Diary* (Lerwick, 1968).

H O U R   F O U R T E E N

13:01   Kobo Abé, *The Box Man* (New York, 1973).

13:02   Wendy Brawley, *Alchemical Transmutations of Magic* (Ottawa, 1985).

13:03   Stephen Parcell, *Rendez vous* in *Parametro* 12 (Bologna, 1983).

13:13   Roland Barthes, "The Jet-Man," in *Mythologies* (Paris, 1957).

13:15   Jean-Jacques Lequeu, *Le Rendezvous de Bellevue*, watercolor part of a manuscript entitled *Architecture Civile* donated by the author to the Bibliothèque Nationale, Paris, in 1825.

13:17   Gaston Bachelard, *El Aire y los Sueños* (Mexico City, 1958).

13:23   Caspar Friedrich, J. M. W. Turner, and Mark Rothko, landscapes (ca. 1818, 1835, and 1953).

H O U R   F I F T E E N

14:02   René Daumal, *Le Mont Analogue* (Paris, 1987).

14:04   Milan Kundera, *The Book of Laughter and Forgetting* (New York, 1980).

14:05   Alfred Kubin, *The Other Side* (Harmondsworth, England, 1969).

14:09   David Coxhead and Susan Hiller, *Dreams* (New York, 1976).

14:15   Daniel Libeskind, *Theatrum Mundi* (London, 1985).

14:20   Max Ernst, *Men Will Know Nothing about It*, painting (1923) and text in Peter Schamoni, *Max Ernst Maximiliana* (Boston, 1974).

14:26   Cennino Cennini, *Il Libro dell'Arte* (Florence, 1859).

14:31   Alberto Giacometti, "The Dream, the Sphinx and the Death of T.," in *Labyrinthe* 2 (Paris, 1946).

14:35   Max Ernst, *Frottages* (ca. 1926).

14:39   Raymond Roussel, *Impressions d'Afrique* (Paris, 1910).

14:40   Max Ernst, *The Elephant Celebes*, painting (1921).

14:51   Salvador Dalí, *Giraffe on Fire*, painting (1937).

14:55   Raymond Roussel, *Locus Solus* (New York, 1983).

H O U R   S I X T E E N

15:04 Bernard Rudofsky, *The Unfashionable Human Body* (New York, 1971).

15:22 Thomas More, *Utopia* (London, 1516).

15:34 Max Ernst, *Erectio sine qua non,* drawing (1919).

15:49 "Asclepius," trans. J. Brashler et al., in *The Nag Hammadi Library* ed. James M. Robinson (New York, 1981).

15:55 Alain Robbe-Grillet, *Djinn* (New York, 1982).

15:57 Ambroise Paré, *On Monsters and Marvels* (Chicago, 1982).

H O U R   S E V E N T E E N

16:04 Jacques Monod, *Chance and Necessity* (London, 1972).

16:08 Jorge Luis Borges on Steiner's theosophy in *The Book of Imaginary Beings* (Toronto, 1974).

16:13 Gaston Bachelard, *La Psychanalyse du Feu* (Paris, 1949).

16:17 James Joyce, *Finnegans Wake* (New York, 1982).

16:20 *Herakleitos and Diogenes,* trans. G. Davenport (San Francisco, 1983).

16:22 Meton Gadelha, "The Anarchitomy of Tec-ture," in *Carleton Book,* ed. Stephen Parcell and Katsuhiko Muramoto (Ottawa, 1986).

16:35 Mario Perniola, "Between Clothing and Nudity," *Zone* 4 (New York, 1989).

H O U R   E I G H T E E N

17:04 Roland Barthes, *Mythologies* (St. Albans, England, 1973).

17:11 Alain Robbe-Grillet, *Project for a Revolution in New York* (New York, 1972).

17:13 "American Collection," *Photography Venezia 79,* exhib. cat. (Venice, 1979).

17:29 Donald Kunze, "Chiastic Practices in Architecture," lecture (1986).

17:37 Edward Hopper, paintings on urban themes (ca. 1928–1944).

17:59 Gregory Henriquez, *Alephville* (Ottawa, 1986).

H O U R   N I N E T E E N

18:08 Donald Kunze, "The Role of the Monster in Architecture," lecture (1986).

18:16 Paul Delvaux, paintings, ca. 1940–1965.

18:26 Constantin Jelenski, introduction, *The Drawings of Hans Bellmer* (London, 1972).

18:44 Georges Bataille, *The Story of the Eye* (New York, 1986).

18:46 Esther Rochon, *Coquillage* (Montreal, 1985).

H O U R   T W E N T Y

19:07 Jorge Luis Borges, "La Biblioteca de Babel," in *El Jardín de los Senderos que se Bifurcan* (Buenos Aires, 1941).

19:13 Geoffrey Steven Kirk et al., "Pythagoras," in *The Presocratic Philosophers* (Cambridge, England, 1983).

19:23 *Malevitch*, exhib. cat. (Collections du Musée National d'Art Moderne, 1980).

19:39 Max Ernst, *Vox Angelica*, painting (1943).

H O U R   T W E N T Y - O N E

20:22 Mina Loy, *The Last Lunar Baedeker* (Charlotte, N.C., 1982).

20:42 Daniel Libeskind, *Letter* (Milan, 1987).

20:43 Kurt Schwitters, *Merz*, (1921).

20:49 Alain Robbe-Grillet, *Recollections of the Golden Triangle* (London, 1984).

20:59 Andrey Bely, *Petersburg* (Bloomington, Ind., 1978).

311

H O U R   T W E N T Y - T W O

21:00 Alain Robbe-Grillet, *Last Year at Marienbad* (London, 1977).

21:02 Kobo Abé, *The Box Man* (New York, 1974).

21:51 John Hejduk, "A Berlin Masque," *Chelsea* 41 (New York, 1982).

H O U R   T W E N T Y - T H R E E

22:05 Alain Robbe-Grillet, *Last Year at Marienbad* (London, 1977).

22:10 John Hejduk, *The Mask of Medusa* (New York, 1985) and "A Berlin Masque," *Chelsea* 41 (New York, 1982).

H O U R   T W E N T Y - F O U R

23:00 Arnold Schoenberg, *Die Gluckliche Hand*, drama with music, in *Arnold Schönberg–Wassily Kandinsky*, ed. Jelena Hahl Koch (London, 1984).

23:16 Georges Bataille, *The Story of the Eye* (New York, 1986).

23:47 Paul Valéry, *An Evening with Monsieur Teste* (New York, 1947).

23:51 Henri von Kleist, "On the Marionette Theater," trans. R. Paska, in *Zone* 3 (New York, 1989).

Jun 12 Alex
1:15 Noah
ed - bread
Sunday morning 9ish